THE SIMON & SCHUSTER
POCKET GUIDE TO
CHEESE

SANDY CARR

A Fireside Book
Published by Simon & Schuster Inc.
New York London Toronto
Sydney Tokyo Singapore

Key to symbols

🐄	cows' milk	see p.8
🐑	ewes' milk	
🐐	goats' milk	

🌓	very soft	see p.9
🌓	soft	
🌓	semisoft	
🌓	semihard	
🌓	hard	

○	sphere	see p.10
⬭	drum	
▱	rectangular loaf	
⬭	wheel	
▱	square	
⬭	roll	

🌱	may be suitable for vegetarians	see p.5

Ⓐ	widely available
Ⓑ	outside country of origin available only in specialist shops
Ⓒ	widely available in country of origin
Ⓓ	rare outside area of production except in specialist shops

★	recommended for excellence and/or interest

Fat content is shown as a percentage (see p.10) and the approximate weight of a whole cheese is given in both kg and lb

A Fireside Book
Published by Simon & Schuster Inc.
Simon & Schuster Building, Rockefeller Center,
1230 Avenue of the Americas, New York, NY 10020

Edited and designed by
Mitchell Beazley Publishers
part of Reed International Books
Michelin House, 81 Fulham Road, London SW3 6RB

Editor Maggie Ramsay
Art Editor Paul Drayson
Senior Executive Editor Anne Ryland
Production Sarah Schuman
Map illustrator Eugene Fleury
Typeset in Gill Sans and Caslon by Kerri Hinchon for Evolution
Originated and produced by Mandarin Offset, Hong Kong
Printed in Malaysia

10 9 8 7 6 5 4 3 2 1
Library of Congress Cataloging in Publication Data available on request
ISBN: 0-671-77899-4

Contents

Introduction

Cheese, according to the ancient Greeks, was a gift from the gods. This may have been another way of saying that nobody could really remember when, where or how it first came into being, or perhaps, unaware of the chemical processes involved, the Greeks believed there was something miraculous about the transformation of milk into cheese.

The true origins of cheesemaking are, and probably always will be, a mystery. Like many inventions, cheese was probably discovered by different peoples simultaneously. Once they had realized that the milk of certain mammals was both appetizing and nutritious, it was only a short step to the observation that sour milk separates naturally into curds and whey, and from there to cheesemaking. Herds of sheep and cattle were raised for milking in Sumeria and ancient Egypt, sheep were domesticated in Mesopotamia about 12,000 years ago and in the Old Testament there are many references to ewes' and cows' milk cheeses. Classical Greek literature provides abundant evidence that, by that time, cheesemaking had long passed the primitive stage. Even in those days cheese was made not only for domestic use but for trade. Recent excavations have uncovered evidence of a cheese market in Jerusalem and a cheese factory in northern Israel, and by the 6th century BC the Romans were importing cheese from all over the Empire.

Then, as now, cheese was prized not only as a staple food (often being, for the peasant, the only form of protein in an otherwise frugal diet) but also as a delicacy worthy of the attention of the most exigent gastronome. Cheese was, and is, all things to all men. It can be robust or delicate, strong or soothing, an abundant meal in itself or a rare and precious morsel to be savoured and treated with the reverence afforded all great miracles of art or nature.

This book seeks to demonstrate above all that *cheese is not one thing*. There are hundreds, maybe thousands, of different cheeses. Some of them are widely available, others only within a few miles of the locality in which they are made.

I have chosen over 1,300 cheeses from all over the world, some of which will already be familiar to you, others mere acquaintances and some complete strangers. The main characteristics of each with regard to taste, texture, etc., are described, together with any idiosyncrasies of temperament. Cheeses can be notoriously temperamental and a chance encounter with a bad example can lead to lifelong antipathy. It is therefore important to know how to recognize a good cheese and how, having found it, to cherish it.

Cheesemaking processes

By the time the milk leaves the animal, a host of factors has already determined the character of the cheese to some extent. The nature of the grazing—whether fresh grass or scrub, hay, clover, corn or manufactured concentrates—influences milk yield and flavour. Soil and subsoil, climate and even micro-organisms present in the air also have a part to play. The animal itself—be it cow, sheep, goat, buffalo, camel, yak, zebu or reindeer— will be a major influence on the eventual cheese. Each cheese type is based on a unique combination of all these factors even before man begins his work. For this reason it is notoriously difficult to reproduce some cheeses outside their area of origin.

Pasteurization is a means of partially sterilizing milk (by raising its temperature to 72-76°C for 10-20 seconds) to destroy potentially harmful bacteria; this makes it possible to mix milk from different herds to allow for large-scale industrialized cheesemaking. But in doing so, some cheese connoisseurs and cheesemakers would argue, it also destroys much of the individuality of the cheese and makes for a blander product. Nevertheless, most of the cows' milk cheese made in the world today is made from pasteurized milk (ewes' and goats' milk is rarely pasteurized). Many cheesemakers around the world consider thermalization—heat treatment at a lower temperature (about 65°C)—a more acceptable alternative.

Unpasteurized cheese made in modern dairies is *not* a health hazard. Good cheese cannot be made from dirty milk, and standards of hygiene and quality control have improved immeasurably in recent years. Besides, most of the pathogens present in milk are destroyed by the cheesemaking process itself. The listeria bacteria which has caused so much worry in recent years may occasionally be found in both pasteurized and raw milk cheeses of the softer types. For this reason it is recommended that pregnant women and anyone whose immunity to disease may be low should avoid such cheeses.

The basic principles of cheesemaking are the same for all cheeses. The object is to extract the water from the milk, leaving the milk solids (fat, protein, vitamins, etc.) behind. There are of course many variations at each stage which all contribute to the character of the finished cheese.

COAGULATING THE MILK

The cheesemaker may choose to use morning milk, evening milk (slightly richer) or a mixture of the two. It may then be partly or fully skimmed or more cream may be added. At this moment the cheesemaker may add a dye (such as annatto) or mould spores (such as *Pencillium roquefortii*) to promote veining, or propionic acid bacteria to encourage the development of holes. The milk is brought up to a uniform temperature (varying from cheese to cheese) and soured by means of a starter (a special culture of sour milk with a high concentration of lactic acid). From now on, until salt is added at a later stage, the acidity of the curds will gradually rise. The cheesemaker tests the level constantly so that he knows when it is time to move on to the next stage. Some cheeses are coagulated entirely by lactic acid (or lemon juice in some simple cheeses) and are known as lactic-curd or acid-curd cheeses. Others require rennet, an enzyme extracted from the stomach of a young calf (or lamb). When the levels of acidity and temperature are right (they vary for each cheese), the rennet is added, causing a reaction in the milk that separates it into firm curds and watery whey.

At one time, plant rennets such as the juice of fig leaves, thistle seeds, safflower, melon and ladies' bedstraw (*caille-lait* in French) were widely used. Some countries, notably Portugal, still use plant rennets for many of their traditional cheese types, and they are also used in kosher cheese and in some Asian types where religious beliefs forbid the eating of cows' meat. Cheesemakers today often choose a vegetarian or microbial rennet (an enzyme produced from yeasts or fungi) to ensure their cheeses are acceptable to vegetarians.

TREATING THE CURDS

The curds are next cut and drained. The size of the cut, the method used and the amount of time expended will determine the moisture content and consequently the softness or hardness of the cheese. For softer cheeses the curds are sparingly cut and ladled into moulds to drain naturally. For harder cheeses the curds are cut vertically and horizontally into tiny pieces, or combed into fine strands. As the curds settle on the bottom of the vat, they may be recut and turned (pitched) or piled in blocks one on top of the other (cheddared) to expel the maximum amount of whey. Sometimes, as in the case of very hard cheeses, the curds are 'cooked' in the whey before being drained, in that the vat is heated to bring the curds up to a specific temperature. For some semihard cheeses the temperature of the vat is also raised, but less high, so that the curds are 'scalded' rather than 'cooked'. Some cheese types also involve the addition of herbs or spices or wine to the curds during this stage.

One important variation in the treatment of curd is that instanced by many Italian cheeses and known in Italy as *pasta filata* and elsewhere as spun-curd or plastic-curd cheeses. The drained curd is immersed in hot water, where it becomes soft and pliable, and then stretched and kneaded until it reaches the required consistency.

The whey drained from the curd can be heated (to collect residual milk proteins and fats etc.) and used to make another cheese, as in the case of Ricotta, Mysost and Broccio, which are all whey cheeses. Albumen cheese (such as Sapsago) is made by heating whole or skimmed milk and is very rare.

MOULDING, PRESSING, FINISHING

The treated curds are spooned, ladled or shovelled into moulds of a vast range of shapes and sizes, perforated to complete drainage. The moulds may be stainless steel drums, wooden hoops, rush baskets or any other suitable vessels. The curds may be left to firm naturally or they may be pressed, either lightly or heavily. Alternatively the curds may be scooped out of the vat in a cheesecloth and moulded by hand.

The cheese may then be soaked in brine, be bandaged or waxed, be sprayed with mould-forming spores or exposed to bacteria. It may be washed with water, brine or alcohol, or buried in ashes or herbs, oiled or painted, smoked, or just left alone to ripen in its own way.

RIPENING

This is the last critical stage in cheesemaking. Its length varies with each cheese type—fresh cheeses are barely ripened at all, while Parmesan may take up to four years. Even within the same cheese type the period of ripening can vary considerably. This means that the process must be carefully monitored throughout by expert cheese graders who are specifically attuned to the qualities of each cheese. The colour, shape, texture, aroma and even the sound of a cheese all indicate whether or not it is *à point*. In some cases the grader 'irons' the cheese: a long, thin, metal cylinder—the cheese iron—is inserted into the centre of the cheese and pulled out, bringing a rod of cheese with it. The colour, smell and texture are examined before it is replaced in the cheese. The Cheshire cheese grader will also hold it to his ear, listening for minute squelching sounds which tell him that there is too much or too little moisture in the cheese. The Parmesan grader thumps the cheese and listens to the vibrations coming from the crust. Each cheese is tested in different ways.

During the ripening period the conditions of temperature and humidity are carefully controlled to promote the development of desirable micro-organisms which help the process and discourage those that hinder it. Some cheeses are ripened from the inside out, while others are ripened from the outside in. For some, the object is to encourage internal moulds, for others to prevent them. All these require different conditions in the cheese store.

It is during the ripening period that special characteristics develop, like the blue veining in Stilton, the holes in Emmental, the red smear on the surface of Limburger and the white mould on a Camembert. This sometimes happens naturally, but there is usually something the cheesemaker can do to help it along. For example, by piercing the cheese with fine stainless steel needles, the cheesemaker can aerate the paste and so help the veins in blue cheeses spread. By turning a holey cheese regularly, the cheesemaker ensures that the holes will be evenly formed and distributed throughout the cheese.

SEASONALITY

Creamery cheeses, made from pasteurized milk collected from many herds, tend to be the same throughout the year. Hand-made cheeses, especially those made from unpasteurized milk, have added interest for the gourmet: not only are they more characterful to begin with, they also reflect the seasons in their colour, texture and taste.

Milk from cows at pasture usually makes better cheese than that made when the cows are milked in their winter stalls. Fresh grass, meadow herbs and flowers undoubtedly affect the finished product, whether the cheese takes two weeks or two years to ripen. Pierre Androuët, France's foremost authority on cheese, said that to find any cheese at its best, you first need to know when the cows are put out to pasture (as early as February in mild lowlands, as late as May in mountainous regions). You also need to know how long it takes to ripen the cheese. Simple mathematics will then tell you when any cheese is in its prime.

Ewes' and goats' milk was traditionally available only during certain months of the year (January to May for ewes, February to November for goats), so again length of ripening determines when each variety is at its best.

Entries within the book for individual cheeses point out if a cheese is particularly good at a certain time of year. (Many farmhouse cheesemakers, however, freeze summer milk or curds to ensure their cheeses are always available. Others adapt their recipe slightly with the seasons, to give a consistent cheese despite richer milk or warmer weather.)

Classification of cheese

The sheer multiplicity of cheeses is, at first sight, quite bewildering. To convert the complexity into manageable proportions, cheeses can be grouped in various ways.

This guide to cheese represents one way in which cheese can be classified—by country of origin. As far as possible, cheeses have been assigned to their country of origin, even though, in many cases, they are made in several other countries as well. Cheese is closely related to climatic, geographical, economic and cultural circumstances. Some people even perceive national characteristics that make one nation's cheeses different as a whole from another's. Other forms of classification relate to the nature of the processing, the type of milk used, texture, fat content, shape, size, colour, flavour, smell and type of rind.

PROCESSING

The various permutations of the cheesemaking process allow a rough and ready classification:

Fresh cheeses Unripened or barely ripened cheeses coagulated with rennet (rennet-curd) or by lactic fermentation (acid- or lactic-curd). Some may be lightly pressed or moulded by hand, but mostly they are simply packed into tubs or crocks.

Ripened unpressed cheeses Curds are minimally cut and allowed to drain naturally. Quick-ripened (about a month) by surface moulds. Includes cheeses with white rind flora and those with orangey washed rinds.

Pressed uncooked cheeses Lightly or heavily pressed and medium-ripened (from two to 18 months).

Pressed cooked cheeses Curds are 'cooked' in the whey before being moulded, heavily pressed and ripened up to four years.

Pasta filata cheeses Curd is immersed in hot water, kneaded and moulded (often by hand). Ripened or unripened.

Whey cheeses Usually made as a by-product of other cheeses. May be fresh, pressed and dried, or caramelized.

Processed cheeses Made by blending cheese with various other ingredients including vegetable oils, butter, emulsifiers, artificial preservatives and flavourings. Such cheese products are outside the scope of this book.

TYPE OF MILK

Milk may be whole, or partly or fully skimmed, and this affects the fat content of the cheese. It may also be pasteurized or unpasteurized (see previous chapter). The flavour of the cheese is determined, above all, by the type of animal that provides the milk. In some cases, even the particular breed is significant.

Cows' milk cheeses Most of the world's cheeses are made from cows' milk. The lactation period of dairy cattle is unusually long: up to ten months in some cases, followed by a two-month dry period. By staggering calf production in a large herd, milk can be made available all year round. The milk changes in character and reduces in yield during the lactation period. The first milk produced after calving is a rich concentrated substance called colostrum or beestings. This is full of nourishment for the newborn calf, but rarely used in cheesemaking. It is followed by the 'new' milk, high in fats and proteins. Both the yield and the fat content gradually reduce until the end of the lactation period, when the milk increases in fats once again. Milk produced towards the end of a milking is also higher in fats than the first flow. (Some cheeses, such as Reblochon, are traditionally made only from this milk.) Cows are milked twice a day, evening and morning, the morning milk being slightly lower in fat. Most cheeses are made of a mixture of the two milkings, but they can also be used separately or sometimes coagulated separately and then mixed. The fodder and nature of grazing also affect the milk and thence the cheese. Cheeses made from summer milk are generally regarded as superior.

Ewes' milk cheeses Sheep can thrive in harsh conditions and on thin pasture that would be quite unsuitable for cattle. The lactation period is short and the yield low, but the use of ewes' milk enables cheesemaking to take place in areas where it would not otherwise be possible. Some countries, notably Spain, Portugal, Pyrenean France and parts of Italy are particularly renowned for their ewes' milk cheeses. The availability of ewes' milk used to be highly seasonal, and in some areas still is. In parts of France, for example, the season lasts from about January to mid-May. Fresh cheeses will be found only in these months; three-month ripened cheeses will be available from April to mid-August. However, new breed management methods (staggered lambing) often mean that a flock can give milk throughout the year. Milk can also be frozen. Ewes' milk cheeses are almost always sharper-tasting than cows' milk cheeses. Ewes' and goats' milk cheeses are becoming increasingly popular among people who are allergic to cows' milk.

Goats' milk cheeses Goats' milk is exceptionally high in fat content and is free from many of the pathogens that affect cows' milk—one reason why it is hardly ever pasteurized. Goats have a high milk yield and can live on difficult terrain, but their lactation period is traditionally short and the milk, therefore, seasonal. Many of the classic pure goats' milk cheeses are available only from the beginning of spring to the end of autumn. As with sheep, however, modern farming means that goats' milk is now available all year. Goats' cheeses generally have a stronger, fuller, barnyard flavour than any others, although many makers prefer their cheeses to be sold mild and young, making them acceptable to a wider public.

Other animals Yaks', reindeer's and camels' milk cheeses do still exist in some remote areas, but are extremely rare. The water buffalo is more important, particularly in Italy and the Balkans, but even there it is being supplanted by the cow.

TEXTURE

The hardness or softness of a cheese is directly related to its moisture content. The harder the cheese the lower the moisture content. The world of cheese is a continuum between very soft and very hard so that any classification is likely to be arbitrary, especially where one group shades into the next. Also, many cheeses lose moisture as they mature. A four-year-old Parmesan is much harder than a two-year-old one. With these reservations, most cheeses fall into one or other of the following groups:

Very soft Spoonable cheeses. Most fresh cheeses, like Quark, come into this category but not all (such as Mozzarella).

Soft Spreadable cheeses like Camembert or Brie.

Semisoft Firmer, often crumbly or springy but still moist. Many blues and some washed rind cheeses come into this category.

Semihard The largest family and what the Germans call *Schnittkäse* (sliceable cheese), such as Cheshire, Tilsit.

Hard Very firm, dense, sometimes grainy cheeses. Sliceable when young and grated when old, like Parmesan, Cheddar, Sbrinz.

FAT CONTENT

Milk contains around 75 per cent water, with fats, proteins, vitamins and minerals in suspension. It is the fats that carry the aroma and flavour through to the end product, along with the fat-soluble vitamins A and D. After draining and pressing, Cheddar cheese contains fat, protein and water in roughly equal proportions. Many countries have legislation about the fat content of different types of cheese, and these are measured as a minimum percentage of dry matter, ignoring the moisture content, which varies with age. Cheeses made from whole (unskimmed) milk are therefore described as having a fat content of about 40-50 per cent. (Double- and triple-cream cheeses are made from milk with extra cream—in France this means a minimum of 60 per cent and 75 per cent fat in dry matter.)

Remember, however, that the actual fat content of a moist cheese such as Camembert will be lower than that of a drier cheese such as Emmental. Although both have a stated fat content of 45 per cent, Camembert contains more water, and therefore less fat (and fewer calories), gram for gram. High fat cheeses should be avoided by people on low cholesterol diets.

Farmhouse cheesemakers are sometimes unable to state precise fat content because it varies in the milk throughout the seasons.

SHAPE AND SIZE

Cheeses come in many shapes and sizes. These may be a result of tradition or of marketing convenience. Often, however, they are directly related to the nature of the cheese and to the ripening process in particular. A Camembert, for example, has to be small and flattish with a large surface area in relation to its volume. If it were not, the surface micro-organisms would not penetrate to the centre before the outside became overripe. Similarly, the convex sides characteristic of many cheeses are a result of gases given off during fermentation. Six basic shapes predominate; sphere, drum, rectangular loaf, wheel or disc, square or cube, roll, log or sausage. Cheeses listed in this book have been assigned to one of these groups wherever possible, and variations on the norm explained wherever applicable. In all cases, it is the traditional shape of the whole cheese that has been cited. Many cheeses nowadays are also available in easily sliceable rectangular blocks.

COLOUR

Natural cheeses range in colour from white through all the shades of yellow to dark chocolate brown. Their colour generally depends on the length of the ripening process combined with the butterfat content of the milk. It deepens during ripening and the richer the original milk, the more golden the cheese. This is, however, complicated by the fact that artificial colouring agents are also used. The most common is annatto (*Bixa orellana*), a plant of West Indian origin, responsible for the deep orange colour characteristic of some cheeses. In the past, saffron, marigold petals, beetroot and carrot juice were used for the same purpose.

FLAVOUR AND SMELL

Cheeses range from mild to strong in both flavour and smell depending on their maturity. Unpasteurized cheeses vary even more: the season, a change of pasture, the weather during cheesemaking will all have their effects, making each cheese you buy subtly different. The following descriptions can only therefore be a rough guide. Taste before you buy wherever possible, bearing in mind that nuances occur when the cheese is accompanied by different food and wine. Smelly cheeses, by the way, are not necessarily strong tasting.

RIND

The rind of a cheese is usually very distinctive. Although fresh cheeses generally have no rind at all, most cheeses fall into one of four groups:

Dry natural rinds Formed by the curds at the edges of the cheese drying out. They may be brushed or bandaged to make them coarse or grainy or they may be oiled to become smooth and shiny. Generally tough and thick.

Soft bloomy white rinds *Penicillium candidum* is sprayed on the soft moulded curds and the resultant growth of white fur is regularly brushed off until the desired thickness of rind is achieved. Pure white and dry to touch when the cheese is fresh, darkening with age. The rind may or may not be eaten.

Washed rinds Cheeses washed with water, brine, wine or beer and sometimes a culture of *Breyibacterium linens* develop a smeary bacterial growth, which varies from yellow to dark red depending on the intensity of the treatment. Usually softish and damp to touch, often smelly. Rarely eaten.

Artificial rinds 'Artificial' in that they do not arise from the cheese itself. The substance may be organic, such as herbs or leaves, or inorganic, such as wax or ashes.

Africa

Most of Africa is totally unsuited to cheesemaking. Violent extremes of climate, and vegetation ranging from desert to jungle typify the bulk of the continent. Cattle are mostly of the zebu type whose already scant yield is not helped by the lack of adequate fodder in periods of drought. These animals were once indicators of wealth and since they were beasts of burden they were not used for milk before the Europeans came. There is no evidence that cheese formed a part of the native African diet, except in the Islamic north, where ewes' and goats' milk types were made by semi-nomadic herdsmen. Colonial administrations introduced cheesemaking where conditions were favourable. In Algeria, South Africa and Kenya, for instance, thriving dairy industries produce mainly copies of European cheeses.

Aoules (Algeria)
Skimmed goats' milk (sometimes diluted with water) and a piece of the previous cheese batch as a starter are placed in an animal skin bag and shaken vigorously to produce lumps of butter fat. The remaining watery liquid is heated and the curds are moulded into small cakes. These are dried until flinty hard, pulverized and used for seasoning.

Blaauwkrantz (South Africa)
Creamy-textured blue-veined cows' milk cheese. Vegetarian.

Drakensberg (South Africa)
Semisoft, mild golden yellow (annatto-coloured) loaf-shaped cheese, made from cream-enriched cows' milk. Made with vegetarian rennet.

Jbane (Morocco)
The word simply means 'cheese' in Arabic. In Morocco it is made from goats' or cows' milk and vegetable or animal rennet, drained in woven rush bowls, and eaten fresh, or moulded into discs and dried.

Numidia (Tunisia)
Potent blue-veined cheese made from ewes' or goats' milk.

Oriental (Tunisia)
White brined ewes' milk cheese similar to Greek Feta.

Rosetta (South Africa)
Creamy, crumbly, ivory-coloured white-veined cheese. Quite sharp and salty. Made with vegetarian rennet.

Sarde (Tunisia)
Pressed, uncooked ewes' milk cheese like Spanish Manchego.

Sicille (Tunisia)
Semihard white cheese with lots of holes made from ewes' milk mixed with a little cows' or goats' milk. Eaten young after one to three months ripening, or aged up to a year.

Takammart (Algeria)
Made with whole goats' milk. The curds are drained on straw mats, then kneaded and moulded into small flat squares and left to dry for two or three days. Stored in goatskin bags until hard and brittle.

Testouri (Tunisia)
Smooth, lightly brined hand-moulded balls of ewes' or goats' milk curds.

ARGENTINA see *Latin America*

Asia

The controlled conditions necessary to ripen cheese successfully present insuperable problems in tropical climates and such Asian cheeses as do exist are mostly fairly primitive fresh types. The Chinese and Indonesians generally regard milk as a repulsive substance quite unfit for human consumption. The Japanese have no indigenous cheesemaking traditions although they now make some foreign types and are passionately fond of processed cheese.

Aarey (India)
Semihard buffalo milk cheese made near Bombay.

Bandal (India)
Acid-curd cheese made from cows' or buffalo milk or cream. Shaped into small balls and eaten fresh, or smoked. From West Bengal.

Chauna, Chhana, Chhena (India)
Acid-curd cows' milk cheese eaten fresh or used in sweetmeats.

Chura (Tibet)
Yaks' milk is a staple of the Tibetan nomads. It is made into butter and the buttermilk is heated, drained, moulded into balls and dried. It becomes a sourish, fatless sort of cheese, used for grating.

Dacca (India)
Made from cows' or buffalo milk or a mixture of the two. Drained in baskets and pressed. Dried for about two weeks and then smoked.

Karut, Krut, Kurt
The nomadic tribesmen of central Asia were certainly among the first cheesemakers. Yet technological advances require settled habits and cheesemaking in that area today is still extraordinarily primitive. Krut is made in Pakistan, Iran, Afghanistan and by the Turkoman tribes of southern USSR, using any available milk. Made by boiling buttermilk and draining and drying the solids. Has to be reconstituted with water before being eaten but it will keep for years.

Kesong Puti (Philippines)
Fresh cheese made from buffalo milk. Wrapped in leaves.

Lighvan (Iran)
White brined cheese made from ewes', cows' or goats' milk.

Paneer, Panir (India)
Fresh acid-curd cows' milk cheese, usually cooked with vegetables.

Panir Kusei (Iran)
Kneaded curd (any available milk) is stored in earthenware pots for three to four months, becoming firm and dry.

Peshavani (India, South East Asia)
Ewes' or buffalo milk cheese coagulated with withania berries.

Seret Panir (Iran)
Thickened sour milk is smoke dried, formed into balls, brined and beeswaxed. Ripened for ten weeks, can be kept for many months.

Surati Panir (India)
Buffalo milk cheese from Gujarat. The curds are drained and then ripened in whey for 12 to 36 hours. Sold in clay pots.

Australasia

The early settlers in Australia found little in the way of agricultural traditions. Nearly two-thirds of the continent is composed of desert and barren scrublands, rich in mineral deposits but poor in pasture. The Aborigine population basically consisted of hunters and gatherers relying on game and wild fruits and vegetables for sustenance. Nevertheless, the modern Australian dairy industry, concentrated in Queensland and New South Wales, is highly productive and efficient, and apart from making enough dairy products to satisfy its own needs, Australia has found ready markets abroad, especially in the Far East. Cheddar is still the most widely produced and consumed cheese. It is sold mild (three months old), semi-mature (three to six months), mature (six to 12 months) and vintage (over 18 months). Cheddars can also be flavoured with 'smoke', cumin, garlic, bacon or port wine; or, in the case of processed Cheddars, with spring onion, ginger, curry, chilli and even peanuts. The Italian connection is evident in the making of rather good versions of Ricotta, Mozzarella, Provolone, Parmesan, Pepato and Romano. Other foreign cheeses catering for nostalgic immigrant communities include Feta, 'Swiss', Gouda, Edam and Leiden, and versions of Brie and Camembert.

Of the early postwar Australian cheeses, Cheedam is no longer made, but as in many other countries, the 1980s saw the renaissance of farmhouse cheesemaking, especially in Victoria, Tasmania and Western Australia. From King Island (Tasmania) comes one of Australia's creamiest Bries and a Tomme Fraîche, as well as Italian-style Peperati (like Pepato), and Pyengana, a firm, lightly pressed cheese rather like a Wensleydale. A producer in the Margaret River area (Western Australia) makes Brie, Camembert, Tomme Fraîche and Margaret River Fine Grade Farmhouse Cheese, a young, creamy, mildly acidic, lightly pressed cheese made in small wheels. Officially, no raw milk cheeses are allowed to be made. Pasteurized cows' milk is still the usual basis, but ewes' and goats' milk cheeses are increasingly seen.

Bass River Red

Leicester-style cheese from Top Paddock, Victoria. More than a mere copy, as they make their cheeses with great care, and have an 18-month-old clothbound Cheddar in their range. Benandale is a Wensleydale type.

Gippsland Blue

A superb veined cheese matured for 10 to 12 weeks, first made in the state of Victoria in 1984. Found in specialist shops (sometimes known as Bunyip Blue) and restaurants, and in ceramic pots on first-class Qantas flights.

Hillcrest Farm Curd Truckle

From the same maker as Gippsland Blue, a firm young cheese with a milky flavour which is also available smoked or lavender-scented.

Jindi Supreme

A neighbour of Hillcrest makes this tender double-cream cheese with a soft white rind.

Kervella

These goat cheses from Western Australia, found in specialist shops, are among the finest in the country. There is a wide range, from

Fromage Frais to Mature Pyramids and including a Coeur aux Herbes, a young cheese coated in herbs made to a French recipe.

Milawa
A small team of cheesemakers in Victoria are known for their superb washed rind cheeses, one simply called Milawa and a smaller cheese known as King River Gold. They also make a blue cheese and, in spring, a small Milawa Goat Blue truckle.

Pasterello
Invented in Sydney by an Italian, Daniele Lostia, a rather delicate softish cheese with a high moisture content, somewhat reminiscent of Fontal although it is drained in wicker baskets like several other Italian cheeses.

St Claire
A widely available Jarlsberg type.

Timboon
This farm in Victoria is run on organic principles: they are making Brie, Camembert (including 30g (1oz) Camembert Berties), Havarti-style Buetten made in wheels, and mould-ripened Timboon Triple Cream (also sold as 100g (3½oz) Tee Cees).

Whitelaw
A small, crumbly white, slightly acid lightly pressed fresh cheese made by Top Paddock, South Gippsland, Victoria. Moyarra is similar, but with an annatto-coloured stripe running through the centre.

NEW ZEALAND

The temperate New Zealand climate is ideal for cattle raising: animals remain out at pasture all year round, and the environment is exceptionally clean and unpolluted. Even so, pasteurization is compulsory, probably because 70 per cent of New Zealand's production is exported to distant lands. Cheddar is still the most important cheese in New Zealand. Cheshire, Edam, Gouda, Feta (some made from ewes' milk), Brie, Camembert, Colby, Blue Vein and many other European styles are made for the home market, and a cheese called Egmont, a Gouda type developed in the 1960s, is a popular export to Japan.

Increasing interest in cheese in the 1980s led to an expansion of the varieties made, from 15 to over 60 in 1990. Farmhouse was developed in 1981 from a Gouda recipe but cured in high humidity, forming a bloomy white rind. It is made in a small factory in Oamaru, near Dunedin. Kapiti Cheeses are a bigger organization based at Paraparaumu, North Island. Over the past few years they have developed several varieties, found in shops and restaurants—most of these are made with vegetarian rennet: Aorangi (Maori for 'white cloud') is a white mould-ripened cheese with a hint of mushroom flavour and when ripe, oozes luxuriously; Kirima is a log-shaped Camembert type; Hipima is a small wheel-shaped ewes' milk cheese with a soft white rind and Camembert character; Kahurangi is like a mild blue Brie; Kapiti is the name of an Italico-type cheese—soft, spreadable, with a slightly lactic flavour— and Kapimana is a crumblier, more acidic variation. Other developments on Kapiti are Aukai (smoked), Montachio (almonds and pistachio flavour), Jalapeno Kapiti and Tupihi (reduced fat). The same cheesemakers produce a mild Saint-Paulin-style cheese called Port Nicholson and some unusually flavoured Bries (one with sun-dried tomatoes and basil) and Cheddars (including Walnut Red and Lindale Sage).

Austria

Austrian cheeses reflect various influences: pungent cheeses with red rind flora, mild buttery types and fresh curd cheeses have affinities with their German neighbours; Swiss types come from the mountains; Liptauer, a cheese spread much liked in Austria, is of eastern European origin. There are also abundant copies of other European types.

Bachensteiner 🐄 🗯 55% ⊖ 250g (9oz) Ⓓ
Unpasteurized pale cheese with irregular small eyes and a light orange washed rind. Ripened for four to eight weeks.

Bergkäse 🐄 🌑 45% ⊖ 8-25kg (18-55lb) ©
Alpine raw milk cheeses. Similar to Swiss Emmental but smaller, with smaller, sparser eyes. Ripened for three to six months.

Bierkäse 🐄 🌑 15% 1.5-4kg (3-9lb) ©
Piquant washed rind cheeses made in wheel or loaf shapes.

Kochkäse ★
Spicy, almost spreadable cheese made from sour-milk curds heated with salt, pepper and caraway. Made in various shapes and fat contents in southern Austria. Also known as Glundner and Steirerkäse.

Mischlingkäse 🐄 🌑 35-45% ⊖ 6-7kg (13-15lb) ©
A pale golden cheese with irregular holes and an orange rind. It has a spicy aroma and a full, sharpish flavour. From western Austria.

Mondseer 🐄 🗯 45% ⊖ 1kg (2lb) ©
Firm, moist, mildly spicy cheese with a few irregular eyes and a soft dry orange rind. Ripened for four to six weeks.

Quargel 🐄 🌑 1% 🌱 ©
Ripened acid-curd cheese hand-moulded into small flat discs and sometimes flavoured with caraway seeds or paprika. Sharp and fairly pungent. Translucent, greyish-yellow, rubbery paste. Originally from Olmütz, Czechoslovakia. Also known as Handkäse.

Rässkäse 🐄 🌑 35-45% ⊖ 3.5-4kg (8-9lb) ©
Spicy washed rind cheese made in the Vorarlberg region.

Schlosskäse 🐄 🗯 35-55% ⊖ 60g (2oz) ©
Rather mild washed rind cheese made in northern Austria.

Selch-Kas
Semihard smoked cheese which looks like a large golden bread roll, made from mixed cows' and ewes' milk. Smooth yellow paste.

Steirischer Bauernkäse
Tangy, rindless white open-textured cheese made from mixed ewes' and cows' milk. Made in a basin-shaped mould or larger wheel.

Tiroler Graukäse ★ 🐄 🌑 0-2% ⊖ 3kg (8lb) 🌱 Ⓓ
A tangy, rather sour-tasting cheese made from pressed sour-milk curds. Grey-green mould spreads inwards from the surface.

Topfen 🐄 🌙 10-40% ©
Fresh cheese used in cooking. Available plain or with various flavours.

Vorarlberger Sauerkäse
Acid-curd, very low fat pale creamy cheese with soft golden rind.

Belgium

The reputation of Belgian cheeses tends to be overshadowed by that of its more famous cheesemaking neighbours, France and the Netherlands, and even its best-known cheese, Limburger, has been effectively appropriated by Germany. Many Belgian cheeses are closely related to French types, especially those from Trappist abbeys with a tradition of cheese (and beer) making. The quality of Belgian cheeses is very high and only the best are allowed to be exported. Ironically, most Belgian cheese exports consist not of its indigenous cheeses but of copies of foreign types: Cheddar goes to England, Asiago, Fontina, Montasio and Canestrato end up in Italy. Apart from these, Belgium also makes Gouda, Emmental, Brie, Camembert and, interestingly, Spanish Manchego. Goat farmers are thriving, making cheeses for restaurant and home consumption.

Abdijkaas see *Fromage de Trappiste*

Beauvoorde 🐄 🌀 50% 3 and 6kg (7 and 13lb) ©
Rounded hexagon with a dusting of grey-white mould over a golden crust. Revived from a traditional recipe, it has a mild but full flavour and fruity aroma.

Boû d'Fagne see *Herve*

Boulette
There are various local types of Boulette (those from Namur, Huy, Charleroi and Romedenne are the best known and most widely available). All are small soft, surface-ripened farmhouse cheeses moulded into cylinders, drums, rolls and balls and variously flavoured with herbs, rolled in crushed spices or wrapped in leaves. Fairly strident in flavour and aroma. Also known as Crau-stoffe. Generically related to the Boulettes of French Flanders.

Bouquet des Moines
A type of Boulette, small, shaped like a tall drum and with a light covering of white rind flora.

Broodkaas 🐄 🌀 40% 🧀 2-4kg (4-9lb) ©
'Loaf cheese', rectangular block with rounded edges. Smooth and mild, similar to Dutch Gouda. May be waxed yellow, red or orange.

Brusselsekaas ★ 🐄 🌀 0% 150g (5oz) ©
Smooth, salty, low-fat cheese made from pasteurized skimmed milk. Regularly washed with tepid water during the three to four month ripening period. It has virtually no rind and is moulded into small irregularly shaped cakes and sold in clear plastic tubs. Fairly strong and tangy with a light spicy aroma. Also called Fromage de Bruxelles

Cassette de Beaumont
A type of Boulette. Smooth, pale, creamy cheese moulded into a rough conical or rectangular shape. Very low fat cheese made from skimmed milk.

Chimay
The Trappist abbey famed for its beer has developed a fine range of cheeses which are now made by a local commercial concern. There are three semihard naturally rinded cows' milk cheeses matured for three to five weeks: Chimay is the mildest, Chimay au lait cru slightly tangier, and Chimay a la bière stronger still. Chimay de Brebis (ewes' milk) is matured for up to four months, and is a hard, rather dry cheese

with a typical ewes' milk tang. Vieux Chimay is a mild tasting, orange coloured Mimolette-style cheese, made in a small ball.

Crameû

Named after the old pottery utensil used to skim off cream for butter-making, Crameû is a soft, thick triple cream cheese, rather like sour cream. Best from March to October.

Crau-stoffe see *Boulette*

Fleur de Fagne   🍶 🐄 48% ⊖ 1.5kg (3lb) ©
Surface-ripened white rind cheese made from raw milk.

Fromage d'Abbaye see *Fromage de Trappiste*

Fromage de Bruxelles see *Brusselsekaas*

Fromage de Trappiste

Semihard cheese, often factory-made from pasteurized milk and inspired by Port-Salut and other French monastery cheeses. There are numerous types variously shaped into flat wheels or loaves and with smooth springy rinds ranging from light golden yellow to black. From mild to slightly nutty or spicy. Often sold as 'Saint-Paulin' or Paterskaas or under brand names such as Affligem, Casse-Croûte de l'Abbaye du Val Dieu, Echte Loo, Petrus, Père Joseph.

Herve ★   🍶 🐄 45-55% ⊂⊃ 50-200g (1¾-7 oz) ⑧
Generic term for a family of strong pungent cheeses, of which Remoudou is the best known, deriving from the town of Herve in northern Liège. It is a washed rind cheese dating back at least to the mid-16th century. Its warm golden crust covers a rich velvety paste ranging from sweet to spicy depending on the length of the ripening period (two to three months). Some is still made from unpasteurized milk, and double-cream Herves are quite common. Traditional drinks with Herve cheese are coffee or port. Two recent additions to the family are Trou d'Sottai and the milder Boû d'Fagne, both made from raw milk.

Limburger see *Germany (Limburger)*

Macquée

Soft fresh cows' milk cheese made from partly skimmed milk. Usually brick-shaped.

Mandjeskaas   🍶 🐄 0% ©
'Basket cheese', named after the process of draining curds in a basket, is thought to have been introduced by the Romans. It is a fresh, mild curd cheese.

Maredret   🍶 🐄 50% 1.8kg (3½ lb) ©
A white-rinded cheese of recent invention, in the shape of a four-leaf clover.

Maredsous   🍶 🐄 45% ▭ 1 and 2.5kg (2 and 5½ lb) ©
Pressed, uncooked washed rind monastery cheese. Smooth, pale yellow with a moist golden rind.

Nazareth   🍶 🐄 45% ⊖ 12kg (26lb) ©
Emmental-like cheese with large holes and a sweet, nutty flavour. Coated in brown wax. Formerly known as Pelgrim.

Passendale ☼ ⬙ 50% 3kg (7lb) ©
Looking like a floury round loaf with a natural crust, inside it is a creamy mild cheese.

Plateau de Herve ☼ ⬙ 45% 1.5kg (3lb) ©
Lightly pressed dome-shaped washed rind cheese, matured for four weeks and wrapped in foil.

Plattekaas
Fresh curd cheese with a 20 to 40 per cent fat content.

Postel ☼ ◗ 48% ◵ 4kg (9lb) Ⓓ
Made on the farm at the Abbey of Postel, Mol, and sold locally.

Princ'Jean ☼ ⬙ 70% ◵ 150g (5oz) ©
Triple-cream variation of Boulette. Available in three versions: unripened (*vers*), rolled in crushed black peppercorns (*met peper*) or ripened with white surface moulds (*geaffineerd*).

Remoudou ★ ☼ ⬙ 45% ▱ 100-400g (3½-14oz) Ⓑ
Belgium's famous 'stinking cheese', a particularly strong type of Herve which originated in Battice in the reign of the Emperor Charles V (1519-58). Usually larger and ripened for longer than the normal Herve, it has a darker, brownish-orange rind. The name is derived from *remoud*, a Walloon word for the exceptionally rich milk provided towards the end of the lactation period. Nowadays mostly factory-made. Double- and triple-cream Remoudou is made.

Saint-Bernard ☼ ◗ 50% ◵ 4kg (9lb) ©
Slightly salty, smooth, straw-yellow cheese with a tough black rind. Ripened for about six weeks.

Trappistenkaas see *Fromage de Trappiste*

Trou d'Sottai see *Herve*

Vacheloo ☼ ◗ 50% ◵ 2.7kg (6lb) ©
Creamy pressed cheese in two varieties: with provençal herbs and a little garlic (black rind), or with pepper (red-brown rind).

Wynendale ☼ ⬙ 50% ◵ 3.5kg (8lb) ©
Soft ripened tender cheese with a yellow-ochre rind and pronounced flavour.

BOLIVIA, BRAZIL see *Latin America*

British Isles

ENGLAND

Geographically and climatically Britain is perfect for cheesemaking. Numerous breeds of sheep, cattle and goats are raised on terrain that ranges from fertile water meadows to coarse scrub, yet until very recently cheese types were oddly limited. The range of textures and tastes is less extensive than that of, say, French or Italian cheeses, possibly because the British have been left alone for centuries to develop their own gastronomic style with a minimum of outside influences. By the 16th century practically every county, if not every parish, had its own cheese. Most of these ancient cheeses are now extinct, but those that remain include one of the most popular cheeses in the world (Cheddar) and one of the most celebrated (Stilton).

There have been several disasters in British cheesemaking history which account, at least in part, for the comparative decline of British cheese. The first was the cattle epidemic of 1860 when thousands of cows were slaughtered. This led to a shortage of cheese and subsequently to massive imports of American factory-made Cheddar which paved the way for the industrialization of cheesemaking along American lines. This, combined with commercial pressures to meet burgeoning demand from the growing urban centres, meant that quantity superseded quality and the small farmer could no longer compete. Nevertheless, many small cheesemakers struggled on into the 20th century until World War II dealt another blow. Food rationing was introduced and with it stringent controls on food manufacture. Most milk was commandeered for the liquid market and so-called 'luxury' cheese varieties and those with minimal keeping qualities were banned. Before the war there were 1,500 farmhouse cheesemakers. In 1945 only 126 remained.

When rationing ended in 1954, the Milk Marketing Board set up the Farmhouse Cheesemakers Scheme to help farmers market their cheese. Independent grading ensured quality control. The scheme covers Cheddar, Cheshire and Lancashire cheese, and a small quantity of other traditional hard varieties—Leicester, Double Gloucester, Caerphilly and Wensleydale. These cheeses may bear the Farmhouse English Cheese symbol, which guarantees that they have been made on English or Welsh farms in the traditional way and are of the highest quality, though few are made from unpasteurized milk, and two thirds of them are made as rindless blocks. The symbol may be used only by farmers who market their cheeses through the Milk Marketing Board's agents. Consequently, many traditional English cheeses (made on farms, often with unpasteurized milk) are not permitted to use the 'Farmhouse' label.

Farmhouse cheesemaking in Britain accounts at present for about five per cent of total cheese production (the rest is made in creameries or factories), but interest in traditionally made cheese is steadily increasing. One of the most encouraging developments of recent years has been the enormous upsurge in cheesemaking by independent cheesemakers in small dairies and farms all over the country. For the first time in centuries there are now genuinely British ewes' and goats' milk cheeses as well as superb traditionally made cows' milk cheeses.

SKYE

COLL

MULL

ISLAY

GIGHA

CORNWALL

20

ORKNEY
ISLANDS

HIGHLAND

Spey
Aberdeen •

HIGHLAND

S C O T L A N D

NORTHERN
Belfast
IRELAND

Dunlop
Edinburgh •
Lanark
Dublin •
STRATHCLYDE
Ayr
(AYRSHIRE)
IRELAND
BORDERS
CLARE
TIPPERARY
Dumfries •
WEXFORD
NORTHUMBERLAND
CORK

CLEVELAND

CUMBRIA
DURHAM
Cotherstone •
SWALEDALE
WENSLEYDALE
YORKSHIRE
MOORS
NORTH
YORKSHIRE
LANCASHIRE
York •
Preston •

ANGLESEY

Chester •
CLWYD
CHESHIRE
DERBYSHIRE
Derby •
LINCOLNSHIRE
Whitchurch •

NOTTINGHAMSHIRE

LEICESTERSHIRE
Leicester •
Stilton •
NORFOLK
WALES
POWYS
HEREFORD
& WORCESTER
E N G L A N D
Cambridge •
SUFFOLK

Carmarthen
Gloucester •
COTSWOLDS
GWENT
GLOUCESTERSHIRE
OXFORDSHIRE
Caerphilly
Newport
ESSEX
GLAMORGAN
Cardiff •
Severn
Bristol •
BERKSHIRE
London •
MENDIP
HILLS
WILTSHIRE
COUNTRY
Cheddar •
SURREY
KENT
SOMERSET
HAMPSHIRE
Dover •
DEVON
DORSET
SUSSEX

500 m
200 m

SHROPSHIRE

PENNINE CHAIN

21

Allerdale 🐄 ❂ ▭ 450g-2.3kg (1-5lb) ❁ Ⓓ
Creamy-textured pressed cheese. Unpasteurized, sometimes made with vegetarian rennet. Clean, sweet, mildly goaty. Coated in natural wax. Sold at two to three weeks, best after six to eight. From Cumbria.

Alston see *High Pennine, Tynedale Spa*

Arcadian see *Roubiliac*

Avalon ♉ ❂ 48% ▭ 2-2.3kg (4-5lb) ❁ Ⓓ
Caerphilly-type cheese with caraway seeds mixed into the curd. Matured for three months. From the makers of Torville, Somerset.

Basing 🐄 ❂ ▭ 1.5 and 4kg (3 and 9lb) ❁ Ⓓ
Caerphilly-type cheese from Kent, with a rice flour coating. The high butterfat content of goats' milk gives this cheese a creamier taste than cows' milk Caerphilly. Sometimes available smoked.

Baydon Hill
One farm near Marlborough has revived the old North Wiltshire cheese, a hard pressed ewes' milk cheese, coloured with annatto to a pale butter yellow. It is rich, smooth and moist, matured for five months and coated in natural beeswax. Baydon Hill Farm also makes a cows' milk version. Both are made from unpasteurized milk, in 450g (1lb) rounds and 2kg (4lb) truckles. Sold in southern England.

Beamerdale 🐄 ❂ 48% 450g and 1kg (1 and 2lb) ❁ Ⓓ
Fresh spreadable cheese (often used for cooking) with a slight lactic tang. Smaller cheeses come in pyramids, larger ones are red wax coated. Unpasteurized, from an organic farm in North Yorkshire.

Beamish ♉ ❂ 50% ▭ 450g-8kg (1-18lb) ❁ Ⓓ
Moist cheese similar to Wensleydale but less crumbly. Clothbound, matured six weeks. Made at Beamish Open Air Museum, Durham.

Bedwardine ♉ ❂ 42% ▭ 450g and 1.7kg (1 and 3½lb) ❁ Ⓓ
From Worcester, a smooth, buttery full fat cheese made in three varieties: plain (with annatto wash), with chives or smoked.

Beenleigh Blue ★ 🐑 ❂ ▭ 2.7kg (6lb) Ⓓ
Made in Devon from unpasteurized milk. Velvety, ivory paste with an even scattering of small blue holes. Cheesemaker Robin Congdon aims to avoid the saltiness so often associated with blue cheeses, and makes Beenleigh Blue from March to August—the cheeses are best after four to five months, from autumn to spring.

Belstone see *Curworthy*

Bewcastle 🐑 ❂ ▭ 225g (8oz) ❁ Ⓓ
Moist lactic creamy raw milk pressed cheese coated in clear wax. Eaten fresh, it can be spread, but it also keeps well. From Cumbria.

Bexton 🐄 ❂ ▭ 250g-1kg (9oz-2lb) ❁ Ⓓ
A mould-ripened log with white surface mould tinged with blue. Soft white cheese with a mild clean flavour, more pungent just under the rind, especially after four to six weeks. From Cheshire.

Blackdown see *Loddiswell*

Blue Cheshire ★ ♉ ❂ 48% ▭ 22kg (48lb) Ⓓ
A blue-veined cheese now made by Long Clawson in Leicestershire.

At one time Cheshires blued naturally but so rarely and unpredictably that it was more a matter of luck than judgement—the resulting cheese was called Green Fade. Nowadays *Penicillium roquefortii* is added to the milk. The cheese is pressed less than ordinary Cheshire and is aerated with steel needles during ripening. Only red farmhouse Cheshires are 'blued', maturing for six to eight weeks. The flavour is exceedingly rich since the saltiness of Cheshire combines with the sharpness of the mould. See *Cheshire*

Blue Stilton ★ 　 ▶ 48% ▢ 2-8kg (4-18lb) ▒ Ⓑ

Velvety, close-textured unpressed cheese with a pale ivory paste, grading to amber at the edges and marbled with greenish-blue veins. The rind is dry, crusty, greyish brown and slightly wrinkled with white powdery patches. The flavour ranges from mild with a sharp edge when young, to rich and tangy when mature. Stilton, known everywhere as the 'King of English cheeses' is one of the few with any reputation in other countries. It already existed in 1727, when Daniel Defoe mentioned 'Stilton, a town famous for cheese'. In fact, Stilton was never made at Stilton, although it was sold there from the Bell Inn to coach travellers on the Great North Road.

Nowadays Stilton is made in seven dairies scattered around Leicestershire, Nottinghamshire and Derbyshire and protected by a certificated trade mark. Milk is collected from neighbouring farms and pasteurized at the dairy. A culture of *Penicillium roquefortii* is added to the milk with the starter and rennet is added a short time later. The curds are cut by hand into small cubes and allowed to settle on the bottom of the vat. They are left to drain until the following morning when they are milled, salted and placed in hoops for three days to a week. The cheeses are turned daily to drain further. Once removed from the hoops each cheese is rubbed down by hand to smooth out creases and seal the edges. The cheeses are then stored in precise conditions of temperature and humidity for an average of three to four months, when the characteristic crust will develop. During the first month the cheeses are turned every day and at eight weeks they are pierced with steel needles to promote veining.

The best Stilton is made from summer milk and is distinguishable by a slightly yellower paste. These cheeses are in the shops from September onwards, and are traditional at Christmas. Obviously as the cheese ages the mould spreads and the flavour deepens, but the rate varies from cheese to cheese. When buying Stilton look for one with evenly distributed veins and a good contrast between the creamy yellow paste and the blue streaks. Avoid a cheese where the paste is dry, cracked or brownish (except at the edges). Stilton is an excellent dessert cheese and is traditionally accompanied by port. Like other cheeses, Stilton has recently been the subject of various marketing experiments: layered with Double Gloucester, it becomes Huntsman or County. See *White Stilton*

Blue Vinn(e)y 　 ▶ 15% ▢ 5.5-6.6kg (12-14lb) ▒ Ⓓ

Genuine Dorset Blue Vinny is not easy to come by. Originally the milk used was that left after the cream had been skimmed off for buttermaking, and the only maker in Dorset today—Woodbridge Farm, Sturminster Newton—follows this practice, adding vegetarian rennet and liquid *penicillium* mould. The cheese is pressed into moulds by hand, matured for four to six weeks, spiked to encourage blueing, then ripened for a further one to four months. It is a very pale, fairly mild, moist cheese, not as sharp as a Stilton. More widely available is the Blue Vinney made by the Long Clawson dairy in Leicestershire.

Blue Wensleydale ★ 　 ▶ 48% ▢ 4.5kg (10lb) Ⓓ

An exquisite close-textured blue-veined cheese. The paste is white with the barest hint of cream and has a delicate, almost honeyed flavour. It is made in the same way as Wensleydale except that *Penicillium roquefortii* is added to the milk. The cheese is pressed for only 24 hours before being transferred to the cheese store, where it is turned regularly, pierced to help the mould develop and matured for at least six weeks. It is, if anything, more temperamental than Stilton and more trouble to make. See *Wensleydale*

Botton ♉ ● 55% ⊟ 7kg (15lb) ✿ Ⓓ

Unpasteurized organic clothbound Cheddar type from Danby in Yorkshire. Matured for four months to a year. A modern cheese made to a traditional Dales recipe and using vegetarian rennet.

Brendon Blue ♦ ● ⊟ 2.5kg (5½lb) ✿ Ⓓ

Firm, lightly veined cheese with a natural crust like Stilton, made from raw goats' milk on a farm near Taunton, Somerset. Made throughout the year, it is aged for three to four months: beginning white, it deepens to ivory, then takes on a brownish tinge.

Burdale ♦ ● 48% ⊟ 1.5kg (3lb) ✿ Ⓓ

Crumbly Wensleydale-type mould-ripened, air-dried goats' cheese with a natural whitish rind. Best at about two months old. From the same organic North Yorkshire farm as Beamerdale and Fotherdale.

Buxton Blue ♉ ● 48% ⊟ 4.5kg (10lb) Ⓒ

Lightly veined, deep russet-coloured cheese with just a hint of a tang. A recent invention, designed to be milder than Stilton.

Cambridge

One of the few traditional soft cheeses still occasionally available—a mixture of plain and coloured curds made from raw or pasteurized cows' milk curdled with rennet. Fresh or ripened for a few weeks.

Capricorn ♦ ● 50% ✿ Ⓒ

White bloomy rind covers a butter-smooth paste with a mild flavour—truly delicious when ripe and runny (about a month old). Made in 100g (3½oz) cylinders and 1kg (2lb) squares. From Somerset.

Caprino see *Mendip*

Carolina

Semihard, fairly strong-tasting ewes' milk cheese with natural rind. Each 2-3kg (4-6lb) cheese is individually pressed, then matured for two months before it leaves the Kent farm; smaller cheeses—450-700g (1-1½lb)—ripen for six weeks. Made with vegetarian rennet. Cecilia is similar but is matured in barrels of hops.

Cerney

Ash-coated flattened pyramid of the French Valençay type made from unpasteurized goats' milk in Gloucestershire. A semihard, sliceable cheese. Ready after five days, it can be kept for three weeks.

Chavannes ♦ ● 50% ⊟ 125g (4oz) ✿ Ⓓ

Camembert-style cheese from the Gedi herd of goats in north London. Deliciously creamy at about six weeks old.

Cheddar ★ ♉ ● 48% ⊟ 5-27kg (11-59lb) Ⓐ

Golden yellow, close-textured cheese ranging in flavour from sweet and mild when young to mellow and nutty when mature. The making of Cheddar, which began near the Somerset village of that name, has spread and it is now the most widely made cheese in the world.

Unfortunately the quality has suffered. Of the millions of people who eat Cheddar daily, only a few will have tasted the real farmhouse product. There are fewer than 20 farms in the West Country of England still producing Cheddar by traditional methods (and only a handful use unpasteurized milk, notably the Montgomerys, the Keens and the Times Past dairy). These farmhouse Cheddars rank among the finest cheeses in the world. The distinctive process is the 'cheddaring' (see Glossary) which takes place after the curds have been cut into tiny pea-sized pieces, scalded in the whey, pitched and cut into blocks. This slow, persistent draining of as much moisture as possible and the subsequent heavy pressing give the cheese its smooth, hard texture that ideally never crumbles when cut.

Cheddars are sold at various stages of maturity. The 'mild' creamery Cheddar is between three and five months old while 'mature' is over five and up to nine months or possibly more. Some good farmhouse cheese is kept longer up to 18 months or even two years.

Cheddars can also be bought with various added flavourings—pizza herbs, ham and mustard, Cajun spices to name a few. While usually clearly labelled, some have also been named by their manufacturers: with paprika and smoky flavouring (Applewood, Charnwood); with port (Vintage) or elderberry wine (Windsor Red); with raisins, hazelnuts and cider (Nutwood); with walnuts (Cheddington, Nutcracker); with garlic, beer and parsley (Rutland, Somerton); with pickles (Yeoman); with Scotch whisky (Glenphilly). Cherrywood, Westmorland and Woodley are smoked Cheddars.

Cheshire ★ ☼ ☻ 48% ▱ 4-22kg (9-48lb) ©

Moist, friable, slightly salty cheese, mild when young but acquiring a more pronounced tang with age. 'White' (pale yellow) or 'red' (annatto-dyed to a deep peach colour), the flavour is the same.

Cheshire is the oldest British cheese. It was mentioned in Domesday Book in 1086, but the evidence of folklore suggests that it is much older, going back, perhaps, even earlier than the Roman occupation. Cheshire can only be made from the milk of cattle grazed on the salty pastures of the Cheshire Plain, either in Cheshire, Shropshire or Flintshire (now more or less renamed Clywd). The Chester produced in France and elsewhere is related to English Cheshire in name only.

Most Cheshire nowadays is creamery-made, but there are still about a dozen farms in the area producing the cheese. It takes only about two to three hours to make. Evening and morning milk are mixed and after coagulation the curds are scalded in the whey for about 40 minutes. The whey is drained off very quickly while the cheesemaker cuts the curd and then tears it into small pieces. It is then salted, milled, put into moulds and pressed for between 24 and 48 hours. Some farmhouse Cheshires (such as Appleby's unpasteurized) are still bandaged in the traditional way with cheese cloths dipped in lard. Others are dipped in wax. The cheeses are usually ripened for between four and eight weeks, but sometimes a particularly fine one will be selected for longer ripening, up to 18 months.

Cheshire is a very even-tempered cheese. It is almost always good and often superb. Choose a farmhouse cheese if possible, even though Cheshire suffers less from factory methods than do most other cheeses. There are no hidden pitfalls in buying Cheshire: if it looks bright and fresh, buy it; if it is dry and cracked or sweating inside a vacuum pack, leave it alone. See *Blue Cheshire*

Chesvit ▼ ▥ 50% ▱ 600g and 1.5kg (1¼ and 3lb) ✿ ⑩

Affineur James Aldridge of Surrey takes Spenwood, washes its rind and matures it for two months. Smooth texture with a sparse scattering of holes. Sweet tasting with fruity overtones. Best from June to January. Rook's Nest is a young oak-smoked Chesvit.

Chiddingly 🔥 🌙 ⊟ 2kg (4lb) 🌿 Ⓓ

Unpasteurized pressed cheese with a natural rind, matured for three to six months. From a farm near Lewes, East Sussex.

Cloisters 🌱 🌙 ⊟ 2kg (4lb) 🌿 Ⓓ

Charles Martell of Dymock, Gloucestershire (renowned maker of Double and Single Gloucester), did some research and found that an order of monks who settled in Dymock in the 13th century were famous for cheesemaking, so he named his cheese in their memory. It is matured for six weeks, with an edible annatto-washed rind.

Coleford Blue 🔥 🌙 55% ⊟ 2.5kg (5½lb) 🌿 Ⓓ

Creamy yellow cheese with pronounced veining and a wrinkly grey-brown crust. Made on the same Somerset farm as Brendon Blue from raw milk, it matures for two to three months, and is made all year.

Coquetdale 🌱 🌒 54% ⊟ 2kg (4lb) 🌿 Ⓓ

Looking rather like a classic French Tomme with a grey rind, this is a mildly nutty mould-ripened cheese. Crumbly at first, it softens from the outside to a delightful creaminess. Pasteurized cheese from the Redesdale Dairy, Otterburn, Northumberland.

Cornish Yarg ★ 🌱 🌙 55% ⊟ 1-3kg (2-7lb) 🌿 Ⓓ

Stunning-looking cheese coated in nettle leaves. Uncooked pressed cheese comparable to Wensleydale in that it is moist and crumbly, but it is a mould-ripened cheese which develops a creamier texture from the outside in. Sold at three to six weeks old, it has a slightly herby taste from the nettles.

Cotherstone 🌱 🌒 48% ⊟ 1-2.3kg (2-5lb) Ⓓ

One of the old Teesdale cheeses made on two farms near Cotherstone, Yorkshire, traditionally from May to the first winter frost. Light yellow, soft, open-textured with a soft golden crust and a rich flavour with a sharp finish. Ripened for one to three months.

Cottage Cheese

Cooked, skimmed cows' milk curds, drained, washed and coated with thin cream to produce a pure white, bland, low-fat granular cheese which is usually sold prepacked in tubs. It is eaten fresh or used in cooking: it can be an acceptable culinary substitute for Italian Ricotta.

Coverdale 🌱 🌙 45% ⊟ 450g-6kg (1-13lb) Ⓓ

Like Wensleydale and Swaledale, this was originally made from ewes' milk by monks who settled in Yorkshire after the Norman conquest. It was reintroduced by Fountains Dairy in North Yorkshire in 1987 and is now a crumbly young white cheese (firmer than Wensleydale) with a distinctive nutty taste. Also made speckled with fresh chives.

Cream Cheese

Unripened rennet-curd cows' milk cheeses made from single or double cream. Eaten fresh or used in cooking.

Cricketer

Somerset Cheddar-style ewes' milk cheese made with vegetarian rennet and matured for seven months. Ivory-coloured and somewhat softer than ordinary Cheddar.

Crofton 🌙 1 and 2.3kg (2 and 5lb) 🌿 Ⓓ

Made from two thirds cows' milk and one third goats' milk at Thornby Moor Dairy, Cumbria. Matured for two to three months, with a natural grey crust, the cheese itself is creamy smooth with a mild tang.

Crusoe ✂ 🌙 50% 150g (5oz) ☘ Ⓓ

A copy of French Boulette d'Avesnes developed by *affineur* James Aldridge. He mixes semi-ripened Tornegus with tarragon and spices, moulds it into a cone and washes the rind for five to six weeks.

Cumberland Farmhouse ✂ 🌑 ⬭ 450g-9kg (1-20lb) Ⓓ

Smooth-textured, with a mature creamy flavour after two to five months ageing. Sold younger, the oak-smoked version is very popular, as are those flavoured with fresh garlic, fresh sage, fennel or dill.

Curd Cheese

Acid-curd unripened cheese made from cows', ewes' or goats' milk. May be low, medium or full fat. Also known as lactic-curd cheese.

Curworthy ✂ 🌙 48% ⬭ 450g-2.3kg (1-5lb) Ⓓ

Unpasteurized milk from a farm near Okehampton, Devon, is used to make this cheese to a 17th century recipe. Aged for three to four months, it has a natural grey rind and a pale, creamy paste with small irregular holes. Light and buttery when young, it is full flavoured and mellow when aged. Belstone is the same cheese made with vegetarian rennet; Meldon is flavoured with wholegrain mustard; Devon Oke is made in 4.5kg (10lb) truckles and matured for five to six months.

Danbydale ✂ 🌙 ⬭ 300g (10oz) ☘ Ⓓ

Unpasteurized full-fat cheese from the same (organic) farm as Botton. Crumbly Feta-type cheese in clear waxed rounds.

Derby ✂ 🌙 48% ⬭ 4-14kg (9-31lb) Ⓒ

Mild, primrose yellow cheese with a close, rather flaky texture. Neither a particularly interesting nor a popular cheese, possibly because it is almost always sold too young at four to six weeks old. Ideally it should be ripened for around six months, but such mature Derbys are rare. The Fowlers of Forest Farm near Solihull have a well-supported claim to be the oldest cheesemaking family in Britain. When they left Derbyshire they renamed their cheese Little Derby, but continued to mature it for six to seven months. See *Sage Derby*

Devon Blue ✂ 🌙 ⬭ 2.7kg (6lb) Ⓓ

Rich, creamy cheese from the maker of the acclaimed ewes' milk Beenleigh Blue. Made all year round from raw milk to which *Penicillium roquefortii* is added. The unpressed cheeses are salted, spiked and put in cradles to mature for four weeks. Then they are foil-wrapped and matured for a further four months.

Devon Garland ★ ✂ 🌙 52% ⬭ 3kg (7lb) ☘ Ⓓ

Moist rich flaky cheese with a band of mixed fresh herbs in the middle. Made from raw milk to a traditional Dales recipe—gently pressed, matured for about six weeks, with a natural rind.

Devon Oke see *Curworthy*

Double Berkeley ✂ 🌙 52% ⬭ 1.3 and 3.5kg (2½ and 8lb) Ⓓ

Red and white marbled cheese, hard pressed but slightly softer and lower in acidity than Double Gloucester. It is made by Charles Martell of Dymock, who says that it was probably originally a plain Gloucester cheese made in the Vale of Berkeley, given a different name because the makers thought it superior. Aged for two months.

Double Gloucester ★ ✂ 🌙 48% ⬭ 4-14kg (9-31lb) Ⓒ

Bright orange waxy cheese with a strong mellow flavour. Originally Gloucesters were made with the milk of Old Gloucester cattle.

Double Gloucester has a tough rind and has been coloured artificially (first with saffron, beetroot or carrot juice and later with annatto) since the 16th century. It acquired the name Double Gloucester in the early 18th century, some say because it was bigger than Single Gloucester, others because it was a 'double cream' cheese, using the cream from the evening milking and the whole morning milk. Most Double Gloucester is now creamery-made and coloured although a few farms make both white and coloured versions. Charles Martell at Dymock uses unpasteurized milk from the original Gloucester cattle and this is creamier even than Guernsey milk. The best Double Gloucester is that made from summer milk and aged for at least four months. It is also available layered with Blue Stilton (sold as County, Huntsman), Caerphilly and onion (Romany), or flavoured with chives and onions (Abbeydale, Cotswold). See *Single Gloucester*

Duddleswell 🐄 🌙 45% ⬚ 2-2.3kg (4-5lb) ✿ Ⓓ

Pressed cheese with a natural wood-brown rind, made in Uckfield, Sussex. Usually pasteurized, it is made all year and matured for at least three months. Sometimes seen under the name Forresters.

Dussatre see *Golden Cross*

Elgar 🐐 🌙 45% ⊖ 450g and 1.7kg (1 and 3½lb) ✿ Ⓓ

Rich, creamy pasteurized farmhouse cheese from Worcester. Open-textured, coated in yellow wax and matured for six to seven months.

Elsdon Goat 🐐 51% ⬚ 800g and 3kg (1¾ and 7lb) ✿ Ⓓ

Smooth and firm, with a less acidic flavour than other goats' cheeses. Pasteurized. Made at the Redesdale Dairy, Northumberland.

Emlett 🐑 🌙 ⊖ 180g (6oz) ✿ Ⓓ

Usually sold as a white mould-ripened cheese at two to five weeks old, with a fruity taste and strong finish. A larger size resembling Camembert is known as Little Ryding. Occasionally seen as a silky-textured fresh cheese, topped with a bay leaf. Unpasteurized; made at Sleight Farm outside Bath, with Mendip, Tymsboro' and Tyning.

Endeavour 🐑 🌙 ⊖ 4kg (9lb) Ⓓ

Made on the same Yorkshire farm as Whitby Jet, Endeavour is made in the winter when the ewes are dry. Pasteurized clothbound cheese matured for about six months—it is moister and creamier than Cheddar.

Exmoor 🐑 🌙 ⊖ 2kg (4lb) Ⓓ

Pale moist raw milk cheese with a fresh flavour. Made to a traditional recipe. Pressed and naturally rinded; sold after about a month.

Forresters see *Duddleswell*

Fotherdale 🐑 🌙 ⊖ 600g (1¼lb) ✿ Ⓓ

Made at the same North Yorkshire farm as Beamerdale and Burdale. Under its yellowy grey crust, this is a very rich, dense firm cheese. Mould-ripened, it matures for ten to twelve weeks.

Golden Cross 🐑 🌙 ⬭ 225g (8oz) ✿ Ⓓ

Dense, creamy cheese made to the French Sainte-Maure recipe, rolled in charcoal and with a white mould growing through the ash. Ripened for three to four weeks. Also known as Dussatre. Laughton Log is a larger version. Made on a farm near Lewes, East Sussex.

Golden Saye

This cheese begins life as a small Wellington, but is transformed by

James Aldridge into a Munster-style washed rind cheese. Matured for five to six weeks, it has a deep orange rind and is very soft but not runny. Sweet when young, it becomes quite pungent.

Gospel Green 🧀 ● 55% ⊟ 1-3kg (2-7lb) 🌿 Ⓓ

Hand-made cheese from the Surrey village of the same name. Something like a Cheddar-Cheshire cross, matured for three months with a natural grey rind and a clean, fresh taste with a lingering tang. The milk is unpasteurized, and the spring and summer cheeses are a deeper shade of gold and slightly softer textured.

Harbourne ★

Goats' milk blue-veined cheese from the maker of Beenleigh and Devon Blue. Harbourne is similar to Beenleigh, with a very white paste and even blueing.

Hereford Hop 🧀 ● 52% ⊟ 2kg (4lb) 🌿 Ⓓ

Creamy smooth pale cheese with a few holes, coated in toasted hops. The curds are scalded and pressed—lightly in summer, hard in winter to force out the whey before the curds cool. Matured for eight weeks.

Hereford Red 🧀 ● ⊟ 450g and 3kg (1 and 7lb) 🌿 Ⓓ

Mild cheese, similar to Leicester but smoother. Notable for its clashing colours—it is annatto-coloured deep orange, and coated in red wax.

High Pennine 🐐 ● ⊟ 450g-2.3kg (1-5lb) 🌿 Ⓓ

White, crumbly, fairly mild cheese from Cumbria. Coated in white wax, or smoked, unwaxed. Sometimes sold as Alston Goat.

Innes

Unpasteurized vegetarian goats' cheeses from a Staffordshire dairy which keeps its own herd. Variously sized rounds are made, the largest being about 10cm (4in) across. Fresh Innes cheese may be plain, ash-coated or covered with dried rosemary, thyme and oregano. Ash- and mould-ripened cheeses are matured for about a month.

Jouvenet 🐐 ◎ 50% ◯ 110g (3¾oz) 🌿 Ⓓ

Matured for up to two months, with a more goaty flavour than the other Gedi cheeses (Chavannes, Roubiliac and Velde). Moillon is similar but slightly larger, at 150g (5oz).

Knowle

A large goats' cheese log made at Nut Knowle Farm, West Sussex. Very much in the French style, they make a smaller version of the same cheese which is known as Sainte-Maure.

Lancashire ★ 🧀 ● 48% ⊟ 4-18kg (9-40lb) Ⓒ

White, slightly salty, crumbly cheese with a full-bodied, slightly acid flavour. Lancashire is underrated, probably because most people know only the creamery type. An infinitely superior version is made from unpasteurized milk on three or four farms in the Preston area. Making Lancashire in the traditional way is a laborious process. The curd made on one day is added to the previous day's curd, which has already been drained, salted and partly pressed. Both curds are then milled, placed in moulds, pressed for 24 hours, bandaged, waxed and ripened for (at best) two months. Lancashire is the softest of the English pressed cheeses. A smoked Lancashire made by a large creamery is known as Longridge Fell. See *Sage Lancashire*

Laughton Log see *Golden Cross*

29

Leicester ★ 🏠 ❱ 48% 🝙 4-22kg (9-48lb) ©

Sometimes unnecessarily called Red Leicester (there is no other kind), this is a hard-pressed grainy cheese with a faint lemony bite. The colour—from bright russet-gold to tomato-red—originally came from beetroot or carrot juice. It is best at six to nine months old, when really mellow and nutty, but creamery versions go out at under three months. One flavoured with herbs and garlic is called Beauchamp.

Little Ryding see *Emlett*

Loddiswell

Blackdown Goat Centre near Kingsbridge in Devon makes cheese for its visitors as well as for local shops and restaurants. Unpasteurized milk and vegetarian rennet are used. Loddiswell Banon is a soft fresh cheese with a smooth texture, available plain or garlic-flavoured with parsley covering. Blackdown is an uncooked hard pressed cheese with a natural rind, matured for five weeks, available mainly in winter.

Longridge Fell see *Lancashire*

Lymeswold

Early 1980s invention: a white rind soft cheese with blue veining. Made in Somerset from pasteurized cows' milk.

Malvern 🍃 ❱ 44% 🝙 400g and 2.5kg (14oz and 5lb) ♻ Ⓓ

Hand-made in the Severn Valley. Smooth, very white with a thin natural rind, it is sold at three stages: mild (two months), medium (four months) and mature (ten months).

Meldon see *Curworthy*

Mendip 🍃 ❱ 🝙 2-3kg (4-7lb) Ⓓ

Most unusual-looking cheese with a bumpy grey-brown rind and close, smooth white interior. Mendip owes its shape to the way it is moulded—in a kitchen colander. Made at Sleight Farm in the Mendip Hills from unpasteurized milk, the curd is washed with hot water before it is moulded. The mould is turned as the cheese matures for at least three months—it is particularly good at six months old, and the best cheeses are made in spring and autumn when the milk is richest. Summer cheeses have a tendency to be dry: these make an excellent grating cheese, sometimes sold as Caprino.

Moillon see *Jouvenet*

Nanny's Goat Cheddar

Made in Somerset, using vegetarian rennet and pasteurized goats' milk; prepacked and sold in blocks in supermarkets as an alternative to Cheddar for people who are allergic to cows' milk.

Nanterrow 🍃 ❱ 🝙 3-3.5kg (7-8lb) ♻ Ⓓ

Made on a Cornish farm to a Caerphilly recipe. Matured for three to four weeks, during which the cheeses are scrubbed with salted water two or three times, forming a thin natural rind.

Nepicar

Semihard pressed ewes' milk cheese, matured for between six weeks and six months. Made in Kent, along with Carolina and Cecilia.

Newbury 🍃 ❱ 🝙 1.5kg (3lb) ♻ Ⓓ

Unpasteurized mild and creamy rindless cheese from Hollam Hill Farm, Hampshire. The only pressure on the cheese is from the curds themselves as they ripen for ten to 14 days. Plain or with a layer of fresh garlic (quite strong) and rolled in mixed herbs.

Nuns of Caens ♥ 🐑 50% 2kg (4lb) 🧀 Ⓓ
Unpasteurized ivory-coloured washed curd cheese with a very creamy fruity flavour. Made in Gloucestershire.

Old York ♥ 🐑 ⊜ 450g (1lb) 🧀 Ⓓ
Unpasteurized crumbly cheese coated in natural wax and available plain or in various herb flavours. Can be eaten after a week, or kept for six to eight weeks. Yorkshire is known mainly for its curd cheese, used in the local sweet cheese tarts.

Perroche 🐐 🐑 15% ⬭ 180g (6oz) 🧀 Ⓓ
Small cheese in the French style, intended for eating young. Raw milk is used. Mild clean flavour, plain or rolled in tarragon, dill or rosemary. Also made as a log. From Kent.

Prince Bonnie
James Aldridge takes Nuns of Caens cheese and matures it for a further five months. The resulting cheese has deep, sweet, complex flavours and a natural rind coated with blue-grey mould, speckled with orange. Ivory to golden paste; close, melting texture.

Red Box 🐐 🐄 ⊜ 800g (1¾lb) 🧀 Ⓓ
Crumbly cheese with a mild yet fresh lactic taste. Two days after pressing it is coated with yellow wax to keep it moist, and it is then matured for about a month. Raw milk from an Essex herd.

Redesdale ♥ 🐄 53% ⊜ 500g-3kg (18oz-7lb) 🧀 Ⓓ
Smooth, sweet-tasting washed curd cheese matured for about three months. Pasteurized. From the Redesdale Dairy, Northumberland.

Ribblesdale
Ashes Farm, high in the North Yorkshire Pennines, uses an original Dales recipe to make cows', ewes and goats' milk (pasteurized) versions of this firm, pressed cheese. They also produce smoked and garlic-flavoured varieties, all waxed in different colours. Made with vegetarian rennet in 1-2kg (2-4lb) wheels, they are sold quite young (three weeks) but can be kept for up to two years.

Ribchester 🐐 🐄 ⊜ 1 and 2kg (2 and 4lb) 🧀 Ⓓ
Full fat pressed cheese coated in yellow wax. It is matured for four to eight months and should be creamy white, close textured and mellow. Some is smoked. Made on a dairy in a village near Preston.

Richmond 🐮 🐄 ⊜ 450g and 1.5kg (1 and 3lb) 🧀 Ⓓ
A smoked cheese, based on Swaledale but pressed slightly more, gently smoked, coated in red wax and matured for three to four weeks.

Rook's Nest see *Chesvit*

Roubiliac 🐐 🐑 50% ⬭ 150g (5oz) 🧀 Ⓑ
A range of fresh logs is sold under this name: plain, garlic-flavoured or coated with black pepper, Provençal herbs or red and green pepper. Made from a herd in north London from pasteurized milk and vegetarian rennet. A chocolate box presentation of small balls in mixed flavours is known as Arcadian. Saint Gedi is an ash-coated log.

Roundoak 🐐 🐑 ⊜ 115g (3¾oz) 🧀 Ⓒ
Mild, rindless, solid but light and smooth. Made on a Wiltshire farm

and sold in small chipwood boxes. To be eaten very fresh: plain or with garlic and herbs or black pepper.

Sage Derby

Derby with green marbling produced by soaking sage leaves in chlorophyll and adding the juice to the curds. This process produces a more subtle flavour than the chopped leaves used in Sage Lancashire. Spinach juice was once used. See *Derby*

Sage Lancashire

Farmhouse Lancashire with chopped sage added to the curds. The flavour of sage is overpowering for some tastes. See *Lancashire*

Saint Gedi see *Roubiliac*

Saint George ⭐ 🌙 ⊖ 225g and 1kg (8oz and 2lb) ✿ Ⓓ

Best known of the goat cheeses made at Nut Knowle Farm, West Sussex, Saint George is a creamy Camembert-style cheese matured for three weeks, or six to eight weeks for the larger cheese.

Sharpham

Soft Camembert-type cheese made in Devon from unpasteurized Jersey milk and vegetarian rennet. Mild and buttery. Matured for six weeks, as 20cm (8in) rounds.

Shropshire Blue 🐄 🌙 48% ⊡ 7kg (15lb) ©

Between Blue Cheshire and Blue Stilton in flavour, an orange-coloured cheese with even blue veining extending from the centre, and a patchy mid-brown rind. Not a classic Shropshire cheese: in the 1970s it was made in Scotland and now comes from the Colston Bassett (Nottinghamshire) and Long Clawson (Leicestershire) dairies.

Single Gloucester

White, open-textured cheese which is softer, milder and lower in fat than Double Gloucester. The processing is conducted at a lower temperature and a lower acidity level than that of Double Gloucester. The curds are cut more finely and the cheese ripened for only about two months. A rarer cheese, at one time it was considered inferior to Double Gloucester because it was made from skimmed evening milk added to the whole morning milk, and was mainly given to farm workers. Extinct before World War II, it was revived by Charles Martell using milk from his Gloucester cattle, although other farms now make it. Also available flavoured with herbs or nettles.

Spenwood ★ 🐑 🌙 50% ⊡ 1 and 2.3kg (2 and 5lb) ✿ Ⓑ

Named after the Berkshire village where it is made, Spencers Wood. Pressed, white, smooth but slightly open-textured cheese with a natural grey-white rind. Matured for six months. Well developed flavour, nutty with a hint of sweetness.

Staffordshire Organic 🐄 🌙 ⊡ 9kg (20lb) ✿ Ⓓ

Traditionally made, muslin-bound unpasteurized farmhouse cheese of the Cheddar type, although quicker maturing. It is sold at various stages, from mild (eight to ten weeks) to fully mature (six months). Also with mixed herbs and garlic, fresh chives or smoked.

Sussex Slipcote 🐑 🌙 ⊖ 125g (4oz) ✿ Ⓓ

Light, moist, soft rindless cheese made to a recipe dating back to Shakespeare's time. Made from raw milk and sold in small wooden boxes. Plain, with herbs and garlic or crushed peppercorns.

Swaledale 🍶 45% ⊟ 450g and 2.7kg (1 and 6lb) 🐄 Ⓑ
Moist creamy white mild cheese made in Swaledale itself. Matured for three to four weeks, it is at its best in late spring, but is good throughout the year. Like Wensleydale it was once a blue ewes' milk cheese. A ewes' milk Swaledale is now being made again.

Tewkesbury 🕮 🌙 ⊟ 450g-11kg (1-24lb) 🐄 Ⓓ
Made on a Gloucestershire farm from unpasteurized milk, this is a pressed cooked cheese with a full flavour and annatto-coloured paste. Large cheeses mature for at least six months, smaller ones for two.

Ticklemore
Semihard goats' milk cheese from the maker of Beenleigh Blue in Devon. Lightly scalded curds are hand moulded into a 2kg (4lb) basket and turned twice a week for two to three months—the finished cheeses have a natural rind showing the lines of the basket

Tornegus 🕮 🍶 50% ⊟ 2kg (4lb) 🐄 Ⓓ
Made in Somerset as unpasteurized Caerphilly, then transferred to Surrey, where it is washed with Kentish wine. After six weeks, it has an orange rind and a springy texture, softer around the edges. Strong flavoured, fruity to begin with, becoming more pungent.

Torville 🕮 🌙 48% ⊟ 3.5-4kg (8-9lb) 🐄 Ⓓ
The Ducketts of Walnut Tree Farm, Somerset, began by making traditional unpasteurized Caerphilly (which they still make). Torville starts life as Caerphilly, then is pressed, washed and finished with cider and matured for four to six weeks. Fruity and flavoursome pale cheese inside a golden brown rind. See *Wales (Caerphilly)*

Tymsboro' 🐐 🌛 225-300g (8-10oz) 🐄 Ⓓ
Medium fat unpasteurized cheese made as a truncated pyramid. White mould ripened for two to three weeks with blue-grey speckles or sometimes ash-coated. Creamy under the rind, with a taste that has been described as lemony and almondy.

Tynedale Spa 🕮 🌙 ⊟ 450g-2.3kg (1-5lb) 🐄 Ⓓ
Pale primrose yellow open-textured Dales cheese from Cumbria. Mild slightly acid yet buttery flavour. It is pressed, waxed after four to five days, then matured for four to six weeks. An unwaxed smoked version has an orange-brown rind. Sometimes sold as Alston, not to be confused with the goats' milk version. See *High Pennine*

Tyning 🐑 🌙 ⊟ 2 and 2.7kg (4 and 6lb) 🐄 Ⓓ
Made on the same farm as Mendip and in a similar way—it shares the 'flying saucer' appearance with its bumpy grey rind. A very dense cheese; aged for six months it develops a full Pecorino-like flavour.

Velde 🐐 🍶 125g (4oz) 🐄 Ⓓ
Mould-ripened flattened ash pyramid from the Gedi herd in north London. At three weeks it becomes beautifully creamy inside.

Vulscombe 🐐 🍶 40% ⊟ 180g (6oz) 🐄 Ⓓ
Rich, smooth and creamy acid-curd cheese which is surprisingly robust as it is pressed for 24 hours, resulting in a texture rather like White Stilton. Matured for one to three weeks. Available plain, with fresh herbs, or crushed peppercorns and garlic.

Wackley
Unpasteurized Coulommiers-style ewes' milk cheese from a Shropshire farm. Made in various sizes and herb flavours.

Walda 🐾 ➊ ⊟ 1-3kg (2-7lb) Ⓓ

Unpasteurized Gouda type, matured for a minimum of 90 days. It develops a fuller flavour as it ages, and after two to three years takes on some of the characteristics of Parmesan, becoming hard and good for grating. Available flavoured with green peppercorns or caraway.

Wealden Round 🐄 ➋ 15% ⊟ 180-225g (6-8oz) 🌿 Ⓓ

Soft moist fresh cheese in a variety of herb flavours. The curds are hand moulded in layers with spring onions, chives, parsley and garlic or black pepper and garlic.

Wedmore 🐄 ➊ 48% ⊟ 2-2.3kg (4-5lb) 🌿 Ⓓ

Wedmore is a small Somerset Caerphilly with a layer of fresh chives in the middle. Lightly pressed with a natural rind, both the cheese and the chives strengthen in flavour as the cheese matures.

Weekender 🐾 ➋ ⊟ 125g (4oz) 🌿 Ⓓ

Fresh cheese from the Severn Valley, available plain, with chives, lemon pepper or garlic and parsley.

Wellington 🐄 ➊ 55% ⊟ 1-4.5kg (2-10lb) 🌿 Ⓑ

Unpasteurized milk from the Duke of Wellington's herd of Guernsey cattle goes into this pressed cheese with a natural grey rind. Made in a nearby village, and matured for six months. Deep golden, close-textured, with a delicately sweet flavour and fruity aroma.

Wensleydale ★ 🐄 ➊ 48% ⊟ 4-6kg (9-13lb) Ⓒ

Until the 1920s, Wensleydale meant the blue-veined cheese we now know as Blue Wensleydale. Now, however, the white unveined version is much more common and is what you will get if you ask for Wensleydale. It is a lightly pressed, smooth-textured cheese with a subtle, milky flavour which is clean and refreshing. Generally eaten young, at about a month old. It is not a cheese that improves with age, though a prize specimen may be matured for a few months longer. The original Wensleydale was a ewes' milk, soft, blue-veined cheese which must have been somewhat similar to Roquefort. This and other cheeses, such as Swaledale, Cotherstone and Coverdale were introduced into England by monastic orders who settled in the Yorkshire Dales after the Norman conquest in 1066. After the Dissolution of the Monasteries in the 16th century, production moved to farmhouses and later to small dairies and the cheeses began to be made from cows' milk. Ashes Farm and Shepherds Purse Cheeses in North Yorkshire are now making ewes' milk Wensleydale, and the Redesdale Dairy in Northumberland makes a cloth-wrapped mixed cows' and ewes' milk version with considerable body. See *Blue Wensleydale*

Westmorland see *Cheddar*

Whitby Jet 🐾 ➋ ⊟ 4kg (9lb) Ⓓ

Firm, nutty, ivory-coloured cheese coated in black wax after maturing in cloth wraps for five months. This ewes' milk cheese is made from March to October; during winter months the Yorkshire farm switches production to the cows' milk Endeavour.

White Stilton 🐄 ➊ 48% ⊟ 6.5kg (14lb) Ⓒ

Bland, close-textured white cheese made in the same way as Blue Stilton except that *Penicillium roquefortii* is not added to the milk and the cheese is sold at about eight weeks old. If left, a White Stilton will blue naturally and this produces a slightly milder flavour than the 'normal' blue. One dairy makes an unusual variation—chopped dried apricots are mixed with the curd. See *Blue Stilton*

Wiltshire White 🐄 🍃 ⊖ 110g (3¾oz) ❦ ©
Organic unrinded smooth mild cheese; plain or with fresh chives.

Windsor Red, Woodley see *Cheddar*

Worcester Sauce Cheese 🍃 ● 45% ⊖ 400g and 3kg (14oz and 7lb) ⑩
Distinctive dark marbled cheese made by adding Lea and Perrins Worcestershire Sauce to the milled curds before they are moulded. Although vegetarian rennet is used, the cheese cannot claim to be wholly vegetarian because there are anchovies in the sauce.

Worcester White 🍃 ● 45% ⊖ 400g and 2.5kg (14oz and 5½lb) ❦ ⑩
Pressed farmhouse cheese with a buttery flavour and distinctive 'bite'. Matured for four to five months, it has a dry pale brown rind.

IRELAND

The lush pastures of Ireland are ideal for dairy cattle, and its moist climate and mineral-rich soil gives the milk a unique character. Cheese production has increased hundreds of times over since the beginning of this century, yet the Irish are not traditionally great cheese eaters, and much of the cheese is exported. Block Cheddar accounts for a high proportion of production, along with creamery copies of Double Gloucester (known as Tipperary), Leicester (Munster), mature Cheddar (Wexford, Old Charleville), Gouda (Aherlow) and even imitation Parmesan (Regato) which is exported to the Mediterranean. However, a host of newcomers demonstrate dedication to the revival of traditional cheesemaking. Many of them have already found a place in good cheese shops throughout Europe.

Aran 🍃 ● 20% ⊖ 4kg (9lb) ©
Reduced fat pasteurized Cheddar matured for three to four months.

Ardrahan 🍃 🍃 ⊖ 1 and 4kg (2 and 9lb) ⑧
Described by its makers as somewhere between a French Tomme and Danish Havarti, the similarity to Havarti becoming more pronounced (along with the flavour) as it matures (two to three months). Lightly pressed, brine-washed rind and a creamy white paste with many small holes. Unpasteurized; hand-made in Co. Cork.

Ballyneety see *Knockanour*

Bay Lough 🍃 ● ⊖ 450g-5.5kg (1-12lb) ©
Named after the lake at the foot of the Knockmealdown mountains in Co. Tipperary, where the cheese is made. Unpasteurized milk is lightly skimmed, cooked and pressed, then waxed. The resulting cheese has some of the characteristics of Cheshire and Derby. Ripened for three months, it has a full flavour which develops further up to eight or ten months. Generally the best cheeses are made in the cooler winter months, although a cool summer makes for truly excellent cheese. Available plain, or with garlic and herbs.

Blarney 🍃 🍃 48-53% ⊖ 5kg (11lb) ©
Factory-made, pale, waxy cheese with small holes and red waxed rind. Mild, sweet and nutty.

Cais Cleire 🌢 🍃 ⊖ 250-400g (9-14oz) ⑩
Smooth and soft with a clean, acid taste, an unpressed moulded cheese. Eaten very fresh (within a week). Not sold in January and

February, when the goats are dry. The name means Cape Clear, the island where the cheese is made, Ireland's southernmost point.

Caora
Semihard Cheshire-style ewes' milk cheese (*caora* means sheep in Gaelic) with a nutty, slightly tart flavour. Farm-made in Co. Down.

Carna 🌱 🌢 45-50% ⊖ 4kg (9lb) ©
Pasteurized Wensleydale type, matured for eight to ten weeks.

Carrigaline 🌱 🌢 ⊖ 400g and 2kg (14oz and 4lb) ©
Gouda type, coated with yellow wax. Unpasteurized; ripened for six to eight weeks. Mild flavour, becoming more piquant. Also made with garlic and herbs. Named after the place it is made, in Co. Cork.

Cashel Blue ★ 🌱 🌢 54% ⊖ 1.5kg (3lb) 🌣 Ⓑ
Ireland's most famous blue cheese is made in Co. Tipperary. Some is made with vegetarian rennet, and most is now pasteurized. The apricot-tinged paste is lightly scattered with blue-grey veining, and the cheeses are foil-wrapped. Cashel Blue has a melt-in-the-mouth creaminess and is less salty than Roquefort, although the flavour strengthens with age. It ripens for about two months, and as the best cheese is made when the cows are at pasture (April to October), try it from June to December.

Chetwynd Blue 🌱 🌢 51% ⊖ 2.3kg (5lb) Ⓑ
Slightly stronger than Cashel Blue, this creamy white cheese has distinct blue veining. Foil-wrapped after about six weeks; continues to mature up to three months. Made near Cork. Pasteurized.

Claddagh 🌱 🌢 45-50% ⊖ 4kg (9lb) ©
Annatto-coloured Leicester-type cheese from Co. Galway. Made on the farm from pasteurized milk and matured for three to four months.

Coolea 🌱 🌢 ⊖ 450g-4.5kg (1-10lb) Ⓑ
Unpasteurized, mild, creamy-tasting cheese, made to a Gouda recipe on a farm in Co. Cork. Sold young (four to eight weeks) either plain or with herbs and garlic, or matured for up to a year (only summer milk cheeses are matured).

Cooleeney 🌱 🌢 45-50% ⊖ 200g and 1.7kg (7oz and 3½lb) Ⓑ
Cooleeney farmhouse Camemberts from Co. Tipperary are hand-made from unpasteurized milk. Small cheeses ripen in six weeks and have a semi-liquid interior and pronounced flavour; large Cooleeneys take 12 weeks to mature, but have a milder, creamy taste.

Corleggy 🌢 🌢 ⊖ 350g and 1kg (12oz and 2lb) 🌣 Ⓑ
Organically produced in Co. Cavan from raw milk and vegetarian rennet. Based on a Gouda recipe, this is a washed curd cheese, pressed for 12 hours and matured for two to three months. Made from mid-February to November. Mildly goaty flavour; Cheddar-like texture.

Corrib 🌱 🌢 45-50% ⊖ 4kg (9lb) ©
Double Gloucester-type cheese made on the same Galway farm as Aran, Carna and Claddagh. Matured for three to four months.

Cratloe Hills ★ 🌢 🌢 2kg (4lb) ©
Unique in appearance: shaped in moulds in the form of a Celtic cross, and finished with clear wax. Although not veined, it has a crumbly, Roquefort-like texture. Pasteurized. Ripened for up to six months. From Co. Clare.

Crimlin ♘ ➌ 40-48% ⊖ 500g and 1kg (18oz and 2lb) Ⓓ

Unpressed, washed rind cheese coated in yellow wax, developed from a Tilsiter recipe by its makers in Co. Sligo. Unpasteurized milk is used, and the cheese is made only from summer to late autumn. Ripened for four to six weeks.

Croghan ◀ ➌ 50-52% ⊖ 1.5kg (3lb) Ⓑ

Lightly cooked and pressed cheese with a high moisture content, ripened for one to two months and smeared with a bacterial culture towards the end of ripening. Made all year round in Co. Wexford, the cheese made from rich autumn milk is particularly runny and Brie-like.

Cushlee ♘ ⟋ 46% ⊖ 1.7kg (3½lb) Ⓑ

Creamery-made washed rind cheese. Pale, smooth paste with irregular small holes, distinctive aroma and full flavour.

Derreentra ♘ ➋ 100g and 200g (3½oz and 7oz) ♚ Ⓓ

Low-fat acid-curd cheese made in Co. Cork to an old Polish recipe, from pasteurized skimmed milk. Firm but smooth, sold in tubs.

Desmond ★ ♘ ➌ 29% ⊖ 3-4kg (7-9lb) ♚ Ⓑ

Bill Hogan, who makes this cheese in West Cork, learned his craft in Switzerland. The curds are scalded at a high temperature as in Gruyère or Emmental, which makes a long-lived cheese—these are ripened for a minimum of four months, up to a year. After light brining, the cheeses are intensively smeared with yeasts and bacteria. Natural, whitish crusty rind; deep cream-coloured close-textured paste; piquant flavour; a very digestible cheese. Made from May to October from raw milk. Some is made with vegetarian rennet.

Dunmore ♘ ➌ 46% ⊖ 2kg (4lb) Ⓒ

Yellow waxed creamery cheese with a creamy, open texture and a mild, aromatic flavour which enriches with age (about four months).

Durrus ♘ ⟋ ⊖ 350g and 1kg (12oz and 2lb) Ⓑ

Made from unpasteurized morning milk, brine-washed and turned for ten days, Durrus has a silky texture and is creamy and mild when young (three weeks), stronger and more like a French Tomme when older (three months). Autumn cheeses are richest. From Co. Cork.

Gabriel ♘ ➌ 31% ⊖ 6kg (13lb) ♚ Ⓑ

Made on the same farm as Desmond, using unpasteurized milk (and sometimes vegetarian rennet). Rock-hard cheese which nevertheless melts in the mouth, with a few small holes, a deep, fruity flavour and mellow aftertaste. After pressing, the cheeses are lightly smeared with a bacterial culture to give a thin, speckled golden natural crust. Made from May to October, matured for many months, up to a year.

Gigginstown ♘ ➌ ☐ 2 and 3.5kg (4 and 8lb) Ⓑ

Naturally rinded, full-flavoured Cheddar type made from unpasteurized milk in Co. Westmeath. Matured six months to a year.

Glen O Sheen ♘ ➌ ☐ 3.5-14kg (8-30lb) Ⓓ

Traditionally made, unpasteurized Cheddar from Co. Limerick. Matured for four to six months. Available plain or coloured.

Gubbeen ★ ♘ ⟋ 48% ◯ 500g and 1kg (18oz and 2lb) ♚ Ⓑ

A washed rind like a wrinkled peach covers a pale yellow, springy paste with a delicious flavour which varies with the seasons. In spring it is creamy and buttery, in summer quite nutty and sometimes rather savoury. Winter cheeses have a firmer texture. The curds are cut with

37

water to balance acidity, gently heated, then moulded and washed and turned in brine for eight hours. Ripened for two to three weeks near the southwest coast of Co. Cork. Pasteurized, sometimes made with vegetarian rennet. An oak-smoked version is also available: semi-hard, matured for three months and coated with wax.

Kerry Farmhouse ⚗ ➊ ⊝ 1-9kg (2-20lb) Ⓑ
Unpasteurized, partly skimmed milk cheese made to a Cheddar recipe on a farm in Co. Kerry. The mild version ripens for two months, mature cheeses for four months. Also available flavoured with nettles, chives, garlic or hazelnuts.

Kilshanny ⚗ ➊ ⊝ Ⓒ
Unpasteurized Gouda type from Co. Clare, matured for two months, and made from February to October. Plain or flavoured with garlic, herbs, pepper or cumin.

Knockanour ⚗ ⚗ ⊝ 2.7kg (6lb) Ⓑ
Unpasteurized hand-made cheese from Co. Waterford. Lightly cooked, clear-waxed and matured for eight to ten weeks, with a mild yet rounded flavour. Also sold oak-smoked. From the same maker, Ballyneety is a washed rind type, ripened for 15 weeks.

Lavistown ⚗ ➊ 51% ⊝ 1.5 and 3kg (3 and 7lb) Ⓒ
Unpasteurized Wensleydale type from Co. Kilkenny, moist and creamy when young, becoming crumbly and sharper after six to eight weeks. Cheeses bought in February, March and April undergo a dra-matic change of character, becoming soft and mushroomy.

Lough Caum ◢ ➊ ⊝ 350g and 2kg (12oz and 4lb) Ⓒ
Pressed, cooked cheese, matured for six to eight weeks, up to a year. Cheddar-like texture; older cheeses are stronger. From Co. Clare.

Milleens ★ ⚗ ⚗ 45% ⊝ 1.5kg (3lb) Ⓑ
Veronica Steele has been making Milleens to great acclaim since 1978 on her farm in Bantry, Co. Cork. An unpasteurized, surface-ripening cheese along the lines of Pont l'Evêque, the rind is brushed with brine every other day for ten days. Clean and acidic when young, it ideally ripens for eight to ten weeks. The perfectly ripe Milleens is translucent throughout (not liquefying) and has a pungent, slightly unclean odour and palate-burning tang. Best in winter months.

Porter Cheese ★ ⚗ ➊ 45-50% ⊝ 450g and 2.3kg (1 and 5lb) Ⓒ
St Patrick's Day or any other celebration is a good reason to buy this striking, brown-marbled Cheddar. The drained whey is replaced with dark porter beer before the curds are finally pressed. The porter and cheese mature together for six months in a brown wax coating. The maker, Davy Cahill of Co. Limerick, applies the same technique to his whiskey cheese (yellow wax) and Ardagh (red wine and red wax), and also makes Ballyporeen (with herbs) and Ballintubber (chives).

Rathgore Blue ◢ ⚗ 45% ⊝ 2.7kg (6lb) ✿ Ⓑ
Made on a dairy in Northern Ireland, milk from local farms is pasteur-ized, coagulated with vegetarian rennet and matured, unpressed, for three months. Velvety smooth, white with blue-green veins.

Ring ⚗ ➊ 48% ⊝ 3.5kg (8lb) Ⓑ
Naturally rinded, deep golden cheese which cuts like Gouda and tastes like a mild yet nutty Cheddar. Matured six months. Made from unpasteurized milk on a farm in Co. Waterford.

Round Tower 🍶 🌓 ⊖ 1-14kg (2-31lb) Ⓓ

Unpasteurized Gouda type made from the milk of a herd in Co. Cork. Cooked, pressed and coated by hand with a natural wax. The youngest cheeses are two months old; very mature ones over a year. Two flavoured versions are made—red pepper and garlic, and herb.

Ryefield 🍶 🌓 45% ⊖ 300g and 5kg (10oz and 11lb) Ⓒ

Raw milk Cheddar type from Co. Cavan, matured for six months and coated with black wax after three. Made by traditional methods.

St Brendan 🍶 🌓 56% ⊖ 1.3 and 2.7kg (2½ and 6lb) Ⓑ

Hand-made Brie from the milk of one herd. Although pasteurized, it has more flavour than factory Brie.

St Killian 🍶 🌓 45-50% 250g (9oz) Ⓑ

Hexagonal Camembert type from Carrigbyrne in Co. Wexford (same farm as St Brendan). Mushrooms and cream taste.

St Martin 🍶 🌓 ⊖ 450g-2kg (1-4lb) Ⓓ

Unpasteurized Gouda type which can be eaten young (four to six weeks) or mature and strong (up to a year). From Co. Clare.

St Tola

Soft log—7.5cm (3in) diameter— of goats' cheese made in Co. Clare (along with Lough Caum) from raw milk. Sold fresh and will mature up to four weeks, becoming firmer and more crumbly.

Shannon 🍶 🌓 48-53% ⊖ 5kg (11lb) Ⓒ

Oak-smoked cheese, creamery-made from pasteurized milk. Smooth, ivory-coloured with a yellow rind. Sweet, creamy with a smoky tang.

Skellig 🍶 🌓 50% ⊖ 1.5kg (3lb) Ⓑ

A washed rind cheese with an orange-red skin which, like Gubbeen, is sold when dry to the touch. The paste is tenderly soft, creamy coloured and fairly mild. Creamery-made from pasteurized milk.

Tara 🍶 🌓 18% ○ 450g and 2kg (1 and 4lb) Ⓒ

Low-fat, low-salt red-waxed Edam type with a mild, light, creamy texture. Hand-made from unpasteurized skimmed milk, the curds are gently cooked and very lightly pressed. Sold young, after four to five weeks ripening. Also available with mixed herbs. From Co. Louth.

SCOTLAND

Scotland has had no great reputation for cheese. Its most important indigenous cheese, Dunlop, takes second place in terms of production and in Scottish affections to Cheddar (dyed with annatto for the Scottish market). Scotland also has the dubious distinction of being the first country to introduce rindless cheese (in 1955) and the 1960s and 70s saw the disappearance of many traditional cheeses in favour of commercially successful rindless blocks. Historical records exist of locally made cheeses (now extinct), among them Island of Coll and Blue Highland (said by some to be 'finer than Stilton'); there was also a much-praised ewes' milk cheese known as Crying-kebbuck which was traditionally eaten to celebrate the birth of a new baby. More recently, however, there has been an awakening of interest in good cheeses both from consumers and producers. Some of this has centred on reviving old cheeses like Caboc and Crowdie, some on Scottish variants of Brie and Camembert (notably at the Howgate dairy in Midlothian, and sometimes known as Lothian and Pentland), but there have also been enterprising inventions.

Arran see *Dunlop*

Ballindalloch ⚜ ❱ 49% ▢ 2.3-2.7kg (5-6lb) ☘ ©

Goats grazing on heather-covered hills above the river Spey are
milked to make this cheese all year round. Plant rennet is added to
unpasteurized milk and the pressed cheeses have a brine-washed
rind. Sold mild (creamy white, about one month old) or mature (deep
creamy colour, full flavoured, at least three months old). Also available with caraway seeds or green peppercorns.

Bonchester ★ ⚙ ❱ 44% ▭ 100g and 300g (3½ and 10oz) ☘ Ⓑ

Coulommiers-style cheese, made from March to December at a farm
in the Borders, with unpasteurized Jersey milk. Small Bonchesters are
made with vegetable rennet. White moulds with light brown flecks
coat the surface of the cheese, which ripens over four to five weeks,
becoming deep yellow with a pronounced flavour, best in early summer. Belle d'Ecosse and Teviotdale are made in the winter by putting
together two or four of the larger Bonchesters. Belle d'Ecosse is a
lightly pressed cheese which, like Bonchester, softens as it ripens,
over about six weeks. Teviotdale (four Bonchesters) is a hard cheese,
although it shares the natural white crust. Ripening over two to three
months, it may soften slightly, but will never become runny.

Bonnet ⚜ ❱ ▭ 2kg (4lb) ☘ ©

Fairly mild, moist cheese made from pasteurized milk, scalded and
pressed overnight, then vacuum packed. From an Ayrshire dairy.

Caboc ★ ⚙ ❱ 67% ▭ 100g (3½oz) ☘ ©

Scotland's oldest recorded cheese, known in the 15th century as
chieftain's cheese, was revived from an ancestral recipe in the 1960s
by Susannah Stone in the Ross-shire Highlands. Made without rennet, from pasteurized double cream, it should be eaten very fresh
(within a week). Primrose yellow cheese rolled in toasted pinhead
oatmeal and packed in Black Watch tartan boxes. Smooth as butter,
rich and creamy, with a nutty taste from the oatmeal.

Clava ⚘ ❱ 39% ▭ 5kg (11lb) Ⓓ

Made in the Nairnshire valley in the Highlands, Clava is based on a
crofter's recipe, but is increasingly made in blocks, and even the
wheels (rindless) are matured in vacuum packs. Matured for at least
five months. Mild flavoured, with stronger undertones.

Creag Mhaol

The West Highland Dairy keeps its own flock of ewes, but also uses
the milk of local goats and bought-in cows' milk to make three versions of Creag Mhaol, a semihard cheese with a mild flavour and
smooth, creamy texture, coated in black wax. Cows' and goats' milk
cheeses mature in six to eight weeks; the ewes' milk version is slower
maturing, taking eight to twelve weeks. All pasteurized.

Crowdie

This ancient soft cheese, unique to crofters in the Highlands and
Islands, was originally made with milk left after the cream had been
skimmed off for butter making. Skimming was not the scientific process it is today, so a little cream was always left. Today it is made by
starting cows' milk with natural lactic bacteria (which gives a slightly
lemony taste) and returning a little fresh cream to the skimmed milk.
Moist, crumbly and slightly grainy; eat as fresh as possible. Sometimes flavoured with wild garlic. Crowdie and Cream is made by
adding one part double cream to two parts Crowdie, and Gruth Dhu is
Crowdie and Cream rolled in oatmeal and crushed peppercorns.

Dunlop 🖤 ➤ 48% 🗇 27kg (59lb)

Often described as Scottish Cheddar, which it closely resembles except that it is softer textured and lacks the characteristic Cheddar 'bite'. Naturally pale, it is often coloured deep orange with annatto. As with many famous cheeses, a woman is credited with its invention. In this case it was Barbara Gilmour, who is said to have brought the recipe from Ireland at the time of Charles II. The name derives from the village in Ayrshire where it was first made. It was also the name of the Ayrshire cows that originally provided the milk and, by a happy coincidence, the name of Barbara Gilmour's subsequent husband.

Dunlop is now mostly creamery-made and vacuum packed in blocks. The Arran creamery makes coloured Dunlop in 1kg (2lb) drums, and Islay creamery produces 500g (1lb) rounds. Gowrie is made in the traditional way, from unpasteurized milk, cloth-wrapped in 6kg (13lb) truckles and matured for seven to nine months.

Dunsyre Blue ★ 🖤 ➤ 52% 🖨 3kg (7lb) 💠 Ⓑ

From the same farm as Lanark Blue, Dunsyre is made with vegetarian rennet and unpasteurized milk from a herd of Ayrshire cows. The cheese is mould-ripened and matured for about three months, with a close, creamy texture and delicious piquancy from the blue veins.

Ettrick 🖤 ➤ 45% 🗇 400g and 1.7kg (14oz and 3½lb) 💠 Ⓒ

A traditional cheese from the Borders, formerly known as Smallholder, now made with pasteurized milk. Lightly cooked and pressed in the Cheshire style, the cheeses are sold at three to five months old, and improve up to about nine months. Sold with a red wax coat, or coloured and black waxed. A new development is a mould-ripened cheese which matures more quickly. Firmer, drier and stronger tasting, it is ready after six weeks, and excellent at four months.

Gobhar ✦ 🖎 🖨 125 and 225g (4 and 8oz) 💠 Ⓒ

Made on the same farm as Ballindalloch, from unpasteurized milk and plant rennet. The mould-ripened cheeses look like Camemberts and taste similar to French Chèvres, although not generally as strong. Can be eaten fresh or aged up to four weeks, when they become softer, deeper in colour and stronger-tasting. Made all year; best in spring.

Gowrie see *Dunlop*

Hramsa

Unrenneted full-fat soft cows' milk cheese flavoured with fresh wild garlic leaves, sold in tartan tubs. Galic is a variation, rolled in flaked hazelnuts and chopped almonds and sold as a 100g (3½ oz) log.

Inverloch ✦ ➤ 2.5kg (5½lb) 💠 Ⓓ

Full-flavoured (but not goaty) pasteurized Cheddar-type cheese, coated in red wax and farm-produced on the Isle of Gigha. The cheeses mature for at least three to four months (and up to a year).

Islay see *Dunlop*

Isle of Mull ★ 🖤 ➤ 48% 🗇 25kg (55lb) Ⓑ

The only dairy on the Isle of Mull makes a totally traditional unpasteurized Cheddar (sometimes known as Tobermory) from its herd of 100 cows. The island's moist climate means that grass and herbs grow vigorously in spring, when the cows go out and most cheese is made. The clothbound cheese is never sold at less than eight months old.

Kelsae ★ 🖤 ➤ 🗇 1.3-6kg (2½-13lb) Ⓒ

Made near Kelso in the Scottish Borders. Unpasteurized milk from the Stichill herd of Jersey cows is started with yoghurt, pressed and matured for at least two months. Similar to Wensleydale, but much creamier in both texture and taste.

Lanark Blue ★ 🍤 🌙 52% ⊖ 3kg (7lb) ✿ Ⓑ

Hand-made on a farm in Lanarkshire from unpasteurized milk and vegetarian rennet. Mould-ripened, with creamy white paste and blue-green veins, the cheese has been favourably compared to Roquefort, and some people have detected a subtle smoky aftertaste.

Langskaill ✿ 🌙 45% ⊖ 400g (14oz) ✿ Ⓓ

Small, flat cheese coated in dark red wax. Made to a Gouda recipe with some of the characteristics of Port-Salut: milky mild at first, ageing after two to three months to a buttery tang.

Lochaber ★ ✿ 🌙 47% Ⓓ

Smoked full-fat creamy cheese from a West Highland smokehouse. It is made in a 125g (4oz) block and a 225g (8oz) wheel, both rolled in oatmeal. Softer than Caboc yet firmer than Italian Mascarpone.

Mull of Kintyre ✿ 🌙 48% ⊖ 500g (18oz) ©

Coloured Scottish Cheddar coated in black wax, 10 months old.

Orkney

Scottish Cheddar made in the Orkney Islands, mostly vacuum packed in creameries. Available plain, coloured with annatto or smoked. The earliest Orkney cheese was well known in Scotland before Dunlop; it was a hard cheese made from skimmed milk, often kept in barrels of oatmeal to prevent its drying out, which added to the flavour. In 1812, two Ayrshire dairywomen introduced their methods to the islands, from which developed the traditional Orkney cheese. Mrs Jean Wallace, who until recently made cheese herself, described Orkney cheese as pressed, 2-3lb cheeses not unlike Wensleydale. Some farmers still make them, but they're seldom sold outside the Islands.

St Finan's

The name is given to a range of unpasteurised ewes' milk cheeses made with vegetarian rennet. The full-fat, uncooked, hard cheeses are pressed slowly over four days in traditional Aberdeenshire granite presses in 3.5kg (8lb) wheels. The plain version is matured for at least three months. Banchory Black is flavoured with peppercorns and coated with black wax. St Finan's Caraway is made to a local recipe and waxed clear. Both mature for a month. The unripened medium-fat soft cheeses, 180g (6oz) wheels, are lightly pressed, giving a creamy, crumbly texture. Available plain or flavoured with herbs, garlic, apricot or cracked peppercorns. Sold widely in Scotland.

Sanday Island 🐟 🌙 40% ⊖ 450g-2.3kg (1-5lb) ✿ Ⓓ

Cheddar-type cheese, usually made with raw milk. It may be eaten at almost any stage, from pale youth to amber-coloured maturity at two to three months, as recommended by its Orkney maker. Though milder when young, at all stages it has a fresh, strong tang.

Stichill ✿ 🌙 ⊖ 1.3-6kg (2½-13lb) ©

Hand-made cheese from the Scottish Borders, made from whole, unpasteurized, creamy Jersey milk. Cheshire-style, matured for a minimum of four months and even better at around 10 months.

Strathrorie

Excellent but rare. From Tain in the Highlands. A hard cheese made in 2-3.5kg (4-8lb) Manchego moulds from mixed raw cows', ewes' and goats' milk with vegetarian rennet. Matured for at least two months. If made from pure goats' milk the cheese is called Strathrusdale.

Swinzie 🦃 🌙 ⊖ 2kg (4lb) ✿ ©
Pale yellow, moist cheese rather like mild Cheddar. Pasteurized. Scalded and pressed overnight, then vacuum packed as rindless rounds.

Teviotdale see *Bonchester*

Tobermory see *Isle of Mull*

WALES

There are several tantalizing historical references to Welsh cheeses. At one time there was a spring-made Newport cheese— thick, creamy and square-moulded, Glamorgan cheese was made from the milk of a special breed of white cattle; a mixed cows' and goats' milk cheese, made in North Wales, once competed with Cheshire. The only traditional cheese of Welsh origin remaining is Caerphilly and even this is often made outside Wales.

Acorn ★ 🦃 🌙 52% ⊖ 2-2.3kg (4-5lb) ✿ Ⓓ
Moist, slightly crumbly raw milk cheese with a delicate flavour and long aftertaste. Mould-ripened and matured for 10 weeks, when the mould is scrubbed off. Made on a farm in Bethania, Dyfed. Best at three to four months old. The pasture is richest in herbs during May and June, so look for cheeses in September and October. This cheese sometimes 'blues' naturally on storage—an interesting variation.

Antyphebi see *Caws Cenarth*

Cadern 🐄 🌙 ⊖ 125g and 2kg (4oz and 4lb) ✿ Ⓓ
Felin Gernos in Dyfed is best known for Caerphilly, but the farm also makes a traditional Cheddar which is oiled, cloth wrapped and matured for six months to a year. Some of the mature cheese is milled together with port and peppercorns to make Cadern, meaning 'strong'. Caethwas is Cheddar milled with garlic, wine and parsley.

Caerphilly ★ 🐄 🌙 48% ⊖ 3-4kg (7-9lb) ©
Moist, crumbly, lemon yellow cheese with a salty, slightly sour butter-milk flavour, Caerphilly dates back only to the early 1800s. It was originally made in dairy farms throughout the Vale of Glamorgan and in the western part of Gwent, from the milk of Hereford cattle. For years it was known in Wales simply as 'new cheese' and most of it was consumed locally both because relatively little was made and also because it did not travel well. Two batches were made daily, one from morning milk and one from evening milk, throughout the summer months. They were ready for sale within a week to ten days. This fac-tor made them a tempting proposition for the Cheddar-makers on the other side of the Bristol Channel. Caerphilly could provide a quick turnover during the long months of waiting for Cheddars to mature and by the beginning of this century it was being made in large quan-tities in Somerset. In World War II the making of Caerphilly was banned completely and Welsh cheesemakers are just begininning to recover from this blow. Caws Cenarth and Maesllyn, from Dyfed farms, are both made traditionally, from unpasteurized milk (and veg-etarian rennet), and can be found in good cheese shops throughout Britain. Walnut Tree Farm and the Times Past dairy (both in Somer-set) also make unpasteurized Caerphilly.

The cheese is rapidly drained and lightly pressed. Its rind is formed by soaking the cheese in brine for 24 hours after pressing and then dried and whitened with rice flour. Caerphilly is traditionally eaten very young—a few days after making. The new makers often keep it longer: its character changes completely if it is kept for 12 weeks.

Caethwas see *Cadern*

Caws Cenarth

Caws simply means 'cheese', but in this instance describes a Caerphilly made on a Dyfed farm. Traditionally made, but ripened for three to four weeks for a fuller flavour. It is then washed and given the traditional rice flour coating. A coffee-flavoured version, and one with curry and herbs (known as Antyphebi) are also made.

Cwmbach ✹ ☾ ⊖ 450g and 2kg (1 and 4lb) ✿ D

Deeper creamy white than most goats' milk cheeses, and given a thin yellow plastic cheese coating to improve keeping. Made to a Gouda recipe from unpasteurized milk, the small cheeses ripen for two weeks, larger ones for six weeks. All are quite mild.

Llanboidy ★ ♨ ☽ ⊖ 4.5kg (10lb) Ⓑ

Hand-made from the unpasteurized milk of a rare breed of cow, the Red Poll, on a farm in Dyfed. Pressed cheese with a very pale, dense paste and a creamier texture than Cheddar. It ripens for ten weeks on the farm, and continues to mature up to eight or nine months. Also available flavoured with freshly cooked laverbread (a type of seaweed).

Llangloffan ♨ ☽ 60% ⊖ 2-16kg (4-35lb) ✿ Ⓑ

Pale yellow with a firm, creamy yet unusual, rather flaky texture. Made from organic, unpasteurized Jersey milk on a farm in Dyfed. Natural rind. Sold mild (about eight weeks ripening), mature (four months or longer), or flavoured with chives and garlic.

Maesllyn

Traditional quick-ripening, moist, creamy Caerphilly, which forms a natural rind and is not rubbed with rice flour. Sometimes known as Felin Gernos Caerphilly, after the farm on which it is made.

Merlin ★ ✹ ☽ 54% ⊖ 200g and 1kg (7oz and 2lb) ✿ Ⓒ

Full-flavoured cheese made to a traditional Cheddar recipe, using raw milk from a herd in Dyfed. Six varieties (mild, mature, with walnuts, garlic and chives, olives, and two-year-old vintage olive) are waxed in different colours, and there is an unwaxed oak-smoked version.

Pant-ys-gawn ✹ ☾ 57% ⊂ 100g and 500g (4 and 18 oz) ✿ Ⓑ

Mild fresh cheese made in the Brecon Beacons National Park, Powys, from pasteurized milk. Natural or flavoured with herbs, black pepper, garlic and chives or citrus pepper.

Penbryn ♨ ☽ ⊖ 1 and 3kg (2 and 7lb) ✿ Ⓑ

Full-flavoured organic Gouda-style cheese, matured for two months, with a natural rind. Made with raw milk from a farm in Dyfed.

Pencarreg ★ ♨ ☾ 58% ⊖ 200g and 2kg (7oz and 4lb) ✿ Ⓒ

Organic (pasteurized) white mould-ripened Brie-like cheese with a unique and complex flavour. It is especially attractive in summer, with a deep golden paste. Ripened between two and six weeks.

Pen-y-Bont ★ ✹ ☽ ⊖ 2-2.3kg (4-5lb) ✿ Ⓑ

A traditional Wensleydale recipe made with raw milk from organic pastures. In winter the cheese is higher in fat, milder and moister. It has a natural grey rind and creamy white smooth paste. Matured for a minimum of three weeks, when it is quite mild, becoming richer as it ages, up to two months. Made near Carmarthen.

Saint David's 🍂 🐄 56% ⊖ 2.5kg (5½lb) 🌱 Ⓑ

Buttery-textured, washed rind cheese with a creamy flavour and delicate tang. Made on a farm in Dyfed, from pasteurized milk.

St Illtyd 🍂 🌓 53% ⊖ 100g and 5kg (3½oz and 11lb) 🌱 Ⓑ

Mature Welsh Cheddar milled with white wine, garlic and herbs to make a strong cheese with plenty of bite. Pale smooth paste speckled with herbs. Large cheeses are coated in black wax, while the small unwaxed version is wrapped in muslin. Made from pasteurized milk in the Brecon Beacons National Park, Powys.

St Ishmael 🍂 🌓 ⊖ 3kg (7lb) 🌱 Ⓓ

A traditional Macsllyn Caerphilly, except that laverbread (cooked Welsh seaweed) is added to the curds before pressing, giving a speckled, pale, slightly salty moist cheese. Coated with clear wax.

St Tyssul 🍂 🌓 ⊖ 400g and 3kg (14oz and 7lb) 🌱 Ⓓ

Another Maesllyn Caerphilly, gently smoked over cherrywood.

Senlac 🐐 🌓 50% ⊖ 2.3kg (5lb) 🌱 Ⓑ

Before David Blunn moved to Dyfed, he made cheese in Sussex, and named his cheese after the site of the Battle of Hastings—now sometimes labelled Caws Senlac. His goats graze on organic pasture and the milk is unpasteurized. Senlac is an uncooked pressed cheese which matures for two to four months. It has a natural rind, and a firm, creamy, non-goaty flavour. Made from March to December.

Skirrid ★ 🐐 🌓 51% ⊖ 2-2.3kg (4-5lb) 🌱 Ⓑ

From the same farm as Acorn. Lightly scalded pressed cheese which is marinated in mead for about 24 hours after pressing. It forms a natural rind and ripens for seven weeks, though it will keep for much longer. Firm and sliceable, with a clean, mild, distinctively nutty flavour. The best cheeses are found in September and October.

Teifi ★ 🍂 🌓 ⊖ 450g-9kg (1-20lb) 🌱 Ⓑ

A superb creamy, full-flavoured Gouda-style cheese from Dyfed. Scalded and lightly pressed, then bathed in brine, dried and turned every day until fully ripe (two weeks for the smallest cheeses, one year for the largest). Creamier and smoother in spring and summer. Made from raw milk, and available plain, or in several herb varieties.

Tudor 🐐 🌓 51% ⊖ 1.3kg (2½lb) 🌱 Ⓓ

Two varieties of Tudor are made on the Acorn farm: a moist, sliceable smoked cheese and a tangy horseradish version. Uncooked pressed cheeses finished in clear wax.

Tyn Grug 🍂 🌓 55% ⊖ 7 and 16kg (15 and 35lb) 🌱 Ⓓ

One of the earliest of the new wave of Welsh farmhouse cheeses, a nutty tasting cooked pressed cheese which is quicker maturing than Cheddar—six months is fine for Tyn Grug. Dougal Campbell learnt his craft in Switzerland and now runs an organic farm in mountainous central Wales. The cheese is normally available from summer to early spring. Made with unpasteurized milk and vegetarian rennet.

BULGARIA, CZECHOSLOVAKIA see *Eastern Europe*. CANADA see *North America and Canada*. CYPRUS see *Greece and Cyprus*. CHILE, COLOMBIA, COSTA RICA, CUBA see *Latin America*. DENMARK see *Scandinavia*.

Eastern Europe

Eastern Europe has been the battleground between Europe and Asia for centuries and political boundaries have been drawn and redrawn countless times. It is surprising, in these circumstances, to find that vigorous, identifiable, national gastronomic traditions have been able to develop and endure. Up to World War II, agriculture was the most important economic activity. Since then, the picture has changed several times. After the devastation of the war, postwar recovery emphasized industrial rather than agricultural development. Large-scale collectivization meant that small farms, except in remote mountain areas, all but disappeared and cheesemaking concentrated on mass market rather than traditional products. Cheddar, Tilsiter, Gouda, Emmental and many other popular European cheese types are mass-produced. Recent reforms (since 1989) have reversed years of state nationalization. Agriculture in Bulgaria, Hungary and Romania has been denationalized and small farms are once more making cheeses in the old way, particularly soft ewes' milk cheeses. In the north, traditional cheeses are generally related to German types such as Quark and the Handkäse varieties. There are also some interesting smoked cheeses not found elsewhere. In the south the Mediterranean influence is strong (a legacy of the Roman and Turkish occupations). Descendants of Caciocavallo and white brined ewes' milk cheeses are prevalent and some buffalo milk cheeses can still be found.

Balaton (Hungary) 🎋 ● 45% 🗇 9-12kg (20-26lb) ©
Firm, hard-pressed, golden cheese with irregular holes and a thin, rather greasy rind. The flavour is mildly acidulous. Ripened for five to six weeks. Named after Lake Balaton.

Balkanski Kâskaval (Bulgaria) see *Kashkaval*

Bijeni Sir (Yugoslavia) ● 35% 🗇 ⓓ
Sharp white cheese made from cows' or ewes' milk and ripened in brined whey. From Macedonia. Factory- and farm-made.

Brynza (Bulgaria), Brîndză (Romania), Bryndza (Hungary, Czechoslovakia, Poland) 🐑 ● 45% ⓑ
Salty white brined cheese made in many parts of eastern Europe, particularly in the Carpathian mountains, usually from ewes' milk but occasionally from cows' or goats' milk. Available in several versions ranging from soft and spreadable to firm and crumbly. Sometimes also smoked. It is made in factories from partially ripened curds supplied by mountain shepherds. The curds are scraped of any rind, broken up, salted, milled and remoulded in blocks or packed into wooden barrels with yet more salt. Eaten cubed in salads or with rye bread, it also features in local cooking and can be used as a base for Liptauer. See *Liptói*

Brîndză de Burduf (Romania) 🐑 ● 45% ©
Strong, pungent, spreadable cheese ripened in an animal skin bag (a *burduf*). Has a yellow paste and a grey rind spotted with mould. Traditionally eaten at the end of Lent.

Dalia (Romania)
Kashkaval made from cows' milk.

Dobrogea (Romania)
Type of Kashkaval made from ewes' milk.

Feta (Bulgaria, Yugoslavia)
Originally a Greek cheese but also made for centuries in other Balkan countries, particularly Bulgaria. Exceptionally good Bulgarian ewes' milk Feta is occasionally exported to the West. If you find any, it is well worth trying—creamier and more delicate than the more commonly available cows' milk types. see *Greece (Feta)*

Gomolya (Hungary), **Homolky, Hrudka** (Czechoslovakia)
White ewes' milk cheese made on mountain farms. Eaten partially ripened or sold to factories for making Bryndza. Sometimes used as a base for Liptauer. See *Liptói*

Gruševina see *Urdâ*

Hajdú (Hungary)
Kashkaval made from cows' milk.

Homolky, Hrudka see *Gomolya*

Kaimak (Yugoslavia, Bulgaria, Albania)
A very rich cream chese made from cows' milk. The milk is boiled and the layers of cream skimmed off, salted and allowed to cool. Often used in pastries.

Kashkaval   45% ⊟ 6-9kg (13-20lb) ©
Made throughout the Balkan lands since Roman times and based on Italian Caciocavallo. The best cheeses are made from ewes' milk, although mixed milk and sometimes pure cows' milk types are found. Like Caciocavallo the processing involves a kneading stage, after which the curds are moulded, brined and aged for about two months. The mature cheeses range from almost white to golden yellow depending on the milk and are generally rather hard and crumbly. The flavour is mild and faintly salty to strong and nutty according to age. Kashkaval is the Cheddar of the Balkans, eaten as a table cheese and also used in cooking. Often it is cubed and fried. Older harder cheeses are used for grating. One of the best types is the Bulgarian Balkanski Kâskaval.

Kefalotir (Yugoslavia)   🐄 🌢 45-50% ⊟ 9-10kg (20-22lb) ©
Hard Macedonian grating cheese with a smooth shiny rind, full flavour and pungent aroma. See *Greece (Kefalotiri)*

Kvargli (Czechoslovakia)
A soft, strong-flavoured cows' milk cheese.

Lajta (Hungary)   🕭 🌢 52% 🖾 1kg (2lb) ©
Piquant pale yellow cheese with numerous elliptical holes and a deep orange, moist, washed rind. Ripened for four weeks.

Liptói (Hungary), **Liptovská Bryndza** (Slovakia)   🐄 🌢 50% ©
Liptov in the Tatra mountains was reputedly the place where Bryndza was first made and its name is still used to denote particularly fine, white, creamy, soft ewes' milk cheeses made from whole unpasteurized milk. Such cheeses were the traditional base for a spread that is now widely known as Liptauer. The soft curd cheese is mixed with ingredients such as paprika, caraway seeds, onions or mustard or sometimes with anchovies and capers.

Mandur, Manur (Yugoslavia)   🐄 🌢 40% ○ 3kg (7lb) ©
Dry grating cheese made from the whey by-product of Kashkaval and Kefalotir mixed with milk or buttermilk.

Moravský Bochnik (Czechoslovakia) 🎋 🌙 45% ⊖ 13kg (28lb) ©
Pressed cooked cheese with holes, modelled on Emmental.

Nasal (Romania)
Low-fat washed rind cheese made from cows', ewes' or water buffalo milk in the hills near Cluj.

Niva (Czechoslovakia) 🎋 🐌 50% ⊟ 2kg (4lb) ©
Crumbly piquant blue-veined cheese made from pasteurized milk. Ripened for two to three months and wrapped in foil.

Njeguški Sir (Yugoslavia)
Hard ewes' milk grating cheese from Montenegro.

Olomoucký Sýr (Czechoslovakia)
The prototype of Austrian Quargel from Olomouc in Moravia. Partially ripened lactic curd cheese (*quarg*) is drained, pressed, milled and moulded into various shapes (usually small discs or rolls). It is then further ripened in conditions designed to produce various bacterial growths on the surface of the cheese. The result is a curious translucent rubbery substance with a very odd uncheese-like flavour and a pervasive smell.

Oštěpek, Oštiepok (Czechoslovakia), Oszczpek (Poland)
Spun-curd ovoid cheeses pressed in carved wooden moulds that produce decorative impressions on the surface of the cheese. After spending a day or so in brine the cheeses are smoked for up to six days and vary in colour from warm golden to dark chocolate brown depending on the length of smoking. Similar cheeses shaped like hams and salamis are also made.

Óvár, Ovari (Hungary) 🎋 🌙 45% ⊟ 3-4kg (7-9lb) ©
A pressed Tilsiter-type made from pasteurized milk.

Parenyica (Czechoslovakia, Hungary)
Sometimes called 'ribbon cheese', long strips of spun-curd cheese rolled up and lightly smoked. Traditionally made with ewes' milk. Now also factory-made from cows' milk.

Peneteleu (Romania)
Kashkaval made from ewes' milk.

Pivny Sýr (Czechoslovakia) 🎋 🌙 47% ⊂⊃ 2kg (4lb) ©
Salty 'beer cheese' similar to German Weisslackerkäse. Straw-coloured with a smeary yellow rind and strong sharp flavour. Ripened for four to six months. Foil-wrapped.

Planinski Sir (Yugoslavia) 14-18kg (31-40lb) ©
Dry Serbian 'mountain cheese' from Kosovo made in summer and stored in brine for winter consumption.

Podhalanski (Poland) 🌙 ⊜ 500g (18oz) ©
Lightly smoked cheese made from ewes' and cows' milk.

Sirene (Bulgaria) 🌙 45% 500g-1kg (18oz-2lb) ©
The most popular and widely produced Bulgarian cheese. Basically similar to Brynza, this white brined cheese is made either from ewes' or cows' milk. Crumbly, sharp and salty although the cows' milk type is milder.

Skuta see *Urda*

Somborski Sir (Yugoslavia)

From Sombor, Vojvodina. Soft, slightly bitter cheese made with ewes' milk or mixed ewes' and cows' milk diluted with a proportion of water. It has a strong-flavoured yellowish paste with medium holes and a thin rind. Ripened for three weeks stacked in wooden vessels during which time gases produced in the cheese expand causing it to rise like yeast dough.

Švapski Sir see Urda

Teasajt (Hungary)   🐑 🐄 45% ▱ 500g (18oz) ©

'Tea cheese', a fairly recent invention. It has a creamy yellow paste with small round holes and a smeary rind. Rather sour. Ripened for two weeks.

Telemea (Romania)

White brined cheese similar to Feta. Made from ewes' or cows' milk, or from cows' milk mixed with buffalo milk.

Teleorman (Romania)

Kashkaval made from mixed cows' and ewes' milk.

Travnički Sir (Yugoslavia)

From the town of Travnik, Bosnia. Made from ewes' or mixed ewes' and cows' milk. It has a softish white paste scattered with holes. The flavour is sour and salty.

Tvaroh (Slovakia), Twaróg (Poland)

White compact fresh curd cheese made of cows' or ewes' milk. In Czechoslovakia it is available in two forms: Mekky is soft and crumbly, eaten both as a spread and in salads and is also used to make cheesecake; Tvrdy is the cheese ripened until it is dry and hard, when it is used for grating. It is one of the main ingredients in the pastry for fruit dumplings. In Poland the aged type (zgliwiaty ser) is often fried with eggs.

Urdă (Romania), Urda (Czechoslovakia, Yugoslavia)

Fresh, unsalted, soft whey cheese. Eaten with herbs as a spread or used in cooking. Similar to Italian Ricotta. Also called Švapski Sir, Gruševina, Skuta.

Warszawski (Poland)

Ewes' milk cheese similar to Kashkaval.

Zlato (Czechoslovakia)   🐑 🐄 50% ▱ 1.5kg (3lb) ©

Sweetish cheese with a golden paste and a dry orange rind.

KEY WORDS

Brîndză (Romania) cheese	**Sir** (Yugoslavia) cheese
Sajt (Hungary) cheese	**Sirene** (Bulgaria) cheese
Ser (Poland) cheese	**Sýr** (Czechoslovakia) cheese

EGYPT see Middle East. EL SALVADOR see Latin America. FINLAND see Scandinavia.

France

Boulogne

PAYS B

Neufchâtel

PAYS D'AUGE
CALVADOS   Pont-l'Evêque
NORMANDIE   Vimoutiers
                   Camembert

Laval
MAYENNE   Entrammes

BRETAGNE

                                    Or
                                  ORLE

ANJOU
                   Loire
                        TOURAINE

VENDEE
                              Poulig
                              Saint-

              POITOU   Poitier
                       Couhé-Verac
              La Mothe
OLERON   AUNIS Saint-Héray

                        CHARENTE
                        PERIGORD
                        DORDOGNE

CORSE

        Bordeaux

500 m
200 m
                        AQUITAINE

                                      QUERC

        LES LANDES

              GASCOGNE Toulouse

        PAYS   BEARN
        BASQUE   Oloron-Sainte-Marie
                        PYRENEES   ARIE

ESPANA
                              ANDORRA

French cheese is undoubtedly the best in the world. Although there
are individual cheeses from other countries which may be as good as,
or even better than, the best of French cheeses, no country offers a
range of cheeses that for inventiveness, consistently high quality,
authenticity and sheer variety of flavour and texture, comes anywhere
near the French selection. A number of foreign cheeses are made in
France but, on the whole, the French prefer to concentrate on their
indigenous cheeses. Local cheesemaking traditions are jealously

guarded. Cheesemakers have endeavoured, often successfully, to
protect their products by legal means for hundreds of years. The
Appellation d'Origine Contrôlée regulations effectively protect some
of France's oldest cheeses by defining methods, areas of production
and type of milk (nearly always unpasteurized and often from a
specified breed).

The efforts of the cheesemakers have also been encouraged by the
enviable reputation that French cheeses have always enjoyed both at

home and abroad—ever since the Romans returned home from France with memories of the excellence of Roquefort and Cantal. During the Middle Ages cheesemaking moved into the monasteries, where so many facets of civilized life were preserved for posterity. Such places nurtured the huge family of French monastic cheeses— Maroilles, Munster, Pont l'Evêque and all the Trappist cheeses are their legacies. During the Renaissance fresh cheeses became fashionable, especially among the rich. (Aged, hard strong cheeses were thought to be food only for workers and peasants.) Jonchées and Caillebottes were essential ingredients of the fabulous desserts and pastries that were the crowning glories of sumptuous banquets.

The extraordinary richness of French cheesemaking is rooted in geographical diversity and maintained by that lively interest in the good things of life that is the mark of French culture generally. One might think that with so many cheeses the French would see neither sense nor profit in inventing more and yet there are no signs that their creativity is flagging. New cheeses appear almost every day. Some are mere affectations, novelties designed to titillate the eye or the imagination rather than the palate, but many are really excellent and well worth investigating. I have included a selection of the latter in the listing alongside the classic cheeses which they complement but by no means replace. Also included are many cheeses that never leave France or even, in some cases, the village where they are made. Dedicated cheesehounds may seek them out.

Abondance   🐄 🌙 45-48% ⊝ 7-10kg (15-22lb) Ⓓ

Firm smooth pressed cooked farmhouse cheese made in Haute-Savoie from raw milk of the Abondance breed of cattle. It has a thin, pale golden rind which is washed and rubbed with salt during four to six months of ripening. The cheese itself is golden, creamy and fruity, with a lingering aftertaste. Best from autumn through to spring.

The same area and breed of cattle produce a quite different cheese in autumn and winter—Vacherin d'Abondance. Weighing 500g-1kg (18oz-2lb), it has a wine-washed rind and is encircled by a strip of spruce bark. See *Vacherin du Haut-Doubs*

Aisy Cendré   🐄 🌙 45-50% ⊝ 200-450g (7oz-1lb) Ⓓ

Brine-washed, then stored for several months in the ashes of vine stems, giving a dusty grey coat with a hint of gold. Strong-smelling once cut, a powerfully flavoured raw milk cheese from Montbard in Burgundy. See *Cendré*

Aligot see *Tomme Fraîche*

L'Ami du Chambertin see *Chambertin*

Amou

Béarnaise sheep used to winter in the Landes, so this cheese (now rare) is a close relation of other Pyrenean ewes' milk cheeses. It has a thin, oiled, golden rind and a smooth firm paste with a slightly tangy flavour, reminiscent of Saint-Paulin when young. See *Pyrénées*

Araules

Fresh cows' (or occasionally goats') milk cheese mixed with chives and garlic. Eaten young or kept until stronger. From the Massif Central.

Ardi-Gasna   🐑 🌙 45-50% ⊝ 2-4kg (4-9lb) Ⓓ

The name means 'sheep cheese' in the Basque country, where it is made on mountain farms from December to June and matured for three to six months. A firm, smooth, pressed cheese with a pronounced sheepy aroma matched by a full mellow flavour; older, harder, sharper cheeses are used for grating. The smaller cheeses are also sold under the name Arradoy. Cheeses made when the sheep are in their summer pastures, from June to September, are given the name Arnéguy or Esterençuby. See *Ossau-Iraty-Brebis Pyrénées*

Arêches see *Grataron*

Arômes
A late-autumn speciality of the Lyonnais. Small flattened cylinders of cows', goats' or mixed milk cheese are ripened in white wine or fermenting wine pressings for a month or longer. The cheeses are firm but tender, smelly and spicy. Sometimes called Demi-Lunois.

Asco
Small round or square Corsican cheese made from ewes', goats' or mixed milk. Eaten from early spring to late autumn after three to four months ripening. Very strong. See *Niolo*

Aulus see *Bethmale*

Aunis see *Caillebotte*

Autun see *Charolais*

Baguette ☼ ⊗ 45-50% ▭ 500g (18oz) Ⓑ
Factory-made cheese from Laon. A type of elongated Maroilles, usually sold boxed. A smaller, milder version is known as Demi-Baguette. Also called Baguette Laonnaise, Baguette de Thiérache.

Banon ★ ⊗ 45-50% ⊟ 100-200g (3½-7oz) Ⓑ
Delicious small cheese from Provence. The original was made from ewes' milk in winter and spring, goats' milk in summer and autumn, but cows have supplanted ewes in Provence and dairies make pasteurized cows' milk or *mi-chèvre* Banons all year round (many of them not even in Provence, but in Dauphiné). Instantly recognizable by its chestnut leaf wrapping and raffia ties. The leaves are previously soaked in eau-de-vie or wine and the parcels are ripened in a cool dry place for two to four weeks. Banon au Pèbre d'Aï (also known as Poivre d'Ane or La Sarriette) is a similar cheese, but after draining it is rolled in sprigs of savory (*sarriette*, or *pèbre d'aï* in Provençal dialect). The Banons coated in other herbs and spices (including curry) are nearly always the pasteurized cows' milk type from Dauphiné.

Baratte 🐟 ⊗ 40-45% ⊟ 30g (1oz) Ⓓ
Tiny cylindrical cheeses pierced with a straw bearing a name flag. Organically produced (even the straw) on a Mâconnais farm.

Barberey ☼ ⊗ 20-30% ⊟ 250g (9oz) Ⓓ
Simple rustic cheese with a rather mellow flavour ripened for a month in wood ash, made from partly skimmed milk in small dairies around Troyes, Champagne. Also called Cendré de Troyes, Troyen Cendré.

Barousse ☼ ⊃ 40-50% ⊟ 1.7-2kg (3½-4lb) Ⓓ
Uncooked pressed cheese with a smooth natural rind, becoming harder and more piquant as it ages. Made on farms in the central Pyrenees and good in autumn and winter. Also known as Ramoun.

Beaufort ★ ☼ ⊃ 48-50% ⊟ 20-60kg (44-132lb) Ⓑ
'The prince of Gruyères' according to Brillat-Savarin. Hard-pressed cooked cheese, moulded into huge golden cartwheels with an unusual slightly concave circumference and ripened for at least six months

in cool cellars. As each cheese needs around 450 litres of milk, Beaufort has always been made in village co-operatives, since as long ago as Roman times. Sweeter and more succulent than the other Gruyères, Comté and Emmental, it has a marvellously fruity aroma, rich flavour and a smooth, creamy, buttery paste with very few, if any, holes or cracks. The best is Beaufort Haute-Montagne, a description legally restricted to cheeses made from summer milk from the herb-rich organic pastures of the high mountains of Savoie, and in season from December to late spring. Never pasteurized, Beaufort is protected by an *appellation d'origine* and known for its excellent keeping qualities. See *Gruyère*

Beauges see *Vacherin des Beauges*

Beaumont ⚗ ⊗ 50% ⊜ 1.5kg (3lb) Ⓑ
Mild, creamy raw milk cheese with a smooth, lightly washed pinkish-brown rind, similar to Reblochon. Created in 1881 in Beaumont, Haute-Savoie, from a recipe supplied by Tamié Abbey. See *Tamié*

Belle Bressane see *Bleu de Bresse*

Belle-des-Champs ⚗ ⊗ 50% ⊜ 2kg (4lb) Ⓑ
Brand name for a hardy, white-rinded factory-made cheese.

Bellocq 🐏 ⊗ 50-58% ⊜ 5kg (11lb) B
Made by Benedictine monks at the Abbey of Bellocq in the Basque country. A rich, nutty cheese with a thin golden rind. Comes within the *appellation d'origine* of Ossau-Iraty. See *Ossau-Iraty-Brebis Pyrénées*

Belval ⚗ ⊃ 40-42% ⊜ 450g and 2kg (1 and 4lb) Ⓓ
Mild pressed uncooked (unpasteurized) cheese with a smooth golden washed rind made at Belval Abbey (established 1892). Also known as Abbaye de Belval, Trappistine de Belval. See *Hesdin*

Bergues ⚗ ⊗ 10-20% ⊜ 2kg (4lb) Ⓓ
Made in Flanders near Dunkerque from skimmed or partly skimmed milk. A tangy, strong-smelling cheese that is washed with beer and brine during its three-week ripening period. Once a 'workers' cheese', popular because of its low price, it is now increasingly rare. Sometimes aged up to two months, and used for grating.

Besace du Berger see *Chèvrefeuille*

Bethmale ⚗ ⊃ 45-50% ⊜ 5-7kg (11-15lb) Ⓒ
A much-copied cheese, the original Bethmale was of ewes' milk, all but ousted this century by cows' milk versions (still made from raw milk). Aged for at least two months, Bethmale is notable for its many tiny horizontal slits. It has a thin golden crust and a rich savour unmatched by most of the black-coated factory-made so-called *fromages des Pyrénées*. It is best in spring and summer. Made on farms in Ariège and often sold under the name of the nearest village, for example Aulus, Ercé, Oust, Saint-Lizier. See *Pyrénées*

Béthune
Known affectionately as 'old stinker' (*vieux puant*), a Fromage Fort made from leftover Maroilles mixed with pepper, herbs and beer, sealed in jars for several months to ferment. Said to have been invented by miners who, no doubt wisely, wash it down with a glass of gin.

Bibbelskäse ⚗ ⊃ Ⓓ
Fresh soft cheese from Alsace, flavoured with horseradish and herbs.

Bicorne see *Chèvrefeuille*

Bigoton 🐐 📙 45% 150g (5oz) Ⓑ
Small oval cheese made from raw milk by a large Orléanais goat farm.
Quite firm when young, after a few weeks it develops a crinkly blue
mould and softens under the skin. Nutty flavour with a lactic edge.

Billy
Small goats' milk cheese made near Selles-sur-Cher. Wrapped in
plane leaves to ripen and packed in stoneware crocks.

Bleu
Generic term for blue-veined cheese, also known as *persillé*. The Juras
and the Massif Central are the best areas for such cheeses. Bleu can
also describe a cheese with a blue-tinged natural rind such as Olivet
Bleu or, occasionally, a Cendré.

Bleu d'Auvergne ★ 🐄 📙 45-50% ⊟ 450g-2.5kg (1-5½lb) Ⓑ
From the Massif Central, particularly the *départements* of Cantal and
Puy-de-Dôme. Since each Bleu takes very much less milk to make
than Cantal—the other great cheese of the area—it was more suited
to the small farmer. The best Bleu d'Auvergne is still made on mountain farms by traditional methods, but a great deal is now also made in
commercial dairies from pasteurized milk. It is a lightly piquant
creamy cheese which has a very pale paste with sharply defined dark
blue veining throughout the cheese. The mould, *Penicillium glaucum*,
is added either at the renneting stage or sprinkled in powder form on
to the moulded curds. After salting the cheese is pierced to develop
the veining and ripened in cool cellars for an initial period of one to
two months, then it is wrapped in foil to mature slowly for another
month or so. Farm cheeses are best during late summer and autumn.
The label should show that it is a legally protected cheese.

Bleu de Bresse, Bresse Bleu 🐄 📙 50% ⊡ Ⓑ
Mildly spicy blue-veined cheese with a rather undignified history. It is
a variation on an imitation. Restrictions on the import of Gorgonzola
during World War II led to the development of a French imitation,
Saingorlon (still available). Bleu de Bresse, invented in 1950, is a more
easily marketable blue cheese with a bloomy white rind. Two factories
make it in sizes between 100 and 500g (3½-18oz). Pipo Crem' is a large
log-shaped version, Belle Bressane is ring shaped.

Bleu des Causses 🐄 📙 45-50% ⊟ 2.5kg (5½lb) B
Similar to Bleu d'Auvergne but more assertive, being blued with *Penicillium roquefortii*. From Rouergue in the midst of the stark limestone
country known as Les Causses which provides the natural caves used
for ripening the cheeses. The name is legally protected.

Bleu de Corse 🐑 📙 45% ⊟ 2.5kg (5½lb) Ⓓ
From the late 19th century until quite recently, most of the ewes'
milk cheese made in Corsica was sent 'white' to the Roquefort caves
to be blued, to meet the demand for Roquefort. Bleu de Corse is the
name for cheese that is ripened in Corsica itself.

Bleu de Costaros see *Bleu du Velay*

Bleu du Forez see *Fourme des Monts du Forez*

Bleu de Gex 🐄 📙 45-50% ⊟ 6-8kg (13-18lb) Ⓑ
The name is now more or less interchangeable with Bleu de Septmoncel and Bleu du Haut-Jura. It has been made since the 14th

century in the high Jura mountain pastures. It blues naturally during its three to six month ripening, giving an interesting gentle flavour with a hint of bitterness. It has a powdery, rather crusty golden rind and creamy yellow paste, well-marbled with deep blue. Now made in small co-operative dairies (where *penicillium roquefortii* may be added), its best eating season is still August to January.

Bleu du Haut-Jura
The *appellation d'origine* for the much sought-after Bleu de Gex and Bleu de Septmoncel.

Bleu de Langeac see *Bleu du Velay*

Bleu de Laqueuille 🐄 🥛 45% 2.3kg (5lb) Ⓑ
A lightly piquant blue from the Auvergne, invented in 1850. The raw milk types with a dry (rather than foil-wrapped) crust are well worth trying. Local practice of warming the curd before salting gives an especially rich, smooth cheese.

Bleu de Loudes see *Bleu du Velay*

Bleu du Quercy 🐄 🥛 45-50% ⊖ 2kg (4lb) Ⓓ
From Aquitaine, a strong blue cheese similar to Bleu d'Auvergne.

Bleu de Sainte-Foy 🐄 45% ⊖ 5-6kg (11-13lb) Ⓓ
Lightly pressed, firm, slightly flaky cheese made from cows' and/or goats' milk. Blueing varies enormously, but in any case the cheese has a strong taste and a rough crust. From the Tarantaise mountains.

Bleu de Sassenage 🐄 🥛 45% ⊖ 3½-6kg (8-13lb) Ⓒ
Lightly pressed blue cheese developed by monks in the 14th century in Villard-de-Lans in the province of Dauphiné. Thought to be the original of Bleu de Gex, to which it is similar, though smoother. Once made from mixed cows', goats' and ewes' milk, now mainly from pasteurized cows' milk.

Bleu de Septmoncel see *Bleu de Gex*

Bleu de Solignac see *Bleu du Velay*

Bleu de Termignon 🐄 🥛 45% ⊖ 14kg (31lb) Ⓓ
A most unusual (and expensive) cheese, the dense green-blue veining is totally natural and takes up to a year to show. The paste is ivory or deep cream and surprisingly firm inside a dry dusty brown rind. Made from raw milk on farms in the Parc de la Vanoise, Savoie.

Bleu de Thiézac 🐄 🥛 45% ⊖ 2-3kg (4-7lb) Ⓓ
A much-prized variation of Bleu d'Auvergne produced exclusively on mountain farms near Aurillac.

Bleu du Velay 🐄 🥛 20-30% ⊖ 500g-1kg (18oz-2lb) Ⓓ
Rustic blue cheese with a natural crust made from skimmed or partly skimmed milk. Aged for one to two months, it is quite strong and firm. Closely related to other Auvergne blue cheeses such as those of Costaros, Langeac, Loudes and Solignac.

Bonbel
Brand name for a factory-made Saint-Paulin. Baby Bel is a small French-made Edam from the same company, Bel.

Bondard, Bonde see *Bondon*

Bondaroy au Foin ♨ 🌙 40-45% ⊖ 250-300g (9-10oz) Ⓑ

Tangy cheese with a smooth greyish natural rind or coated with white mould. Traditionally made from the spring flush of milk and ripened in hay for about five weeks. Some of the hay (*foin* in French) clings to the cheese. From Orléanais. Also called Pithiviers au Foin.

Bondon ♨ 🌙 50% ⊂⊃ 100g (3½oz) Ⓑ

Originally a farmhouse cheese produced almost entirely for domestic consumption but now increasingly made in small dairies and factories. It has a thick covering of white rind flora and comes from Neufchâtel in the Pays de Bray in Normandy, noted for its cider. The name Bondon reflects the shape of the cheese, which is similar to the *bonde* or bung of a cider barrel. Also called Bonde or, when twice the size, Bondard or Double-Bonde. Ripened for a minimum of ten days, considered best at around three weeks. Occasionally even larger ones are made on some farms, ripened for several months and served at New Year celebrations, by which time they are very piquant and the white rind has darkened to a brownish red. Cheeses like this have been made for at least 1,000 years. See *Neufchâtel*

Borgo see *Corsica*

Bossons Macérés 🌶 🌙 45% Ⓓ

A ferocious cheese from eastern Languedoc. Small goat cheeses steeped in olive oil, white wine or eau-de-vie with herbs and spices.

Bougnat ♨ 🌗 50% ⊖ 450g-3kg (1-7lb) Ⓓ

The name is Auvergnat for coalman, describing this black-coated cheese flavoured with peppercorns. Also called Poivre d'Auvergne.

Bougon

Formerly the trade name of a mild Camembert-style goat cheese, now used by the creamery for its many forms of pasteurized *chèvre*.

Bouille, La ♨ 🌙 60% ⊖ 225g-1kg (8oz-2lb) Ⓑ

Full-flavoured double-cream cheese from Normandy. Ripened for between two and three months. Covered with a thick downy white mould tinged with pink. Fairly strong fruity smell.

Boule de Lille, Boule du Pays see *Mimolette*

Boule des Moines see *Pierre-Qui-Vire*

Boulette d'Avesnes ♨ 🌙 45% 150g (5oz) Ⓑ

Originally a low-fat Fromage Fort from northern France made by heating buttermilk and draining and seasoning the resultant solids with pepper, cloves, tarragon and parsley. This mixture was then hand-moulded into small cones or balls and ripened for at least three months in a humid environment, during which time the cheeses were regularly washed, usually with beer. Nowadays usually made with unripened Maroilles curds rather than buttermilk solids as a base; creamery versions are ripened for about a month. Very tangy and strong-smelling with bright red rinds, either from annatto or a dusting of paprika. Also known as Boulette de Thiérache. Boulette de Papleux is stronger still; Boulette de Prémont is slightly milder.

Boulette de Cambrai ♨ 🌙 45% 300g (10oz) Ⓓ

Fresh hand-moulded ball or cone-shaped cheese, farmhouse-made using skimmed or whole milk curds flavoured with pepper, parsley, tarragon and sometimes chives. Pale, speckled with green.

Boursault ♉ 🍥 75% ⊟ 200g (7oz) Ⓑ

Small factory-made, triple-cream cheese, very rich and creamy with a soft bloomy rind which becomes tinged with pink if kept. Named after its inventor and made in the Ile de France. Choose the raw milk version (with a gold label) rather than the pasteurized silver-labelled Boursault if possible. Sometimes called Lucullus.

Boursin ♉ 🍥 75% ⊟ 100-225g (3½-8oz) Ⓐ

Factory-made triple-cream cheese using pasteurized milk. Available plain or flavoured with garlic and herbs, or crushed peppercorns.

Bouton-de-Culotte

Literally 'trouser button'. A tiny goats' milk (or *mi-chèvre*) cheese from Burgundy, dried and stored for winter use. Extra sharp with a dark greyish-brown rind, often grated or used in Fromage Fort. Slightly larger cheeses may be called Bouchons or Chevretons de Mâcon.

Bressan

Very small cone-shaped farmhouse goat cheese from Bresse, southern Burgundy. May be sold young and soft, but quickly becomes hard and dry. Sometimes *mi-chèvre*. Also known as Petit Bressan.

Bresse Bleu see *Bleu de Bresse*

Bricquebec

Saint-Paulin type created in Normandy at the abbey of the same name. Now dairy-made and sold under the brand name Providence.

Brie ★ ♉ 🍥 40-60% ⊜ 1-3kg (2-7lb) Ⓐ

After Camembert, the most famous and most imitated of all French cheeses. It is, in fact, a much older cheese than Camembert and can be documented by name at least as far back as the 13th century. The term Brie covers a small family of cheeses, nowadays much depleted, but all of which at one time carried the name of the particular place where they were made. All are soft, unpressed, naturally drained cows' milk cheeses with white rind flora, moulded into large flat discs and ripened for at least three weeks. The family name is that of the area in the *département* of Seine-et-Marne where they originated and where the best ones are still made, from April to October. Nowadays Brie is made all over France and in many other countries. These commercial pasteurized Bries have snow-white rinds, and paler, blander interiors than their originals. There are numerous modern variations on the traditional cheese, such as herb- and pepper-flavoured Bries and versions with blue and/or white internal moulds.

All Bries should be full-flavoured, fruity and mildly tangy. Ideally, the paste is rich, glossy and straw-coloured. It should be plump and smooth but not runny. Avoid cheeses with a hard chalky centre and any that are liquefying. The rind should be firm but tender, not hard or sticky. The smell should be clean and pleasantly mouldy. Cheeses that smell of ammonia are overripe and should not be eaten.

Brie de Coulommiers see *Coulommiers*

Brie de Meaux ★ ♉ 🍥 45% ⊜ 2.5-3kg (5½lb-7lb) Ⓑ

Brie made and matured in specified zones from unpasteurized milk. Ripened for four to six weeks. The rind gradually becomes golden with rosy tinges. Very fruity, golden straw-coloured interior. Protected by an *appellation d'origine*.

Brie de Melun Affiné ♉ 🍥 45% ⊜ 1.5-1.7kg (3-3½lb) Ⓑ

Brie made and matured for six to ten weeks in the Ile de France from unpasteurized milk. Dark red-gold rind with traces of white. Fairly firm, golden paste, strong-smelling and tangy. The strongest of the Bries, it is the original from which all the others have descended. Protected by an *appellation d'origine*.

Brie de Melun Frais 🍥 ☽ 45% 🖵 2.5kg (5½lb) Ⓓ

Brie de Melun eaten unripened, sometimes available *bleu*, which means that it is coated with powdered charcoal.

Brie de Montereau 🍥 40-45% 🖵 400g-1kg (14oz-2lb) Ⓓ

A variety of Brie de Melun Affiné but smaller in size and ripened for six weeks. Also called Ville-Saint-Jacques.

Brillat-Savarin 🍥 🕥 75% 🖵 500g (18oz) B

The name was first given to a gloriously rich and buttery triple-cream cheese made in Normandy and ripened for three to four weeks, when the bloomy rind became rosy gold. Other makers of triple-cream cheeses used the name for some years, but have now been legally obliged to rename their cheeses—Vatel, Brillador, Brivarin, Saulieu—since the right to the name was claimed by a company in Champagne. Pierre-Robert, made in the Brie region, is closest to the original.

Brin d'Amour 🕥 45% 600-800g (1¼-1¾lb) Ⓑ

Firm, aromatic, white cheese from Corsica, coated with sprigs of rosemary and savory. May be made from ewes', goats' or mixed milk and shaped into round-cornered squares or logs. Another maker calls his cheese Fleur du Maquis, *maquis* being the Corsican name for the herb-rich scrubland on which the animals graze.

Brique du Forez 🕥 45% 🖘 250-350g (9-12oz) Ⓓ

Small flattish bricks of cows', goats' or mixed milk cheese made in Auvergne. Ripened for two to three weeks, the rind may be white, grey, blue or pinkish gold, with a smooth, rich, nutty interior. Also called Cabrion, Cabriou, Brique du Livradois or Brique d'Ambert.

Briquette see *Neufchâtel*

Brisegoût

Whey cheese made in Savoie as a by-product of the making of Beaufort. It is eaten either fresh or ripened when it becomes hard, brittle and extremely piquant. Also called Brisco, Brisego.

Brivarin see *Brillat-Savarin*

Broccio, Brocciu

Fresh Corsican cheese once made from the whey by-product of Sartenais but which now increasingly uses a proportion of whole or skimmed milk. Made from ewes' milk in winter and spring, goats' milk in summer and autumn. It looks and tastes very much like Italian Ricotta. It can also be ripened for several months, when it becomes dry, sharp and tangy. Also called Bruccio, Brucciu.

Brocotte, Brokott

Low-fat whey cheese produced as a by-product of Munster. Soft and lactic tasting, served with potatoes. Also called Chigre, Schigre.

Brouère, Le 🍥 🌓 52% 🖵 12kg (26lb) Ⓓ

Recently developed mountain cheese from the Vosges, similar to Beaufort except that it is smaller and has a striking concave edge decorated with relief pictures of birds and pine trees (carved into the wooden moulds). Matured for four to seven months.

59

Brousse

Fresh cheese made mostly on farms in Provence. Snowy white, very mild and creamy. Drained and usually sold in wicker baskets. Traditionally made from whey or skimmed ewes' milk (winter and spring) and goats' milk (spring and summer) with a proportion of whole milk. Today often made from cows' milk.

Bruccio see *Broccio*

Bûcheron 🐐 🥛 45% 1.5kg (3lb) Ⓑ

Pasteurized log from a large Poitevin co-operative. May have a blue or white mould rind.

Butte ☒ 🥛 70% 🧀 300g (10oz) Ⓑ

Rich double-cream cheese with white rind flora made in the Ile de France from unpasteurized milk. Particularly rich in autumn.

Cabécou 45% 40g (1½oz) Ⓑ

The name, a diminutive of *chèvre*, applies to several tiny, flat, goats' milk cheeses made in Aquitaine and Languedoc. They are ripened for two to three weeks and range from semisoft to firm. Cailladou is sometimes used to refer to fresh Cabécou. The flavour is generally fairly pronounced. Occasionally made with ewes' milk, or a mixture of cows' and goats' milk. Local names include Cajassou, Cujassous.

Cabri 🐐 🥛 45% ▭ 90-225g (3-8oz) Ⓑ

Farm-made cheese from Touraine. Sold fresh and white or ripened with a gold or blue-tinged crust.

Cabrion, Cabriou see *Brique du Forez*

Cachat

Goats' or ewes' milk cheese from animals grazed on the slopes of Mont Ventoux, Provence. Sometimes used to describe delicate fresh cheeses, which are also called Tommes de Mont Ventoux. Cachat more often means a Fromage Fort, kneaded with eau-de-vie, olive oil or wine and kept in a sealed pot for several weeks. Cacheille is a similarly strong sticky cheese enriched with cream and traditionally fermented in sealed pots over winter, to be eaten in spring.

Caffuts

Cambrai term for out-of-condition cheeses pounded with herbs and spices and shaped into flattened balls.

Caillada de Vouillos see *Tomme de Brach*

Cailladou see *Cabécou*

Caillé

Fresh, usually unsalted, cottage or curd cheese. In the Basque country it will be ewes' milk, in Brittany cows' milk, in Poitou probably goats' milk. Farmhouse made, particularly in summer.

Caillebotte

Fresh, soft, rennet-curd cheese, an ancient speciality of Poitou, once made from ewes' milk but now mainly from cows' or goats' milk. The name is a combination of *caillé* (curdled milk) and *botte* (the mat on which the curds are drained. Also called Jonchée (*jonchée* means strewn, relating to the scattering of rushes or rush mats). Caillebotte d'Aunis is a rare version shaped into a small triangle. See *Oléron*

Caillotte de Brebis
A sort of potted Roquefort (other ewes' milk cheese may be used).

Caisse
Soft cows' milk cheese from Flanders ripened in chests (*caisses*) lined with walnut leaves. Can be even stronger and smellier than Munster.

Calenzana   ♦ 🐄 45% 150 and 450g (5oz and 1lb) Ⓓ
Corsican raw milk cheese made in small round or large square basket moulds. Firm but supple, with a greyish washed or salt-rubbed crust. Usually aged for five to six months, with a strong, sharp flavour hinting at the herb-rich pasturage. The large ones are sometimes aged for a year, to become the strong Corsevieux; younger, milder cheeses are sold as Montegrosso.

Camarguais   ♥ 🐄 45% ⊖ 60-500g (2-18oz) Ⓓ
Made in the Camargue in winter and spring. Topped with thyme or savory and a bay leaf and eaten fresh. Also called Tomme Arlésienne, Tomme de Camargue, Le Gardian.

Cambrai see *Boulette de Cambrai*

Camembert ★   🐄 45-50% ⊖ 250g (9oz) Ⓐ
One of the three great Normandy cheese, Camembert, in name at least, is relatively young in cheesemaking terms—a mere 280 years old. As a type it is certainly much older. The Pays d'Auge, still the best source of good Camembert, was known for its cheese as far back as the 11th century. In 1702, 90 years before Mme Harel is credited with the 'invention' of Camembert, it was mentioned, along with Livarot, as being sold in the market at Vimoutiers. But Mme Harel refined the recipe and launched it into the wider world. She passed her secrets on to her daughter, whose husband, Victor Paynel, presented one of his wife's best cheeses to Napoleon III. With the royal seal of approval, the future of Camembert was assured. But two further developments were essential to its subsequent spectacular commercial success. One was the invention of the chipwood box in the 1890s. (Previously the cheeses were wrapped in sixes in paper and straw and rarely survived distances farther than Paris.) The second was the introduction in 1910 of *Penicillium candidum*, the snowy white mould which is sprinkled or sprayed on the surfaces of the cheeses. Previously, Camembert rinds were often blue.

Camembert is now made in enormous quantities all over the world. In France it accounts for over 20 per cent of total cheese production. Most of this is factory-made from pasteurized milk; such cheeses simply do not compare with the traditional hand-made Normandy cheeses using raw milk from local herds. These are in season from the end of spring through to the autumn. Check the label for the words *fromage fermier, lait cru* or *non pasteurisé* and the initials V.C.N.—*Véritable Camembert de Normandie*. If it also says Pays d'Auge, so much the better. The rind should be creamy white, flecked with red, not cracked or sticky, with a lightly fruity smell with no trace of ammonia. The paste should be plump and pale golden with no chalky or greyish patches. It should not be runny or sunken in the middle. The flavour is lightly fruity.

Cantal ★   🐄 45% ⊟ 35-55kg (77-120lb) Ⓑ
Probably the oldest French cheese (c. 2,000 years), made in the Auvergne, traditionally from the milk of Salers cattle, and protected by an *appellation d'origine*. Unfortunately, good Cantal is rarely found outside France, because the basic *appellation* allows pasteurization and has a low minimum maturing period of 45 days—which suits the large dairies which make Cantal all year round. However, there is a

superior *appellation*, Salers, which must be made in *burons* (mountain huts) during the summer *transhumance* in the high mountain pastures, from raw milk, with a minimum ripening of three months, which is usually extended to six or eight months. The finest old cheeses are available in winter and spring. Always choose a Cantal *fermier* or Salers to avoid disappointment. Cantal is a pressed uncooked cheese with a dry grey or golden rind and a smooth, dense, pale yellow paste with a rich, nutty flavour. Some people can detect a slight metallic edge from the volcanic soil which is rich in bitter herbs. The *appellation* also covers two smaller cheeses: Le Petit Cantal, 20-22kg (44-48lb) and Le Cantalet, 8-10kg (18-22lb). Also called Fourme du Cantal.

Cantalon see *Fourme du Rochefort*

Caprice des Dieux ♉ ⚭ 60% 150g (5oz) Ⓑ
Factory-made, oval, double-cream cheese with white rind flora and a mild flavour. Sold boxed.

Carré de Bonneville see *Pavé d'Auge*

Carré de Bray see *Neufchâtel*

Carré Breton see *Nantais*

Carré de l'Est ♉ ⚭ 40-50% ⊂⊃ 200g (7oz) Ⓑ
Camembert type from Champagne and Lorraine. Mostly factory-made from pasteurized milk. Mild but slightly salty. The white rind flora should be smooth with no red or grey streaks. There is also a raw milk, washed rind variant with the same name.

Caserette ♉ ⚭ 50% ⊖ 125g (4oz) Ⓓ
One of the oldest cheeses of the Pays de Bray, Normandy, an unsalted fresh white cheese.

Cendré
Generic term for small soft cows' or goats' milk cheeses ripened in wood ash, shaped as discs, truncated cones or pyramids with greyish-black rinds. They are often strong and pungent. Traditionally made in the Orléanais and Champagne to use up the spring glut of milk (partly skimmed) and kept for workers during the harvest and grape picking seasons, but now often made in large dairies and sold after two to three months. The best ashes for ripening are said to be from *sarments* (vine prunings).

Cendré des Ardennes see *Rocroi*

Cendré d'Argonne
Now very rare, a typical strong spicy *cendré* made from partly skimmed cows' milk in Champagne. Local farmhouse variations include Noyers-Le-Val, Heiltz-le-Maurupt, Cendré du Barrois or Eclance.

Cendré de Champagne, Cendré des Riceys see *Riceys, Les*

Chabi(s), Chabichou 🐐 ⚭ 45% 100-180g (3½-6oz) Ⓑ
An ancient Poitevin cheese shaped like a small flattened cone or cylinder and emphatically goaty in flavour and aroma. The farmhouse type, in season from the end of spring until late autumn, has a firm pale blue rind streaked with red or gold. Chabichou Laitier, made in small dairies, has a white bloomy rind. Best in summer. Both types are ripened for between one and four weeks and labelled according to their maturity. The name comes from a local dialect word for 'goat'

derived from the Arabic *chebli*. There is also a Chabichou Cendré. Such cheeses are made from Anjou down to Aquitaine; locally they are often eaten unripened.

Chambarand 🏠 🌓 25-45% ⊖ 160g (5½oz) Ⓓ

Made by nuns at the Monastère Notre-Dame-de-Chambarand in Dauphiné. They follow a Reblochon recipe but use pasteurized milk and ripen for just 12-15 days, making a gentle cheese with a creamy yellow paste and smooth golden rind. Also called Beaupré de Roybon.

Chambertin, L'Ami du 🏠 🌓 45% ⊖ 300g (10oz) Ⓑ

Brand name for a hand-made Epoisses washed in *marc de Bourgogne*, the local grape spirit, during ripening. Strong and savoury.

Chamois d'Or 🏠 🌘 62% ⊖ 2.3kg (5lb) Ⓑ

Modern white-rinded cheese with a firm ivory interior. Bland and creamy, with a long shelf-life.

Champenois see *Riceys, Les*

Chaource 🏠 🌓 50% ⊡ 200-500g (7-18oz) Ⓑ

Milky white, smooth-pasted cheese which can be difficult to mature evenly because of its depth—it is often salty and dryish rather than creamy. Ripened for between two and eight weeks. It has a thin covering of white rind flora tinged with gold. Named after a small village near Troyes, where it has been made since at least the 14th century. Best in summer and autumn. Protected by an *appellation d'origine*.

Charol(l)ais, Charolles

Small, soft, cylindrical or cone-shaped cheese made from goats' milk in spring and summer, and cows' milk or a mixture of the two in other seasons. Raw milk is used, made between the towns of Autun and Charolles in Burgundy. Eaten fresh or ripened for a couple of weeks, when the rind becomes grey-blue and the flavour more nutty.

Chaumes 🏠 🌘 50% ⊖ 2kg (4lb) Ⓑ

First made in 1971. A cheese with a rich golden creamy paste and a yellowy brown edible washed rind. Made from pasteurized milk it has a smooth, springy consistency and a pleasant full, buttery flavour. Gourmelin is similar, but made from raw milk.

Chaumont 🏠 🌘 45% 200g (7oz) Ⓓ

Farm-made washed rind cheese from Champagne. Russet-coloured, cone-shaped and ripened for two months, it has a rather tangy flavour.

Chécy see *Frinault*

Chèvre

The generic term for goats' milk cheeses, of which there are innumerable local shapes and variations. By law, cheeses described as *chèvre* or *pur chèvre* must be made entirely of goats' milk and must contain at least 45 per cent fat. Cheeses using a minimum of 50 per cent goats' milk mixed with cows' milk are described as *mi-chèvre*.

Chèvre à la Feuille see *Mothe-Saint-Héray, La*

Chèvrefeuille 🌢 🌘 45% 225-300g (8-10oz) Ⓑ

Name shared by several shapes of rich young hand-made cheeses from Périgord, including Lingot (ingot-shaped), Palet Périgourdin (larger loaf), Bicorne (two-cornered hat) and Besace du Berger (shepherd's purse). Sometimes with a thin grey-blue rind or herb-coated.

Chevret
Small square soft goats' milk cheese or *mi-chèvre* with a thin blue rind, from Bugey. Also called Tomme de Belley, Saint-Claude.

Chevreton
Used in Burgundy and Auvergne for *chèvre* or *mi-chèvre* cheeses.

Chevreton de Mâcon see *Bouton-de-Culotte*

Chevrette 🐐 🌀 Ⓑ
Two versions exist, both flavoured with garlic and herbs. The Dauphiné Chevrette des Neiges is a small, soft, double-cream cheese, while the Norman Chevrette is presented as a lower-fat log.

Chevrette des Beauges 🐐 🌀 45% ⊖ 800g-1.5kg (1¾-3lb) Ⓓ
Pressed, uncooked cheese from Savoie. Not too strongly goaty, with a smooth pinkish washed rind.

Chevrotin des Aravis 🐐 🌀 45% ⊖ 400-700g (14oz-1¼lb) Ⓑ
A lightly pressed cheese with a thin pinkish washed rind made in Haute-Savoie. With Chevrette des Beauges and many other goats' milk cheeses made in the area it is often sold simply as Tomme de Chèvre or Tomme de Chèvre de Savoie.

Chevroton du Bourbonnais 🐐 🌀 40-45% 100-250g (3½-9oz) Ⓓ
Small flattened cone eaten fresh or ripened for a couple of weeks, when it develops a thin pinkish crust streaked with blue. Mildly acidic to fairly strong depending on age.

Chevru 🌀 🌀 45% 500g (18oz) Ⓓ
Surface-ripened cheese similar to Coulommiers, but deeper and of smaller diameter. Made in the Ile de France from raw milk. Usually sold young, wrapped in bracken. See *Fougéru*

Chigre see *Brocotte*

Cîteaux 🌀 🌀 45% ⊖ 1kg (2lb) Ⓓ
Pressed, washed rind cheese made in the monastery of the same name in Burgundy. Made from unpasteurized milk, it has a clean, fairly tangy flavour. Lightly dotted with holes. Has been compared to Reblochon, but is deeper, and the savoury crust is drier.

Claquebitou
Burgundian fresh goat cheese flavoured with herbs and garlic.

Clochette 🐐 🌀 45% 250g (9oz) Ⓑ
Bell-shaped cheese from Poitou, ripened for a month with a pronounced goaty flavour and a natural gold-tinged crust, becoming blue.

Coeur d'Arras
Heart-shaped, strong, washed rind cheese, similar to Maroilles.

Coeur de Bray see *Neufchâtel*

Coeurmandie 🌀 🌀 60% 200g and 2kg (7oz and 4lb) Ⓑ
Factory-made heart-shaped cheese with white rind flora.

Combe de Savoie see *Tomme au Marc*

Comté ★ 🌀 🌀 45% ⊖ 40-45kg (88-99lb) Ⓑ
One of the French Gruyère family, a hard-pressed cooked cheese

with a smooth pale golden paste lightly scattered with holes. A good Comté can be judged almost entirely by the size, shape and condition of these holes or 'eyes'. They should not be too numerous or too close together. They should be perfectly round, no bigger than a hazelnut and just moist and glistening. Comté has a dark, tough, brushed rind and is stronger than Emmental with a rich, fruitier flavour. It is matured for a minimum three months, but can be aged much longer. Made in Franche Comté since ancient times, it developed out of the need for isolated farm communities, with distant markets, to make a cheese that would keep in good condition for as long as possible. Since such cheeses also required more milk than could possibly be yielded by small herds it also necessitated pooling the milk from several herds and making the cheeses co-operatively. Farmers transported their milk to these local co-operatives (*frutières*) each day, a custom which persists today. Usually sold in France as Gruyère de Comté. Protected by an *appellation d'origine* which demands raw milk and specifies the breeds of cattle and their feeding.

Cornilly 🐄 🍶 45% ⬭ 250g (9oz) Ⓑ
Sold fresh or after three weeks with a thin natural soft blue rind. Not too strong. Made on farms and in small dairies in Berry.

Corsevieux see *Calenzana*

Corsica 🐑 🍶 50% ⊖ 400g (14oz) Ⓑ
Made in round basket moulds with a natural pale mould-coated crust, Corsica is the brand name used for a cheese made by Société (of Roquefort fame). It has a mild, not too salty taste and a velvety texture. Occasionally blues naturally. A development of the ancient Borgo cheese, made in summer while the sheep (or goats) are in their mountain pastures, which is altogether softer and creamier.

Couhé-Vérac 🐄 🍶 45% ⬭ 200g (7oz) Ⓓ
Farm-made around Couhé-Vérac in Poitou. Sharp and smelly it is ripened for three to four weeks. Wrapped in chestnut or plane-tree leaves. Occasionally a flat disc shape.

Coulommiers ★ 🐄 🍶 45-55% ⊖ 350-500g (12-18oz) Ⓑ
Sometimes called Petit Brie or Brie de Coulommiers and now made mostly in large dairies, in the same area as Brie. Much smaller in size and eaten younger, preferably as the surface mould is beginning to appear (after ripening for a month). At this stage the flavour is quite mild and delicate: allowed to ripen further it becomes increasingly reminiscent of Camembert. Farmhouse Coulommiers is traditionally made with the richest milk of the area. Try to get a raw milk version, made with spring milk. See *Chevru*, *Fougéru*

Crottins de Chavignol 🐐 45% ◯ 75g (2½oz) Ⓑ
The name is hardly inviting: *crottin* means 'dung'. Strictly speaking it should apply only to the well-aged, hard, dry cheeses with black or grey-brown mouldy rinds made in the Sancerre area. They are horribly sharp, often very salty and somewhat intimidating to all but the most dedicated. However, the *appellation d'origine* granted in 1976 embraces much younger, more approachable cheeses made in the area, which have a light covering of gold or blue mould.

Croupot 🐐 🍶 75% ⊖ 400g (14oz) Ⓑ
Soft, rich, modern triple-cream cheese eaten young. Made in the Brie region from unpasteurized milk.

Curé see *Nantais*

Dauphin 🎏 🌑 45-50% 150-500g (5-18oz) Ⓑ

Small washed rind cheese similar to Maroilles but flavoured with pepper, cloves, tarragon and parsley. Moulded in various shapes—bar, oval, fish, crescent, heart, shield—it has a smooth brick-red rind and strong spicy flavour. Ripened between two and three months. Made in Flanders and Thiérache.

Demi-Baguette see *Baguette*

Demi-Lunois see *Arômes*

Demi-Sel 🎏 🌙 40% 🗩 60g (2oz) Ⓑ

Originating in the Pays de Bray in 1872, a smooth, white, slightly acidic factory-made, fresh rennet-curd cheese from pasteurized milk.

Doux de Montagne

Creamery-made, large round shiny brown-coated mild cheese with many apertures, made from pasteurized cows' milk.

Dreux à la Feuille 🎏 🌑 30-45% 🖴 300-500g (10-18oz) Ⓑ

Rich, fruity cheese with white rind flora spotted with red and wrapped in chestnut leaves. Made from partly skimmed (or occasionally whole) milk in small dairies in the Ile de France. Also called Feuille de Dreux, Fromage de Dreux.

Eclance see *Cendré d'Argonne*

Echourgnac 🎏 🌑 45% 🖯 300g (10oz) Ⓓ

Mild, flowery, raw milk cheese made by nuns in Périgord. Pressed, uncooked pale yellow paste with pinpoint holes and a buff-coloured washed rind. Also called La Trappe.

L'Edel de Cléron 🎏 🌑 50% 🖯 300g and 2kg (10oz and 4lb) Ⓑ

Commercial imitation of Mont d'Or, a lusciously creamy cheese encircled with a strip of spruce, with a white bloomy rind.

Emmental Français 🎏 ● 45% 🖯 60-100kg (132-220lb) Ⓒ

More Emmental is made in France than in any other country including Switzerland, much of it from pasteurized milk in factories in the Vosges mountains. A superior version, Emmental Grand Cru, is made from raw milk in Franche Comté and Savoie. Aged between two and six months, it should have a pale primrose paste with well-spaced walnut-sized holes, with a hint of the mountain pastures in the flavour. See *Switzerland (Emmental)*

Entrammes ★ 🎏 🌑 40-50% 🖯 225g (8oz) Ⓑ

The archetypal monastery cheese, lightly pressed with a golden washed rind and a supple apricot paste. The flavour is full and mellow with a slight edge but not so tangy as other washed rind cheeses. Made from raw milk by monks at the abbey in the village of Entrammes in the *département* of Mayenne. In 1815 a group of Cistercians, returning from exile in Switzerland, were allowed to use the abbey, which they renamed L'Abbaye de Notre Dame du Port-du-Salut. Their cheeses became well-known in Parisian markets and demand was so great that they were widely imitated. The monks took steps to protect their product and in 1874 the name Port-du-Salut was registered as a trade mark; imitators had to use the name Saint-Paulin. The name of Port-du-Salut was sold after World War II to a commercial enterprise but the monks continued making their own cheeses, sold under the name Entrammes. See *Port-du-Salut*

Epoisses 🐄 🐐 45-50% ⊟ 250g (9oz) Ⓑ

Smooth, pungent, washed rind cheese made in Burgundy. It has a rich orange-red rind which is washed in salted water for three weeks, then in white wine or eau-de-vie-de-marc for a further two to three weeks. The interior is a tender creamy yellow which, though tangy, should not be sharp. Factory versions are neither wine- nor marc-washed, but coloured with annatto. A popular hand-made (raw milk) Epoisses is presented in a wooden box on a bed of paper leaves.

Ercé see *Bethmale*

Esbareich see *Pyrénées*

Esterençuby see *Ardi-Gasna*

Etorki 🐑 🐐 50% ⊟ 4.5kg (10lb) Ⓑ

Factory-made Pyrenean cheese with an amber rind and tangy flavour. See *Pyrénées*

Explorateur ★ 🐄 🐐 75% ⊡ 250g (9oz) Ⓑ

Rich triple-cream cheese invented in the 1950s and made in small dairies in Seine-et-Marne. Virtually odourless with a light covering of snowy white mould. Mild creamy flavour. Ripened for three weeks.

Feuille de Dreux see *Dreux*

Fleur de l'Ermitage 🐄 🐐 52% ⊟ 1.5kg (3lb) Ⓑ

White, mould-ripened, pleasantly flavoured factory-made cheese.

Fleur du Maquis see *Brin d'Amour*

Fontainebleau 🐄 🐐 60% Ⓒ

White and fluffy, unsalted fresh cheese, made from milk mixed with whipped cream. Served for dessert with sugar or fruit.

Foudjou

A Fromage Fort from the Vivarais mountains. Dry and fresh goat cheeses mixed with garlic, salt and pepper and eau-de-vie and sealed to ferment for two or three months. In another version the fresh cheese is left whole and layered with seasonings, eau-de-vie and oil.

Fougéru ★ 🐄 🐐 45% ⊟ 700g (1½lb) Ⓑ

Developed from Chevru, Fougéru is ripened for five to six weeks in fronds of bracken (*fougère*). Both raw and pasteurized versions are made.

Fourme

The old word for cheese is still widely used in the Auvergne: if you ask for plain '*fourme*' you are likely to be offered Cantal or Salers, Laguiole or Rochefort. It is most widely applied to the blue cylindrical cheeses made in the same area, with an equally long history.

Fourme d'Ambert ★ 🐄 🐐 45-50% ⊡ 2kg (4lb) Ⓑ

Looks like a tall slim Stilton and has a similar rough brown-grey crust. A lightly pressed creamy white cheese marbled with dark blue-green veining. The paste should be smooth and fairly moist, tasting quite rich and tangy but not too bitter. Best in summer and autumn at about three to four months old. Formerly blued naturally, but now often injected with mould, the factory-made pasteurized cheeses are also wrapped in foil, which does not produce the same crust. Like Stilton, it should be cut horizontally. Made in the Livradois, Auvergne. Protected by an *appellation d'origine*.

Fourme de Brach see *Tomme de Brach*

Fourme des Monts du Forez, Fourme de Montbrison, Fourme de Pierre-sur-Haute
All similar in most respects to Fourme d'Ambert. Fourme du Forez can be used generically to cover these and other related cheeses.

Fourme de Rochefort 45% 3-10kg (7-22lb) Ⓓ
Like Cantal but smaller. Made on mountain farms in the Auvergne. Also known as Cantalon, Fourme de Rochefort-Montagne.

Frinault 50% 125g (4oz) Ⓑ
Created in the 19th century by a Monsieur Frinault at Chécy, Orléanais and still made at the same dairy, although now pasteurized. Like Olivet it has a downy blue rind and is also available *cendré*. Ripened for three or four weeks, with a spicy flavour.

Fromage Blanc, Fromage Frais
The French tend to use the former term for the fresh (unripened) soft white acid- or rennet-curd cheese made from skimmed or whole cows' milk. Low-fat versions may be described as *maigre*, but will usually state their fat content. Some are very light, with almost a pouring consistency and are the basis for many local and family dishes. Sold by weight or in tubs under a variety of brand names, of which Jockey is perhaps the best known. The words *battu* (beaten) or *lisse* (smooth) may appear on the carton. Often eaten for dessert, with sugar or fruit.

Fromage à la Crème
Fromage Blanc with cream, sold in small pots.

Fromage du Curé see *Nantais*

Fromage Fondu
The generic term for processed cheese with a minimum fat content of 40 per cent. Often sold as *crème de ...* or *fromage à tartiner*.

Fromage Fort
This is not cheese as such, but a preparation usually based on dessert cheese that is, perhaps, not quite perfect or that has become too old for consumption in the normal way. These cheeses are mashed up with various herbs, spices, alcohol (often white wine or eau-de-vie), grape must or oil, sealed in jars and macerated for varying amounts of time. The longer the fermentation period the stronger the flavour but even the mildest of them are impossibly fierce. For locals it is a case of the stronger the better. Eaten after meals or as a snack with a tot of some equally explosive beverage. Different cheeses are used in different parts of the country: goat cheeses in Burgundy and Lyonnais, Maroilles in Artois, Gruyère and Bouton-de-Culotte in Beaujolais. In Dauphiné (cows' or goats' milk) it is called Pétafine (derived from the verb *pétafiner*, meaning to knock someone flat on the back).

Fromage Grand Murol(s) see *Murol*

Fromage de Monsieur see *Monsieur Fromage*

Fromage à la Pie
Fresh cheese made from skimmed or partly skimmed cows' milk, interchangeable in some areas with Caillebotte. In the Ile de France a term for an unripened Brie or Coulommiers.

Gardian see *Camarguais*

Gaperon (Gapron) ★ ♨ 🐄 30-45% 300-500g (10-18oz) Ⓑ

Looking like an upturned basin and tied with raffia, a lightly pressed cheese flavoured with garlic or sometimes peppercorns. Made in a region of the Auvergne known for its garlic, these cheeses used to be made in farms from buttermilk (without rennet) and were consequently low in fat. They were hung to ripen from the beams of the farmhouse kitchen. Now made in small dairies from lightly skimmed, renneted milk: some are still unpasteurized. Le P'ail is a recently introduced larger version, made in a ring shape.

Gérômé ♨ 🐄 45-50% ⊖ 1.5-6kg (3-13lb) Ⓑ

Washed rind cheese similar to Munster but traditionally larger. Made on the western slopes of the Vosges, mostly from pasteurized milk. Also known as Gérardmer, and often flavoured with cumin or aniseed. Sometimes sold fresh locally, under the name Lorraine.

Gien 🐄 40-50% ⊡ 200g (7oz) Ⓓ

Farmhouse cheese using goats' or mixed cows' and goats' milk. It has a dry, blue-grey rind and is sometimes wrapped in plane-tree or chestnut leaves. It may also be matured in wood ash. Ripened for a month, it has a pronounced nutty flavour. From Orléanais.

Golo

Hard ewes' milk cheese from Corsica. Now made by Société, a large company best known for Roquefort, as a golden-crusted Pyrenean type, mild and supple at three months, hard and piquant after six.

Gourmelin see *Chaumes*

Gournay ♨ 🐄 45% ⊖ 100g (3½oz) Ⓑ

A type of Neufchâtel from the Pays de Bray, ripened for no more than a week. The rind has a light down and the flavour is fairly mild. Strictly speaking this is Gournay Affiné; in its freshest state it is often sold as Malakoff. Some *lait cru* farm-made versions can be found.

Graçay 🐐 🐄 45% 450g (1lb) Ⓓ

Flattened cone-shaped cheese with a natural charcoal-covered rind and pure white interior. It has smells mildly goaty and has a nutty flavour. Ripened for about six weeks. From the Arnon valley, Berry.

Grand Mogol ♨ 🐄 75% ⊖ 200g (7oz) Ⓑ

Mild, melt-in-the-mouth triple-cream cheese from the makers of Gratte-Paille and Jean-Grogne. Raw and pasteurized versions exist.

Grand Murol(s) see *Murol*

Grand Rustique ♨ 🐄 45% ⊖ 1kg (2lb) Ⓑ

Raw milk cheese with downy white rind. The paste is buttery yellow and almost foamy in consistency with a delicate flavour. Looks like a small Brie; sometimes sold as Camembert *non pasteurisé*.

Grand Vatel see *Brillat-Savarin*

Grataron d'Arèches 🐐 🐄 45% ⊡ 200g (7oz) Ⓓ

Pressed, uncooked, tangy cheese from Savoie. Dull brown, smooth washed rind, moist paste. Ripened for one month.

Gratte-Paille ♨ 🐄 70% ▱ 350g (12oz) Ⓑ

Cream-enriched white-rinded cheese with a rich, almost fruity flavour. Of recent invention. Available pasteurized or *au lait cru* from a Seine-et-Marne dairy.

Grignette � 🌢 50% ⊖ 180g (6oz) Ⓑ
Raw milk cheese with a soft white rind. Hand-made in a Lyonnais dairy.

Gris de Lille ☇ 🌢 45% ⊂⊃ 800g (1¾lb) Ⓓ
A type of Maroilles, extremely strong and pungent, ripened twice as long with regular washing with brine or beer. Made in Flanders. Also called Vieux Lille, Puant de Lille, Puant Macéré.

Gruyère
Gruyère in France can mean any of the hard cooked alpine cheeses—Emmental, Beaufort or Comté—made in Franche Comté and Savoie. Savoie also produces its own Gruyère and some smaller Gruyères des Bauges. See *Beaufort, Comté, Emmental; Switzerland (Gruyère)*

Heiltz-le-Maurupt see *Cendré d'Argonne*

Henri IV ☇ 🌢 60% ⊖ 1.5kg (3lb) Ⓑ
Modern factory-made Brie-type cheese. Uniform paste, never chalky, never runny.

Hesdin ☇ 🌢 40-42% ⊖ 450g (1lb) Ⓓ
Made at Belval Abbay in Artois, and ripened for two months by *affineurs* who wash the rind with white wine, producing a stronger tasting cheese. See *Belval*

Igny ☇ 🌢 40-45% ⊖ 1.3kg (2½lb) Ⓓ
Pressed uncooked cheese with a washed rind, scraped smooth during its month of ripening. Mild, slightly acidic flavour; elastic texture. Made by monks in Champagne from unpasteurized milk. Also called Abbaye d'Igny, Trappiste d'Igny.

Iraty see *Ossau-Iraty-Brebis Pyrénées*

Jean-Grogne ☇ 🌢 75% ⊖ 500g (18oz) Ⓒ
Triple-cream cheese enriched with crème fraîche. A brother of Gratte-Paille from the same maker (available raw or pasteurized).

Jehan de Brie ☇ 🌢 75% ⊖ 250g (9oz) Ⓑ
Unctuous triple-cream cheese eaten fresh or after a few weeks with a soft white rind. A recent invention, made from unpasteurized milk.

Jonchée see *Caillebotte*

Laguiole ★ ☇ 🌢 45-50% ⊡ 30-50kg (66-110lb) Ⓓ
Superb pressed uncooked cheese, related to Cantal. A much sought-after cheese with smooth, firm light golden yellow paste, pleasant aroma and a wonderful full, slightly tart fruity flavour. The rind is dry, hard and gold, amber or brown depending on age. The best Laguiole is made in summer in *burons* in the Aubrac mountains of Auvergne. Aged for at least four months, although particularly good specimens are sometimes ripened for a further three months to produce a strong robust flavour. Also called Laguiole-Aubrac. Protected by an *appellation d'origine*.

Langres ☇ 🌢 45-52% 200g (7oz) Ⓑ
Strong, spicy, small, orange-brown cheese shaped like a sunken drum, made in Champagne. Ripened for two to three months and washed with brine and annatto. The brine collects in the hollow top and slowly seeps into the cheese, making it distinctively rich and smooth. In season from the end of spring to late autumn.

Larron d'Ors ✿ 🌙 30% 🗀 250-700g (9oz-1½lb) Ⓓ
A rare type of Maroilles made from partly skimmed milk. Quick ripening, about six to seven weeks. Strong-smelling and tangy.

Laruns
Béarnaise town in the Vallée d'Ossau famous for its annual cheese fair (on the first Saturday in October). Local cheeses of the pressed, uncooked Pyrenean type may be made from cows', ewes' or goats' milk (usually unpasteurized), but only the ewes' milk types are eligible for the *appellation d'origine*. See *Ossau-Iraty-Brebis Pyrénées*

Laumes ✿ 🌙 45% 🗀 1kg (2lb) Ⓓ
Rare Burgundian cheese like a larger, square Epoisses. During the three-month ripening the rind is washed with brine or white wine. When made on farms it was occasionally washed with coffee, giving it an oddly smoky flavour.

Levroux 🐐 🌙 45% 250-300g (9-10oz) Ⓓ
Mild, slightly nutty, flattened pyramid with a thin bluish rind. Similar to Valençay, from Berry.

Lezay 🐐 🌙 45% ◯ 2kg (4lb) Ⓑ
From Poitou, cheese with a smooth, medium-flavoured white paste and a firm creamy skin.

Livarot ★ ✿ 🌙 40-45% ⊖ 300-500g (10-18oz) Ⓑ
One of the great Normandy cheeses and one of the oldest. It is usually bound with five strips of sedge, a tradition which began as a support to prevent weaker cheeses from collapsing. Farmhouse production has now been almost entirely superseded by factory-made cheese. A washed rind cheese with an assertive flavour and a smell to match, made from a mixture of skimmed evening and whole morning milk. Ripened in a warm, humid, unventilated environment for about two months. The rind should be a smooth, shiny brown and just moist, neither too dry nor too sticky. The paste should be golden and fairly springy. Avoid cheeses that are runny or sunken in the middle. Protected by an *appellation d'origine*.

Lormes 🐐 🌙 45% 250g (9oz) Ⓓ
Small blue-grey flattened cone with a delicate, pleasant flavour. Similar to Valençay, but from Nivernais. Occasionally *mi-chèvre*.

Lorraine see *Géromé*

Lou Palou ✿ 🌙 50% ⊖ 4kg (9lb) Ⓑ
Brand name for an almost white cheese with a mild lactic flavour and many small eyes. It is ripened for 21 days and is given its black plastic coat after two weeks. Made in the eastern Pyrenees from June to December from pasteurized cows' milk. (The rest of the year the same factory makes the ewes' milk Etorki.) See *Pyrénées*

Lucullus
A term used for several triple-cream cheeses made in Normandy and the Ile de France. See *Boursault*

Lusignan 🐐 🌙 45% ⊖ 200g (7oz) Ⓓ
Small, mild *chèvre*, barely ripened, creamy and smooth, pure white in colour. Also sold *affiné* (after about two weeks) with a thin blue crust and nuttier flavour. From Poitou.

Malakoff see *Gournay*

Mamirolle 🐄 🔪 40% 🧀 500g (18oz) ⑧

Created at a dairy school in Franche Comté using pasteurized milk. A lightly pressed, washed rind cheese. Reminiscent of German Limburger but somewhat gentler.

Maroilles ★ 🐄 🔪 45-50% 🧀 200-800g (7oz-1¾lb) ⑧

The *pater familias* of Flemish washed rind cheeses. Certainly one of the most ancient cheeses, invented in the 10th century by one of the monks at the abbey of Maroilles. Since then it has acquired a string of admirers and as many variations and imitations. The rind is reddish with a light damp sheen and should not be too sticky or too dry. The paste is a smooth pale yellow and, while certainly tangy, is rather more subtle in flavour than other similar cheeses. It should not be bitter or chalky in texture. The smell is strong and full. The ripening period lasts about four months. Most Maroilles are now made in large dairies from heat-treated milk. Smaller versions are sold under the names Maroilles-Sorbais, -Mignon and -Quart. Protected by an *appellation d'origine*. See *Gris de Lille*, *Dauphin*

Meilleraye, La 🐄 🥛 45% 🧀 2kg (4lb) ⑩

Lightly pressed, uncooked, fruity, slightly lactic tasting cheese from the Abbey of Melleray in Brittany. Based on the Entrammes recipe.

Mimolette 🐄 🥛 40-45% ⭕ 2.5-4kg (5½-9lb) ©

Made in Flanders and now in other parts of France, a direct copy of Dutch Edam with annatto colouring. Often eaten young, but best after at least six months, when it can be called Demi-Vieux or Demi-Etuvé. When fully matured (Vieux or Etuvé), at nine months to two years, it becomes much harder and nuttier, with a thick grey crust. Also called Boule de Lille. Boule du Pays is smaller.

Monsieur Fromage

Rich, delicate, double-cream (60 per cent fat) cheese with a thin bloomy white rind and a creamy velvety yellow paste with a superb fruity flavour. Invented in the last century by the appropriately named Monsieur Fromage of Normandy, production ceased in the 1970s, but some double- and triple-cream cheeses are still being sold under this name. Also called Fromage de Monsieur.

Mont-des-Cats 🐄 🔪 40-45% 🧀 2kg (4lb) ⑩

Monastery-made in Flanders. Similar to Saint-Paulin.

Mont d'Or see *Vacherin du Haut-Doubs*

Montegrosso see *Calenzana*

Montoire 🐐 🥛 45% 100g (3½oz) ⑩

Small, blue-grey flattened cone with a mild goaty aroma and mellow flavour. A farmhouse cheese from the Loire valley. A local co-operative makes a raw milk version sold fresh, coated with charcoal.

Montrachet 🐐 🥛 45% 🧀 75g (2½oz) ⑧

Small cylindrical goat cheese ripened for about a week in vine or chestnut leaves. From the *département* of Saône-et-Loire.

Montréal

A kind of Epoisses made on a small scale in the Serein valley.

Morbier 🐄 🥛 45% 🧀 3-9kg (7-20lb) ⑧

An odd-looking cheese made during the winter in the Juras. The pale yellow smooth paste is divided horizontally by a band of blue-black soot, ash or, more often these days, vegetable colouring. Traditionally the cheese was made from morning and evening milk coagulated separately. The soot protected the morning curds until the evening curds were placed on top. A mellow cheese, virtually odourless, with a light grey, dry rind. Ripened for two to three months. Best in spring.

Mothe-Saint-Héray, La   🔥 🍷 45% 200g (7oz) Ⓑ

One of several fine cheeses made in a variety of shapes in the Poitevin town of the same name. It is ripened for a couple of weeks and has a fairly pronounced flavour and a downy white rind. A farm-made version has a thin bluish rind and is occasionally presented on a vine or plane leaf—known as Mothais, Chèvre à la Feuille.

Moyaux see *Pavé d'Auge*

Munster ★   🍷 🍷 40% 🌀 450g-1.5kg (1-3lb) Ⓑ

An ancient cheese from the eastern Vosges mountains, supposedly first made by Irish monks who settled in the area in the 7th century. The cheese is red-skinned, very spicy and tangy with an emphatic aroma. The paste is buttery yellow, very rich and creamy. In Alsace itself it is often eaten when younger and milder. The farmhouse type (Munster Fermier) is made in summer in the *hautes chaumes* (high mountain pastures), and in winter on farms lower down the slopes. Munster Laitier is made all year round from pasteurized milk. The ripening period is one to three months depending on size. Best between May and November. Protected by an *appellation d'origine* which it shares with Lorraine's Géromé. See *Germany (Münster)*

Murol   🍷 🍷 45% 450g (1lb) Ⓑ

A mild, pressed, ring-shaped cheese with a small hole in the middle. The washed rind is pinkish-brown and fairly resilient. A variation of Saint-Nectaire from Auvergne. Also called Grand Murols. A raw milk version is sometimes available.

Nantais   🍷 🍷 40% 🗀 200g (7oz) Ⓑ

The most important Breton cheese, introduced during the French Revolution by a priest from the Vendée. A pressed, uncooked washed rind cheese with a full flavour and pronounced smell. Golden to light brown smooth rind. Usually pasteurized. Also called Curé, Fromage du Curé. Carré Breton is a factory-made version.

Neufchâtel ★   🍷 🍷 45% Ⓑ

Famous white bloomy rinded cheese moulded in a variety of shapes—heart, roll, loaf, square, known as Coeur, Bondon, Briquette and Carré—from the rich dairy country of Bray, Normandy. The process is a particularly laborious one, resulting in a white, soft, smooth cheese with a distinctively lactic flavour. Nowadays mostly factory-made although *lait cru* versions can be found. Some people keep the cheese longer than the usual three weeks, when the flavour becomes more pronounced and rather salty, and the rind shows traces of red-brown pigmentation. Protected by an *appellation d'origine*.

Niolo, Niulincu   🍷 45-50% 🗀 500-700g (18oz-1½lb) Ⓓ

Farm-made in the mountains of northern Corsica from raw ewes' or goats' milk. A fiercely strong cheese with a spiciness from the *maquis* herbs, juniper and wild honeysuckle. The freshly made cheese is dried for one or two weeks, bathed in brine, then ripened in humid cellars for at least three months, being regularly washed and scraped. It has a smooth, greyish rind and a firm yellow paste with a melt-in-the-mouth texture. Can be eaten fresh and mild but more often aged until hard and sharp. Similar to Asco and Venaco.

Noyers-le-Val see *Cendré d'Argonne*

Oelenberg 🏵 ⟆ 45% ⊝ 1.3kg (2½lb) Ⓓ
Gentle cheese with an elastic, golden yellow paste and a smooth pale golden rind. Ripened for two months. Made all year round from raw milk, by monks of the Abbaye de Notre Dame d'Oelenberg, Alsace.

Oléron 🐑 ⟆ 45-50% Ⓓ
A rare survivor of the ewes' milk Caillebottes of Poitou. Very mild, white and creamy. Farm-made on the island of Oléron and in Vendée.

Olivet Bleu ★ 🏵 ⟆ 45% ⊝ 300g (10oz) Ⓑ
A light, almost sweet-flavoured cheese reminiscent of Coulommiers. The white rind flora has a blue tinge and arises naturally during the one-month ripening period. Sold wrapped in leaves. There is also a much stronger Olivet Cendré, which is cured for three months in the ashes of vine stems. Olivet au Foin is ripened in hay. Named after a town near Orléans where the cheeses used to be sold.

Oloron-Sainte-Marie
This Béarnaise town is famous for its cheese market, where various farmhouse cheeses are sold under the local name. See *Pyrénées*

Orrys, Les 🏵 ⟆ 45% ⊝ 10-12kg (22-26lb) Ⓓ
Pressed, fruity, aromatic cheese once made on the Ariège mountains in summer. Reminiscent of good Swiss Raclette, now very rare.

Ossau-Iraty-Brebis Pyrénées ★ 🐑 ⟆ 50% ⊝ 2-5kg (4-11lb) Ⓑ
The firm Basque cheeses known as Ardi-Gasna and Iraty and the Béarnaise cheese from the Vallée d'Ossau have been recognized with the *appellation d'origine* of Ossau-Iraty-Brebis Pyrénées. To qualify they must be made by traditional methods, although there are many imitations. Lightly pressed, uncooked with a pale to golden supple compact paste. The thin rind is smooth orange-yellow to various shades of brown or grey, the flavour delicately lactic to full and mellow according to age. Ripened for at least three months, they can be kept much longer for a harder, sharper cheese. See *Pyrénées*

Ourde see *Pyrénées*

Oust, Oustet see *Bethmale*

P'Ail see *Gaperon*

Palet de Balbigny 🏵 ⟆ 52% 100g (3½oz) Ⓑ
Small oval cheese made from raw milk in Lyonnais. Soft and creamy when young, darker, firmer and slightly crumbly after a few weeks.

Palet Périgourdin see *Chèvrefeuille*

Pannes Cendré 🏵 ⟆ 20-30% ⊝ 300g (10oz) Ⓓ
Made from skimmed milk and ripened in wood ash for three months. Similar to Olivet Cendré and made in farms and dairies in Orléans.

Passe-l'An 🏵 ⟆ 28-32% ⊡ 35-40kg (77-88lb) Ⓒ
An imitation of Italian Grana developed during World War II when imports of Italian cheese were proscribed. The name derives from the fact that the cheeses must be aged for at least a year.

Patay 🏵 ⟆ 20-45% ⊝ 500g (18oz) Ⓓ
Similar to Olivet. Blued naturally or ripened in wood ash. Now rare.

Pavé d'Affinois ⚕ 🌑 45% ⬚ 150g (5oz) Ⓑ
Soft smooth cheese in a thick white coat. Made by a large creamery in the Loire *département* south of Lyon.

Pavé d'Auge ⚕ 🌑 50% ⬚ 600g (1¼lb) Ⓑ
Washed rind cheese which looks like a deep Pont l'Evêque. Fairly firm yellow paste with lots of small elliptical holes. Strong and spicy, almost bitter. The rind may be deep russet or a paler pinkish gold, with a pronounced aroma. Ripened for two to four months. Largely hand-made, from raw milk, in the Pays d'Auge. (*Pavé*, 'slab' or 'paving stone'). Also called Pavé de Moyaux, Carré de Bonneville.

Pavé Blésois ⬧ 🌑 45% ⬚ 250g (9oz) Ⓓ
Lightly nutty, with a thin blue rind. Made near the town of Blois on the river Loire. Also known as Pavé de la Sologne.

Pavé de Moyaux see *Pavé d'Auge*

Pavin ⚕ 🌑 45% ⊖ 500g (18oz) Ⓒ
A type of small, pasteurized Saint-Nectaire.

Pélardon ⬧ 45% ⊖ 60-125g (2-4oz) Ⓑ
Small, thin, disc-shaped cheeses from the Auvergne, Cévennes and Gévaudan mountains and northern Languedoc. May be sold soft, fresh and white or aged for two to three weeks with a blue-grey crust. Odourless, with a very agreeable nutty flavour and the typical goaty aftertaste. Some are coated in black pepper or herbs. All are basically simple rustic cheeses and are still made almost entirely on local farms.

Pérail, Péral ⬥ 🌑 45-55% ⊖ 100-250g (3½-9oz) Ⓓ
Flat pale to deep golden discs with smooth aromatic paste. Sold young and white or ripened for up to three weeks. Made with raw milk in Rouergue, from December to July.

Persillé des Aravis ⬧ 🌑 45% ⬚ 500g-1kg (18oz-2lb) Ⓓ
Blue-veined farmhouse cheese from Haute-Savoie. It has a rough grey-brown natural rind and is very savoury and sharp. Ripened for about two months. Probably the best of the few blue-veined goat cheeses. Also called Persillé de Thônes, Persillé du Grand-Bornand, Persillé de la Clusaz.

Persillé du Mont-Cenis 🌑 45% ⬚ 8kg (18lb) Ⓓ
Blue-veined cheese using a mixture of cows' and goats' milk. Lightly pressed with a firm greyish crust. Ripened for about three months. Farmhouse-made in Savoie.

Pétafine see *Fromage Fort*

Petit Bessay ⚕ 🌑 40-45% ⊖ 200g (7oz) Ⓓ
Bourbonnais farmhouse cheese with a thin natural rind, mild lactic smell and gentle fruity flavour. Sold locally in summer and autumn.

Petit Brie see *Coulommiers*

Petit Lisieux
Flatter, raw milk version of Livarot. Ripened two months, some find it milder than Livarot, but still a fruity tasting cheese.

Petit-Suisse ⚕ 🌙 60% ⊖ 30-60g (1-2oz) Ⓐ
Fresh double-cream cheese made with pasteurized milk. Unsalted, bland, with a moist consistency. Invented in the mid 19th century by

Charles Gervais, a Swiss cheesemaker, who added cream to a Neufchâtel Bondon and sold the cheese unripened. There is also a triple-cream version. Now made all over France, often to a completely different formula: partly skimmed milk is separated by centrifuge instead of renneting, giving a lower fat, watery product.

Picadou

Speciality of Quercy. Dry Cabécou fermented in pots and served in vine leaves. Very strong flavour.

Picodon   🐐 🌙 45-50% ⊖ 50-100g (1¾-3½oz) ©

These tiny sharp (Picodon comes from *piquer*, to prick) cheeses are so greatly esteemed in their area of production (Dauphiné and Vivarais) that there is an annual festival to celebrate and enjoy them, held in Saoû (Dauphiné) around 21 July. Pidance and the Picodon de Valréas are mildest, sold after 12 days. The Picodons of Ardèche and Saint-Agrève (from Vivarais) and of Drôme (Dauphiné) are rich, strong and nutty, developing a white bloom which turns golden or powder blue with time. Representative of the old style of Picodon, which used to be stored in pots with eau-de-vie or wine, is the Picodon de Dieulefit. This is ripened for at least a month, and is regularly washed with wine. It has an alcoholic smell, truly piquant flavour and a red-gold rind. Protected by an *appellation d'origine*.

Pierre-Qui-Vire   🍄 🌙 45% ⊖ 200g (7oz) Ⓓ

Annatto-coloured brine-washed smelly tangy cheese from the Benedictine monastery of La Pierre-Qui-Vire, Burgundy. Can be eaten fresh. Similar to Epoisses. A larger version is sold as Le Trinquelin. The fresh curd may also be rolled into a ball with herbs and sold as La Boule des Moines. All organic and unpasteurized.

Pierre-Robert see *Brillat-Savarin*

Pierre-sur-Haute see *Fourme des Monts du Forez*

Pipo Crem' see *Bleu de Bresse*

Pithiviers au Foin see *Bondaroy au Foin*

Poivre d'Ane see *Banon*

Poivre d'Auvergne see *Bougnat*

Pont l'Evêque ★   🍄 🌙 45-50% ▭ 300-400g (10-14oz) Ⓑ

Probably the oldest of the Normandy cheeses, known to the author of the *Roman de la Rose* (1236) as Angelot. Since the 1600s it has been called Pont l'Evêque after the market town in Calvados which became the principal distribution point. Still made mostly on farms from unpasteurized milk, although factory production is beginning to gather momentum. It is a tender golden-yellow cheese with a ridged rind that is yellowy gold or light tan depending on the finishing. The milk should be coagulated as soon as possible after milking, ideally warm from the cow. The curds are lightly cut and drained for ten minutes before being placed in square moulds. After five days they are salted, then transferred to the humid curing room. Over the next four to six weeks the rind may be brine-washed (smooth golden finish) or brushed (paler, pink tinged, slightly rougher). The smell should be full and savoury but not offensive and the flavour rich and tangy without being sharp or bitter. Best from summer to early winter. Avoid cheeses where the rind is brittle or cracked. Protected by an *appellation d'origine*.

Port-du-Salut, Port-Salut ♉ 🐄 45-50% ⊝ 225g-2kg (8oz-4lb) Ⓑ
Lightly pressed cheese with a tawny washed rind and smooth, springy paste. The flavour is mellow, not as tangy as other washed rind cheeses. Port-du-Salut originated in the early 19th century at the abbey of Entrammes, but in the 1950s the monks sold the right to the name to a large dairy who switched production to Lorraine, using pasteurized milk. See *Entrammes, Saint-Paulin*

Pouligny-Saint-Pierre 🐐 🐄 45% 225-250g (8-9oz) Ⓑ
Pyramid-shaped with a blue-grey rind and a tangy flavour. Nicknamed La Tour Eiffel because of its tall thin shape. Ripened a month, sometimes wrapped in leaves. Protected by an *appellation d'origine*.

Pourly 🐐 🐄 45-50% ☐ 300g (10oz) Ⓓ
Delicate, sweetly nutty goat cheese made in small dairies in Burgundy. It has a blue grey natural rind and a smooth white paste. Ripened for a month.

Poustagnac
Fresh cheese made from cows', ewes', or goats' milk and flavoured with garlic, peppercorns or pimento. From Les Landes.

Prince de Claverolle, Prince de Navarre see *Pyrénées*

Providence see *Bricquebec*

Puant de Lille, Puant Macéré see *Gris de Lille*

Pyrénées
The mountains dividing France from Spain are known for two main styles of cheese, either of which may be sold as *fromage des Pyrénées*, with varying degrees of authenticity. The firm Basque and Béarnaise ewes' milk cheeses have a history dating back over 4,000 years. The main cheesemaking season is from Christmas to July, after the ewes have given birth and before they are in lamb again, but cheeses are also made during the summer *transhumance*, when flocks are taken to the high mountain pastures. Béarnaise farmers have a long tradition of keeping cows as well as sheep, and their cheeses may be made from either milk, or mixed. Goats are a more recent introduction to the region's dairying. All these cheeses are typically uncooked pressed 2-7kg (4-15lb) drums or wheels, with a thin natural golden to brown crust formed during the minimum three-month ripening when they are regularly turned and rubbed with salt or a brine-soaked cloth. Kept longer, they become harder and more piquant. The ewes' milk cheeses (*fromages de brebis*) in particular have a distinctive nutty piquancy and only pure ewes' milk cheeses are entitled to the Ossau-Iraty-Brebis Pyrénées *appellation*. Cows', goats' and mixed milk cheeses and those made outside the AOC area may bear the name of their place of origin, such as Esbareich, Laruns, Ourde; others are branded—for example the pasteurized Prince de Claverolle.
  The western Pyrenees produce *fromage des Pyrénées Ariégoises*, the best known of which is Bethmale, nowadays generally a cows' milk cheese. The pale, supple paste is punctuated by many tiny horizontal slits, mild when young, developing a melt-in-the-mouth richness after several months. Some farmhouse cheeses have a black coat, which may come from ripening on slate shelves, walnut juice, grape pressings or other natural stages in manufacture. Factory versions, coated in black plastic, are often a bland travesty of the original—many do not even use Pyrenean milk. See *Abbaye de Belloq, Ardi-Gasna, Bethmale, Ossau-Iraty-Brebis Pyrénées*

FRANCE

Ramequin de Lagnieu
Small cylindrical farmhouse goats' cheese made in Bugey. Eaten after two or three weeks' ripening, when it is firm and tangy, or aged further and used for fondue or making Fromage Fort.

Ramoun see *Barousse*

Reblochon ★ 🐄 🥛 45-50% ⊖ 250-500g (9-18oz) Ⓑ
One of the magnificent cheeses from the mountains of Haute-Savoie, in particular the Aravis Massif centring on Thônes. Reblochon uses the pasteurized or unpasteurized milk of Abondance or Tarentaise cattle and is made by farms, *fruitières* and large dairies. It is a lightly pressed, scalded cheese with a supple creamy paste and firm pinkish-brown washed rind patched with white mould. The flavour is mild, fruity and absolutely delicious—although it can be bitter if old or badly made. Usually ripened for about five weeks. Sold between two paper-thin wooden discs. The name comes from a dialect word for second milking which refers not to the second milking of the day but to the particularly rich milk that is left in the cow towards the end of a milking. When the farm owner had checked the milk yield, cowherds would milk the cows again, using the rich milk to make their own cheese, namely Reblochon. Protected by an *appellation d'origine*.

Riceys, Les 🐄 🥛 20-40% ⊖ 250-300g (9-10oz) Ⓓ
Made in Bar-sur-Aube, Champagne from whole or skimmed milk and ripened in the ashes of vine stems for one to two months. Fairly strong. Also called Cendré des Riceys, Champenois. See *Cendré*

Rigotte 🥛 40-50% ⊡ 40-90g (1½-3oz) Ⓑ
Very small round cheese made in Lyonnais and the Auvergne from cows' milk or a mixture of cows' and goats' milk. Usually ripened for no more than a week—kept longer it hardens and is used in the local Fromage Fort. Fairly mild to tangy in flavour depending on the milk and the finishing. Some are ripened naturally, some steeped in white wine or oil. Some are artificially coloured. The name is probably a corruption of *recuite* ('recooked'), or of the name Ricotta, meaning the same in Italian, indicating that the cheeses are, or at least were, whey cheeses—nowadays full milk is used. Rigotte de Condrieu, Rigotte des Alpes and Rigotte de Pélussin are the best known.

Rocamadour 🥛 45-50% ⊖ 30g (1oz) Ⓓ
Tiny flat cheeses made in Quercy from ewes' milk in spring, goats' milk in summer and autumn and ripened for one week. Delicate bluish skin and nutty taste.

Rochefort see *Fourme de Rochefort*

Rocroi 🐄 🥛 20-30% 350g (12oz) Ⓓ
Square or disc-shaped farmhouse cheese made from skimmed milk in Champagne. Ripened in wood ash for one to two months. Fairly strong to very strong depending on age. Also called Cendré des Ardennes, Rocroi Cendré. See *Cendré*

Rogeret des Cévennes 🐐 🥛 45% ⊖ 90g (3oz) Ⓓ
Tangy, even fierce, small cheese with a strong goaty smell, made in Languedoc in summer and autumn. Ripened for about a month in cool damp cellars, when the sticky reddish skin forms.

Rollot 🐄 🥛 45-50% 200g (7oz) Ⓑ
Round or heart-shaped cheese from Picardy, similar to Maroilles. Soft, supple, strong-smelling and tangy. Ripened for two months.

Romans 🐄 🐏 50% ▱ 250g (9oz) Ⓑ

Rich, dense yet melting textured nutty-tasting cheese with a slightly sour note. Matured for three weeks, it ripens from the outside, giving the crust a rippled appearance. Gold mouldy rind, becoming blue-grey. From the Dauphiné area. Also called Tomme de Romans.

Roquefort ★ 🐑 🐏 52% ▱ 2.5kg (5½lb) Ⓑ

A cheese with champions as diverse as Pliny, Charlemagne and Casanova arouses formidable expectations. Even people who do not like blue cheeses generally like Roquefort. At its best it is extraordinarily delicate, with none of the harsh overtones which typify many other blues. It has been made in Les Causses for thousands of years and its makers have regularly ensured that their product is legally defined and protected. They were first granted a monopoly on its making in 1411 and this has been confirmed at frequent intervals ever since. It is now protected by an *appellation d'origine*.

Roquefort is made from the milk of the Lacaune breed of sheep and ripened in the caves of Combalou. For nearly 100 years, Corsica and the Pyrenees sent ewes' milk cheeses to be ripened here, extending the availability of the cheese over the whole year, but since the 1980s the Roquefort area has supplied its own needs. (Even so, the best cheeses are those bought from April to November—others will have been subjected to cold storage, not *affinage*, in Roquefort.) The caves, ventilated by currents of air known as *fleurines*, provided ideal conditions for the development of the mould now defined as *Penicillium roquefortii*. This mould, which once grew naturally, is now partly induced by being sprinkled in powdered form on the curds as they are ladled into the moulds. The cheeses are then pierced with steel needles during the three-month ripening period. For the final part of this time the cheeses are closely wrapped in tin foil so that the finished product has virtually no rind. The veining (more green than blue) should be evenly distributed throughout the cheese and the paste should be creamy white and rather buttery. The sheepish origins of the cheese should be easily detectable in both flavour and aroma—the milk is never pasteurized. Unfortunately many exported Roqueforts tend to be oversalted to improve their keeping qualities.

Roulé

Modern rich cheese 'Swiss roll' made with vegetarian rennet. Following the success of the ubiquitous garlic and herb flavour the inventors have come up with many variations: exotic spices, salmon and dill, blue cheese and mushroom—even strawberry.

Rouy 🐄 🐏 50% ▱ 225g (8oz) Ⓒ

Like a small Munster. An early 20th century invention, made in dairies and factories.

Royal Paillaud 🐄 🐏 60% ▱ 200g (7oz) Ⓑ

Like a small, thick Olivet au Foin, with wisps of hay clinging to a bloomy white rind. From a large dairy in Berry.

Ruffec 🐐 🐏 45% ▱ 250-300g (9-10oz) Ⓓ

Poitevin goat cheese which develops a natural dry bluish rind after one month's ripening. It has a smooth, fairly nutty-tasting paste. Sometimes eaten fresh.

Sableau 🐐 🐏 45% 200-300g (7-10oz) Ⓓ

Fresh white triangular cheese from Vendée. Moist and mildly goaty. Also called Trois Cornes, Trébèche.

Saingorlon see *Bleu de Bresse*

Saint-Agur ☼ 🍥 60% 2.3kg (5lb) Ⓑ
Modern octagonal blue-veined cheese. Designed to be mild, but the prepacked portions often develop a salty tang.

Saint-Albray ☼ 🍥 50% 2kg (4lb) Ⓑ
Invented in 1976. Notable for its shape, like a flower with a hole in the middle, the rind is rubbed with annatto, with patches of bloomy white *penicillium candidum*. Ripened for two weeks. Cream-coloured mild paste aerated with small holes.

Saint-André ☼ 🍥 75% ▢ 1.7kg (3½lb) Ⓑ
Dairy-made triple-cream drum, with white downy rind.

Saint-Benoît ☼ 🍥 40% ▢ 400g (14oz) Ⓓ
Farmhouse-made from partly skimmed milk in Orléans. Pale yellow with a thin rind and fruity flavour. Ripened two to four weeks.

Saint-Christophe 🍢 🍥 45% ▭ 300g (10oz) Ⓑ
Sainte-Maure type with straw, made by a co-operative in Berry. Full-flavoured. Sold fresh and white or charcoal coated.

Saint-Claude see *Chevret*

Saint-Félicien 🍢 🍥 45% ⊟ 90-125g (4-5oz) Ⓓ
Irregularly shaped rustic Vivarais cheese with a thin, pale gold or blue rind and a tender rich interior. Prone to over-saltiness. Sometimes also *mi-chèvre*. A cows' milk version is made in Lyonnais and Dauphiné.

Saint-Florentin ☼ 🍥 45-50% ⊟ 450-500g (16-18oz) Ⓑ
Meltingly soft, washed rind cheese from Burgundy similar to Epoisses. Ripened for two months. It has a rich, ruddy colour, a strong smell and a spicy tang. Farm versions are now rare, and the factory-made cheeses are often annatto-coloured rather than washed.

Saint-Gelais 🍢 🍥 45% ▭ 250g (9oz) Ⓓ
Farmhouse *chèvre* from Poitou, presented on a plane leaf. Ripened for six weeks, with a thin blue crust streaked with red.

Saint-Gildas ☼ 🍥 75% ▢ 200g (7oz) Ⓒ
Triple-cream with soft white rind made by a dairy school in Brittany from pasteurized milk. Mild and creamy, matured for two weeks.

Saint-Lizier see *Bethmale*

Saint-Maixent 🍢 🍥 45% ▭ 250g (9oz) Ⓓ
Poitevin cheese with a natural blue-grey rind, strong flavour and a penetrating goaty smell. Ripened six weeks.

Saint-Marcellin ★ ☼ 🍥 50% ⊟ 90g (3oz) Ⓑ
Used to be made with goats' milk but now a cows' milk cheese from Dauphiné. Fairly mild but rich, especially the best *lait cru* types. Ripened for a month—dry cellars will produce a blue rind, damp ones a reddish rind. Some are matured in white wine, others are wrapped in chestnut or Swiss chard leaves. It is *à point* when the paste just clings to the blade of the knife. Best between April and September.

Sainte-Marie ☼ 🍥 45% ▢ 400g (14oz) Ⓓ
Rare fresh white cheese from Burgundy. Bland, slightly lactic.

Sainte-Maure ★ 🍢 🍥 45% ▭ 300g (10oz) Ⓑ
Made in Poitou and Touraine, a soft and creamy cheese with a full

goaty flavour. Both *fermier* and *laitier* types are available. Crusted with a downy white rind tinged with pink. Recognizable by the length of straw through the centre of the cheese (not always present in the factory-made variety). There is also a Sainte-Maure Cendré.

Saint-Nectaire ★ 🏠 🌓 45% ⊖ 1.5kg (3lb) Ⓑ
From the Dore mountains in the Auvergne, an ancient cheese made twice a day from morning and evening milk separately. Pressed for 24 hours and ripened on rye straw for two to four months. A flattish disc with bulging sides and a greyish crust which should show patches of red, white and yellow moulds. It has a firm, golden paste with a gentle mellow flavour. The *fermier* type is infinitely superior in flavour and has an oval plaque on the crust, while the pasteurized *laitier* version has a rectangular plaque; it can be difficult to distinguish them once the plaques are covered with mould. Its best season is from mid-August to December. Protected by an *appellation d'origine*.

Saint-Paulin 🏠 📎 40-50% ⊖ 1.5-2kg (3-4lb) Ⓐ
A factory-made imitation of Port-du-Salut made from pasteurized milk throughout the year all over France and in other countries. It has a thin, smooth, bright orange rind and a mild, bland buttery yellow interior. A pressed uncooked cheese, the curd is washed during the cheesemaking process to soften it, making a rather dull cheese. It is ripened for about two months. See *Entrammes*, *Port-du-Salut*

Saint-Rémy 🏠 📎 40-50% ▭ 200g (7oz) Ⓓ
Lightly pressed washed rind cheese similar to Munster. It has an orange-brown rind, springy pale yellow paste, pronounced smell and a spicy flavour. From Franche Comté and Lorraine.

Salers see *Cantal*

Sarriette, La see *Banon*

Sartenais, Sarteno 🌓 45-50% ○ 1-1.5kg (2-3lb) Ⓓ
Rustic south Corsican ewes' or goats' milk cheese ripened for three months or aged further for grating. It has a firm, close texture and a rich, piquant taste. Sometimes smoked.

Saulieu see *Brillat-Savarin*

Savaron 🏠 📎 45% ⊖ 1.5kg (3lb) Ⓓ
A pressed, uncooked cheese similar to Saint-Nectaire Laitier.

Schigre see *Brocotte*

Selles-sur-Cher ★ 🍃 📎 45% ⊖ 150g (5oz) Ⓑ
Sweet, nutty cheese from Berry, ripened for ten days and covered with powdered charcoal and salt. The surface is blue-black and the paste white, smooth and close-textured. Sometimes made in a heart shape. Protected by an *appellation d'origine*.

Semussac
Small, rich, creamy fresh cows' milk cheese from the village of the same name, north of Bordeaux.

Sorbais see *Maroilles*

Sospel
A semihard cheese from Nice, like a huge Tomme de Savoie. May be made from cows', ewes' or goats' milk. Also called Tomme de Sospel.

Soumaintrain ☼ ⑨ 45% ⊖ 250-350g (9-12oz) Ⓓ

Washed rind cheese from Burgundy, between Saint-Florentin and Munster in flavour and aroma. Ripened for six to eight weeks. Also eaten younger when white and creamy. Annatto-coloured creamery versions are more widely available.

Tamié ☼ ⑨ 45% ⊖ 500g and 1.5kg (18oz and 3lb) Ⓑ

Made at the Abbaye de Tamié near Annecy to the ancient Reblochon recipe, Tamié has a washed, pale ochre to pink rind and a pale, creamy interior which ripens to a richly flavoured unctuousness.

Tartare

Factory-produced soft cream cheese made in Périgord from cows' milk. Flavoured with garlic and parsley, horseradish or walnuts.

Taupinière ✦ ⑨ 45% 125-250g (4-9oz) Ⓓ

Low dome-shaped cheese from Charente—the name means 'mole-hill'. The slightly wrinkled crust has a soft blue mould and the interior is richly nutty. Best from late spring to late summer.

Tavaillon ☼ ⑨ 48% ⊖ 1.5kg (3lb) Ⓑ

Unusual raw milk cheese of modern invention. Like a Vacherin, it is encircled with a strip of bark—in this case larch, which gives a distinctive earthy flavour. Rich creamy golden paste in a washed crust. Unlike other Vacherins it is made all year round (in Beaumont, Haute-Savoie) and is best from May to September.

Tome, Tomme

The word is derived from the Greek *tomos*, meaning a part or fraction, and was originally used for small cheeses made from part of the milking. It became the custom in Savoie to make semihard *tommes* in winter, when there was not enough milk to make the larger Alpine cheeses (other mountain farms have always made goats' milk *tommes*). In Dauphiné the word more often refers to soft young cheeses made from goats' or cows' milk, the best-known of which is the *tomme* of Romans. (Others come from Combovin, Crest and Vercors.) As usage spread over a wider geographical area, the word has come to describe many cheeses of a deep disc shape, and the diminutive *tommette* is increasingly seen.

Tomme d'Abondance see *Abondance*

Tomme d'Aligot see *Tomme Fraîche*

Tomme des Allues ✦ ⑨ 45% ⊖ 3-4kg (7-9lb) Ⓓ

Made in the Tarentaise mountains of Savoie. A pressed, uncooked, mild cheese with a dull yellowy grey smooth rind and smooth buttery paste. Tomme de Courchevel is similar, slightly smaller.

Tomme Arlésienne see *Camarguais*

Tomme de Belley see *Chevret*

Tomme Blanche

Soft, open-textured cows' milk cheese coated with soft white mould. From Auvergne and widely imitated. Also known as Tomme du Velay, Tomme des Neiges.

Tomme de Brach ✦ ⑨ 50% ⊖ 600-800g (1¼-1¾lb) Ⓓ

Rare farmhouse ewes' milk cheese ripened for two to four months. Sometimes blue-veined. Smooth crust, firm paste, rather coarse, fatty taste. Also called Caillada de Vouillos, Fourme de Brach. From Tulle, between Auvergne and Périgord.

Tomme de Camargue see *Camarguais*

Tomme de Courchevel see *Tomme des Allues*

Tomme au Fenouil
Fennel-flavoured semihard *tommes* are traditional in Savoie and Dauphiné, but now rare.

Tomme Fraîche
An unripened or partly ripened Cantal or Laguiole. Used in local Auvergne cuisine. Also called Tomme d'Aligot.

Tomme Grise
Cheeses similar to Tomme de Savoie made elsewhere in France.

Tomme au Marc 🐄 🌙 20-40% ⊟ 1.5-2kg (3-4lb) Ⓓ
Not to be confused with Fondu or Tomme au Raisin, the processed version of this cheese. The authentic Tomme au Marc is a pressed cheese made from partly skimmed raw milk. It is ripened for a total of six months, partly in vats of fermented grape must. Has an overpowering flavour and smell. Also known as La Combe de Savoie.

Tomme de Mont Ventoux see *Cachat*

Tomme de Romans see *Romans*

Tomme de Savoie ★ 🐄 🌙 20-45% ⊟ 2-3kg (4-7lb) Ⓑ
Generic term for the countless pressed cheeses made in Savoie from whole or partly skimmed milk by farms, *fruitières* and creameries. They are firm, smooth cheeses with a yellowy paste and a dry, hard, powdery rind varying from greyish-white to pinky brown. Well-speckled with mould, the rind lends an earthy aroma. Matured for one to two months. The flavour is usually fairly mild and nutty. .

Tomme de Sospel see *Sospel*

Tomme de Valdeblore 🐑 🌙 45% 9-12kg (20-26lb) Ⓓ
Typical of the *tommes* made from the milk of sheep grazing on the hills behind Nice. Pressed uncooked cheese with a natural pinkish grey crust. Matured for three to six months, when young the flavour is slightly lactic, mild and creamy; older cheeses are much stronger in both flavour and aroma. Other local Tommes come from Tende, Vésubie and Valberg.

Toupin 🐄 🌙 45% ⬜ 6kg (13lb) Ⓓ
Pressed cooked cheese from Savoie, ripened for four to eight months. Resilient greyish rind; full-flavoured golden paste.

Trappe, La see *Echourgnac*

Trébèche, Trois Cornes see *Sableau*

Trinquelin see *Pierre-Qui-Vire*

Troyen Cendré see *Barberey*

Vachard 🐄 🌙 25-40% ⊟ 1.5kg (3lb) Ⓒ
Cheese similar to Saint-Nectaire made on farms in Puy-de-Dôme.

Originally made from milk that had been partly skimmed for butter-making. Tangy with a smooth grey crust.

Vacherin d'Abondance see *Abondance*

Vacherin des Beauges ★ ♨ 🕭 45% ⊖ 2kg (4lb) ©
Soft washed rind cheese made in Savoie, similar to Mont d'Or. Bound with a strip of spruce bark. Also called Vacherin des Aillons.

Vacherin du Haut-Doubs ★ ♨ 🕭 50% ⊖ 500g-3kg (18oz-7lb) ⑧
Formerly known as Vacherin du Mont d'Or, but this name has been claimed by the Swiss for their pasteurized version of the cheese. (The French Vacherin, made from raw milk, may also be called simply Mont d'Or.) A superb cheese from Franche Comté, its *appellation d'origine* allows it to be made between August and March and it is in great demand at Christmas. Shaped in cloth-lined moulds, then encircled with a strip of spruce bark and washed with brine for at least three weeks. The spruce imparts its resinous flavour to the pale interior of the cheese which becomes almost liquid as it matures. The undulating golden crust, tinged with pink, shows faint cloth markings. To eat the cheese, some experts recommend removing the rind and spooning out the paste. See *Switzerland (Vacherin Mont d'Or)*

Valençay ★ 🍢 🕭 45% 250-300g (9-10oz) ⑧
A flattened pyramid shape with a deep blue-grey surface covered with wood ash. Ripened for about a month, the paste is smooth and white with a delicate, by no means overpowering, goaty flavour. The *fermier* type is made in Berry from the end of spring until autumn. The commercial version, Valençay Laitier, is made all year round using frozen curds or powdered milk out of season. Ripened for a shorter time and coarser and stronger than the farmhouse type.

Venaco
Ewes' or goats' milk cheese from the mountains of north Corsica. Some tasters have found it milder than Niolo, but it is made in the same way and has a similarly strong spicy flavour. See *Niolo*

Vendôme Bleu ♨ 🕭 50% ⊖ 200-225g (7-8oz) ⑩
From the Loire valley, a pleasant, fruity flavoured cheese similar to Coulommiers but with a natural light blue-white rind. Ripened for about a month. Vendôme Cendré is the same cheese ripened in ashes, drier and stronger than Vendôme Bleu. Both are very rare and most Vendômois cheeses are of goats' milk, charcoal-coated.

Ventoux see *Cachat*

Vercorin ♨ 🕭 50% 300g (10oz) ⑧
Rather salty washed rind raw milk cheese from a Dauphiné dairy.

Véritable Trappe ♨ 🕭 40% ⊖ 300g-1.7kg (10oz-3½lb) ⑧
Made by nuns at Laval, sister house of the Entrammes monastery. They follow the original Port-du-Salut recipe, although now use pasteurized milk. See *Entrammes*

Vermenton 🍢 🕭 45% 50g (1¾oz) ⑩
Now very rare, cone-shaped, blue-rinded cheese from Burgundy.

Vieux Lille see *Gris de Lille*

Vieux Pont ♨ 🕭 50% ⊂⊃ 300g (10oz) ⑩
Small Pavé d'Auge, washed in Calvados and cured for a month.

Vignotte ☼ ♨ 72% ▢ Ⓑ

Meltingly soft, bloomy-rinded cheese made by a large dairy in Champagne. A smaller version of the cheese is sometimes sold as Véritable Fromage des Vignerons.

Ville-Saint-Jacques see *Brie de Montereau*

Yolo

Drum-shaped hard ewes' milk cheese from the western Pyrenees, made from pasteurized milk by Société, who also make Roquefort.

KEY WORDS

Abbaye abbey. Denotes a monastery-made cheese, almost always using traditional methods and unpasteurized milk. See name of abbey in listing

Affiné ripened, cured, aged, as opposed to fresh

Affineur specialist cheese store where cheeses from various farms are taken for ripening

Appellation d'origine label of origin carried by cheeses conforming to legally defined conditions as to type and origin of milk, area of manufacture, production methods, physical characteristics. Guarantee of authenticity, but not necessarily of quality

Artisanal cheese made by hand rather than by machine

Biologique organic

Bondon see main listing

Brebis ewe, ewes' milk cheese

Brique brick (-shaped)

Bûche log (-shaped)

Buron small mountain chalet where cheese is made by traditional methods

Carré square (-shaped)

Cendré see main listing

Chèvre see main listing

Cœur heart (-shaped)

Crème cream *Crème de . . .* on labels indicates a processed cheese where the named cheese is the basic ingredient

Cru see *Lait cru*

Double-crème minimum fat content of 60 per cent

Ecremé skimmed

Fermier farmhouse-made from unpasteurized milk; ripened on the farm or at an *affineur*

Feuille leaf; ripened or wrapped in leaves

Foin hay; ripened in hay

Fourme word denoting cheese, particularly that mountain-made in the Auvergne

Fondu see *Fromage Fondu* in main listing

Frais, fraîche fresh, unripened

Fromage cheese

Fromage Fort see main listing

Fruitière small co-operative dairy using milk (usually raw) from local farms, particularly in Savoie, Franche Comté and remote mountain areas

Haute montagne high mountain; cheeses so labelled are better than the same cheese made in the valley since milk from summer pastures is used

Lait cru raw milk given no heat treatment; particular 'growth' of milk, from a specifically defined locality, with all its idiosyncrasies intact

Laitier made in a large dairy from pasteurized milk

Lingot ingot (shaped like a squared log)

Maigre low fat; less than 20 per cent

Mi-chèvre see *Chèvre*

Pasteurisé pasteurized

Pavé slab (-shaped)

Persillé parsleyed; refers to blue-veined cheeses, mainly from Savoie and Dauphiné

Pur chèvre see *Chèvre*

Trappiste monastery-made cheese. See *Abbaye*

Triple-crème Cheese made from whole milk with added cream. Minimum fat content of 75 per cent

Vache cow; its derivatives Vachard and Vacherin denote cows' milk cheese. It may stand alone in areas where ewes' and goats' milk cheese predominate

Germany

Germany is one of the leading dairying nations, trailing only France, the United States and the USSR in terms of cheese production. Germans are inordinately fond of cheese, a fact which was noted centuries ago by Julius Caesar himself and is confirmed by modern marketing surveys. Even so, German cheeses have a limited international reputation. Most of them are scarcely known outside Germany and many Germans are themselves hard put to name more than three or four genuinely indigenous varieties. One of the reasons for the paradox is that a considerable proportion of the huge domestic production is taken up with foreign cheese types and cheeses for processing. Another reason is that the most important indigenous cheese is Quark, a fresh curd cheese which, until the advent of modern refrigerated transport, could not be successfully exported. Of the ripened types, the various kinds of Sauermilchkäse are generally so strong and pungent as to require a degree of acclimatization that most consumers are unprepared to concede to new and untried foodstuffs. In fact, with one or two exceptions German cheeses tend to be either rather bland or rather strong.

Cheese is made all over Germany (almost entirely from cows' milk; there are few notable ewes' or goats' milk cheeses), but the most important area is the Allgäu, where the Alps straddle the Swiss-German border. The word Allgäuer on a cheese label is a reliable guarantee of a quality product. As one might expect, quality control in cheesemaking is highly developed: German regulations and strictures on labelling are among the most detailed and precise in the world. There are no fewer than eight official categories of fat content:

Mager	less than 10%	low fat
Viertelfettstufe	10-20%	quarter fat
Halbfettstufe	20-30%	half fat
Dreiviertelfettstufe	30-40%	three-quarter fat
Fettstufe	40-45%	fat
Vollfettstufe	45-60%	full fat
Rahmstufe	50-60%	cream
Doppelrahmstufe	60-85%	double cream

Abertamerkäse see *Schafmilchkäse*

Alpenkäse see *Bergkäse*

Alte Kuhkäse see *Handkäse*

Altenburger Ziegenkäse ★ 🐏 20-45% 🧀 250g (9oz) Ⓓ
Made in Thuringia from a mixture of unpasteurized cows' and goats' milk. A rare connoisseur's cheese with a rich yellow paste punctuated with a few irregular eyes and flavoured with caraway seeds. Very strong-tasting and aromatic. Treated with both *Penicillium camemberti* and coryne bacteria during the ripening period, it is a temperamental cheese and one that is very difficult to make successfully.

Ansgar
A milder sweeter version of Tilsiter.

Backsteiner 🐄 🐏 38% 🧀 200g (7oz) Ⓒ
'Brick' cheese; a washed rind, surface-ripened, Limburger-type cheese made from partly skimmed milk.

Bauernhandkäse see *Handkäse*

Bavaria Blu see *Blue Brie*

Bergkäse ♨ ● 45% ⊜ 20-50kg (44-110lb) Ⓑ
'Mountain cheese', a hard-pressed cooked cheese with small round eyes, similar to Emmental but smaller in size and slower-maturing, with a darker rind and a stronger, more aromatic flavour. Made in the Allgäu from raw milk. Also called Alpenkäse.

Berliner Kuhkäse see *Handkäse*

Bianco ♨ ● 55% ⊜ 4kg (9lb) Ⓑ
Trade name (from Italian, meaning 'white') for a pale, mild creamy cheese, with lots of small holes, similar to Tilsiter.

Biarom ♨ ● 45% ⊜ 1kg (2lb) Ⓑ
Trade name for a Bavarian cheese similar to Danish Esrom.

Bierkäse see *Weisslackerkäse*

Biestkäse
Freshly made from beestings. Also called Kolostrumkäse.

Blue Brie ♨ ◐ 60-70% ⊟ Ⓐ
The Germans discovered the marketing possibilities of a mildly 'blued' cheese with white rind flora in the 1970s and it has proved an immensely successful export. Made from pasteurized milk with added cream. Sold under brand names such as Bavaria Blu, Cambozola.

Bodenfelder see *Handkäse*

Bruder Basil ♨ ● 45% ⊟ 1kg (2lb) Ⓑ
Brand name for a traditionally made version of the Bavarian smoked processed cheese one finds almost everywhere. Smooth, firm, yellow cheese with a dark mahogany-coloured rind. Creamy with a pleasantly smoky flavour. There is also a variation flavoured with chopped ham.

Butterkäse ♨ ◐ 50% Ⓒ
A smooth, bland and, as the name suggests, buttery cheese made throughout Germany and Austria. The paste is a clear, pale yellow with or without irregular holes, and the rind is golden to reddish in colour. It comes either in a loaf or a sausage shape weighing 450g-2kg (1-4lb). It is delicate, odourless and quite inoffensive. Also called Damenkäse (ladies cheese).

Buttermilchquark
Fresh lactic-curd cheese made with a mixture of buttermilk and skimmed milk.

Cambozola see *Blue Brie*

Caramkäse
Smooth, bland, elastic cheese, occasionally smoked.

Doppelrahmfrischkäse see *Rahmfrischkäse*

Edelpilzkäse ★ ♨ ◐ 45-50% 2-5kg (4-11lb) Ⓑ
A fine blue-veined cheese with a pale ivory paste and very dark veins travelling vertically through the cheese. It has a strong fruity flavour. The name means 'glorious mould cheese' and it is sometimes sold outside Germany as 'German Blue'. It can be drum- or loaf-shaped.

Edelschimmelkäse
A term which refers to cheeses that have blue veins or white rind flora or both.

Emmental 🐄 ➤ 45% ⊖ 40-90kg (88-198lb) Ⓑ
Although Emmental is definitely Swiss, Allgäuer Emmental has been made in Germany for centuries. Made from raw milk, at its best between six and eight months old. See *Switzerland (Emmental)*

Faustkäse see *Handkäse*

Friesischer Schafkäse see *Schafmilchkäse*

Frischkäse
Generic term for fresh unripened cheeses made from pasteurized milk and coagulated with or without rennet. See *Quark, Rahmfrischkäse, Schichtkäse*

Frühstückskäse 🐄🐐 10% 100-180g (3½-6oz) Ⓒ
'Breakfast cheese'. Cheese is an important ingredient of the German breakfast, especially the *Zweites Frühstück*, the 'second breakfast' taken mid-morning, which fills in the gaps left by the first one. This cheese is a small version of the Limburger type made from whole or partly skimmed milk and eaten either fresh or after a short ripening period, when the surface becomes smeared with coryne moulds.

Gaiskäsle (Gaiskäsli) 🐐 50% ⊖ 100g (3½oz) Ⓓ
A rare cheese made in the Allgäu from a mixture of unpasteurized goats' and pasteurized cows' milk. It is an unpressed surface-ripened cheese in two variations: one a brownish washed rind cheese with a coryne smear, the other milder with white rind flora. The ripening period is between two and three weeks.

Geheimratskäse 🐄➤ 40-60% 500g (18oz) Ⓑ
Small loaf- or wheel-shaped Edam-type cheese with a few small round holes in the pale close-textured paste. May be waxed.

Handkäse ★
Generic term for small, traditionally hand-moulded cheeses made from sour milk curds, descendants of the earliest, most primitive form of cheesemaking. They come in a wide range of shapes—bars, rolls, discs, squares—and vary in flavour from delicate to powerfully sharp. Many are additionally flavoured with herbs or spices. They can have smooth rinds or be covered in mould smears and are white, buff or yellowy orange in colour. All of them are low in fat and high in protein. The innumerable variations are often found under specific (usually regional) designations including Harzer, Mainzer, Rheinischer, Odenwalder, Faustkäse, Bauernhandkäse, Bodenfelder, Berliner Kuhkäse, Korbkäse and Alte Kuhkäse. In Hesse eaten with 'Musik', an onion and vinegar garnish. See *Spitzkäse, Stangenkäse*

Hartkäse
Generic term for hard cheeses such as Emmental.

Harzer see *Handkäse*

Hauskäse
A small cheese similar to Limburger.

Holsteiner Magerkäse
Made in Schleswig Holstein from skimmed milk sometimes mixed

with buttermilk. Also called Lederkäse ('leather cheese', a pretty accurate description).

Holsteinermarschkäse see *Wilstermarschkäse*

Hopfenkäse see *Nieheimer Hopfenkäse*

Klosterkäse
A soft surface-ripened cows' milk cheese similar to Limburger.

Kolostrumkäse see *Biestkäse*

Korbkäse see *Handkäse*

Kräuterkäse
Generic term for cheeses flavoured with herbs

Kühbacher
Soft cheese made near Munich from a mixture of whole and partly skimmed milk.

Kümmelkäse
A small, soft, washed rind, low-fat cheese made from partly skimmed cows' milk and flavoured with caraway seeds.

Labfrischkäse, Labquark
Fresh curd cheese coagulated with rennet (from *Lab*, rennet). Sometimes used as the basis for *Sauermilchkäse*. See *Quark*

Lederkäse see *Holsteiner Magerkäse*

Limburger ★ ♨ ⬭ 20-50% ⬮ 200-600g (7oz-1¼lb) Ⓑ
Of Belgian origin, but adopted by Allgäuer dairymen in the 19th century. A washed rind, surface-ripened cheese with a slightly moist, typically reddish-brown skin and a creamy rich yellow paste. After moulding and draining, the cheeses are salted in brine for seven to 24 hours depending on the size of the cheese and then washed at intervals with coryne bacteria. After about a month the yellowy mould begins to develop, becoming darker and firmer over the next eight weeks or so. Despite the many jokes surrounding the notorious ferocity of Limburger it should not, at least in appearance, be in the least menacing. As far as flavour goes, its decidedly aromatic bark is considerably worse than its bite. If the paste is runny or the rind slimy it means that the cheese is overripe and well past its best. It is available with various fat contents: the lower the fat the firmer the cheese.

Mainauerkäse ♨ ⬭ 40-60% ⊟ 1.5kg (3lb) Ⓒ
A Münster type named after an island in Lake Constance.

Mainzer see *Handkäse*

Marschkäse see *Wilstermarschkäse*

Mecklenburger Magerkäse ♨ ⬤ ⊟ Ⓒ
Hard-pressed, skimmed milk cheese, coloured with saffron.

Münster ♨ ⬭ 45-50% ⊟ 125 and 500g (4 and 18oz) Ⓒ
Another 'borrowed' cheese, this time from Alsace. Munster (without an umlaut) is French; Münster (with an umlaut) is German. The cheese has a smooth, softish, yellow paste with a yellowish red surface and a mildly piquant flavour.

Nieheimer Hopfenkäse

Similar but not identical to Hopfenkäse. Both are made from sour milk curds partially ripened then broken up, remoulded, and allowed to ripen for a further period packed in boxes between layers of hops. In both, the curds are mixed with caraway seeds, but the Hopfenkäse curds, after the initial ripening, are mixed with fresh curds whereas for Nieheimer Hopfenkäse they are mixed with full milk or, occasionally, beer before being remoulded by hand into small cakes. Dry cheese good for grating.

Odenwalder see *Handkäse*

Quark ★

A fresh unripened curd cheese with varying fat contents, made from skimmed milk, lactic starter and rennet. Quark accounts for almost half the German cheese production and is eaten in vast quantities and in innumerable ways. The name, incidentally, simply means 'curds'. See *Buttermilchquark*, *Labquark*, *Speisequark*

Radolfzeller Rahmkäse

Surface-ripened cheese similar to Mainauer, drained on straw mats, dry salted and ripened for about a month.

Rahmfrischkäse 🌢 🌙 50%©

Fresh unripened cream cheese usually sold in small foil-wrapped cubes. Made by adding more cream to Speisequark. For Doppelrahm-frischkäse (double-cream cheese) even more cream is added, bringing the fat content up to 60 per cent.

Räucherkäse

Generic term for smoked cheese which, in most cases, does not mean that the cheese has been literally smoked but that artificial 'smoky' flavouring has been added to the milk.

Rheinischer see *Handkäse*

Romadur 🌢 🌙 20-60% 🧀 75-150g (2½-5oz) Ⓑ

Similar to Limburger but softer and milder. Also a washed rind, sur-face-ripened cheese with a yellowish-brown skin and a rich golden paste which has a scattering of irregular holes. Made either from whole or partly skimmed milk and in various grades of fat content. The brining and ripening periods are shorter than those for Limburg-er, about four hours and two weeks respectively, and the flavour and aroma are consequently less assertive. It should be kept quite cool and not allowed to become overripe. Like Limburger, it originated in Belgium, where a similar cheese is known as Remoudou.

Rotschmierkäse

Generic term for cheeses like Limburger, Romadur and Münster which have reddish skins produced by the action of coryne bacteria on the surface of the cheese during ripening.

Sauermilchkäse

Generic term for cheeses made from sour milk curds, in other words from milk coagulated with a lactic acid starter rather than rennet. Includes all the Handkäse types.

Schafmilchkäse

Generic term for ewes' milk cheese. Only Schnittkäse can officially be made from ewes' milk in Germany. Two good cheeses are Aber-tamerkäse and Friesischer Schafkäse.

Schichtkäse
A fresh unripened curd cheese combining layers (hence the name 'layer cheese') of skimmed milk and whole milk curds.

Schimmelkäse
Sauermilchkäse treated with moulds.

Schnittkäse
'Sliceable cheese', one of the official categories of cheese covering semihard varieties like Tilsiter and Trappistenkäse.

Speisoquark
Quark made from skimmed milk curds mixed with some of the skimmed fats, graded according to the proportion of fat replaced.

Spitzkäse
'Sharp cheese'; a roll- or bar-shaped Sauermilchkäse made from skimmed milk curds mixed with caraway seeds. It has a clear buff-coloured surface smear and is fairly piquant.

Stangenkäse
'Bar cheese', actually shaped like a thin sausage; a type of Sauermilchkäse, tangy and flavoured with caraway seeds.

Steinbuscherkäse ★ 🐄 🌙 30-50% 200-700g (7oz-1½lb) Ⓑ
A yellowy brown cube-shaped washed rind cheese with a smooth, firm, pale straw-coloured paste, mildly piquant in flavour and fairly strong smelling. First produced in the mid 19th century in Steinbusch (now Choszczno, in Poland). Ripened for two to three months.

Steppenkäse 🐄 🌙 35% ▱ 7-12kg (15-26lb) Ⓑ
Rich buttery greyish-yellow cheese with a pronounced full-bodied flavour. Originally made in the USSR by German immigrants from whole milk coloured with annatto and cured in cool humid conditions for about three months.

Tieflanderkäse
A hard-cooked cheese with eyes, similar to Emmental.

Tilsit(er) ★ 🐄 🌙 30-50% Ⓑ
Named after the town of Tilsit (now Soviet Sovetsk), where it was first made by Dutch immigrants in the mid-19th century. It has a lovely buttery yellow paste with many small elliptical holes. The consistency is springy and elastic yet rather moist and creamy and the flavour is mild and delicate with spicy undertones. Made from whole or skimmed milk and the skimmed milk type is sometimes flavoured with caraway seeds. The curds are lightly scalded in the whey before being moulded in stainless steel hoops and, in some places, very lightly pressed. The initial ripening period lasts for about a month, during which time the cheeses are regularly washed with brine. Afterwards they are stored for about five months before being sold. The traditional shape for Tilsiter is a large wheel but the loaf shape tailored to the demands of slicing machines is becoming increasingly common. Also known as Tollenser.

Trappistenkäse
A mild yellow cheese full of tiny holes and shaped like a fat sausage or a rectangular block. Made in southern and central Germany.

Weichkäse
Generic term for soft surface-ripened cheeses.

Weinkäse ★ 🍷 🌙 30-50% ⊖ 75g (2½oz) ©

A small, round, creamy, mild cheese whose name derives from its particular affinity with wine. Has a superb glossy paste and a thin, smooth, pinkish skin.

Weisslackerkäse 🌙 📿 40-50% ⊂⊃ 60g (2oz) ©

The shiny white surface of this Bavarian cuboid cheese is presumably responsible for the name, which means 'white lacquer'. It is a surface-ripened cheese, developed about 100 years ago, and is extremely pungent with a powerfully piquant flavour, becoming even more pronounced with age. Made from a mixture of skimmed evening and whole morning milk, it is salted, dry or in brine, for two to three days before being placed in conditions of high humidity for a few more days, the cheeses just touching, for the surface flora to develop. They are then separated and ripened for up to seven months. Also called Weisslacker Bierkäse.

Wilstermarschkäse 🍷 📿 45-50% 🗩 3-6kg (7-13lb) ©

An ivory-coloured slightly sour-tasting cheese from Wilster in Schleswig Holstein and, like Tilsiter, said to have been invented by Dutch immigrants. It can be made from whole or partly skimmed milk and is ripened for about four weeks. Also called Holsteiner-marschkäse, Marschkäse.

Ziegenkäse

Generic term for goats' milk cheese.

KEY WORDS

Alt old, mature	**Reif** mature, ripe
Frisch fresh, young	**Schaf** sheep
Hart hard	**Scharf** strong
Jung young	**Schmelzkäse** processed cheese
Käse cheese	**Weich** soft
Kuh cow	**Ziege** goat
Rahm cream	

Greece and Cyprus

The cradle of Western civilization is, in some ways, a bleak and barren land where only the most resilient of plant and animal life can survive: the hardy olive and the equally tenacious sheep and goats. Meat always was, and still is, something of a luxury in Greece, so that cheese has provided a major source of protein for thousands of years in an otherwise often frugal diet. Consumption of cheese in Greece is one of the highest per head in the world. Demand is so great that large-scale producers of Graviera and Kefalotiri are using cheap imported powdered cows' milk. Haloumi and Kefalotiri sold outside Greece often come from Cyprus; Feta—in varying degrees of authenticity— is made in many cheese-producing countries.

Anari
Ewes' or goats' milk white whey cheese made in Cyprus. Spreadable, or can be sliced and served with fruit or salad.

Anthotiri   🍶 35% Ⓓ
A fresh, white, unripened cheese made in Crete from ewes' or goats' milk. The name means 'flowery cheese'; it is in fact usually flavoured with herbs or sweetened with honey.

Fet(t)a ★   🍖 20-50% 🧀 Ⓑ
Sharp, salty, white cheese, either soft or firm and crumbly. Versions made outside Greece often use pasteurized cows' milk, but Greek Feta must be made entirely from ewes' milk; if cows' milk is used it is sold as 'soft white cheese'. It has been made by more or less the same method for thousands of years. Milk is curdled by lactic fermentation and the curds and whey are then reheated together causing the remaining fats and proteins in the whey to flocculate. The curds are drained and then turned and lightly pressed. When firm they are cut into blocks and salted in brine for varying amounts of time. The longer the salting, the harder the cheese becomes. The saltier kinds are best soaked in a little milk or water to temper the flavour.

Galotiri   🍖 🍶 Ⓓ
A 'home-made' cross between Feta and Mizithra. Fresh ewes' milk is allowed to ripen for an hour or so and then boiled to separate the curds and whey. The curds are scooped out, salted, stirred from time to time during the following few days and then placed in animal skins to drain. The next day's milking will be treated in the same way and added to the first batch. Eaten after three months.

Graviera   🐄 🍖 50% 🧀 20-40kg (44-88lb) Ⓒ
The second most popular cheese in Greece after Feta, this Greek version of Gruyère is yellowish in colour, with small holes and an exceptionally hard rind. It is a rich, creamy cheese, eaten as an hors d'oeuvre, after a meal or as a side dish. The Cretan version, made with ewes' milk, is much sought after.

Hal(l)oumi ★   🍖 40-45% 🧀 Ⓑ
Creamy white cheese with a somewhat fibrous texture, generally less salty than Feta even though it is also soaked in brine during processing. Firmer than Feta and less brittle, it can be sliced but not crumbled. In Cyprus the cheese is dipped in hot water, kneaded with chopped mint, rolled out like pastry and cut into bars. It is either eaten soon after making or ripened for about a month. Originally made from ewes' or goats' milk; about ten per cent of the Haloumi now produced is made with cows' milk. It should be washed in lukewarm water or milk before using.

Kas(s)eri 🐄 ⟩ 40% ⊖ 9kg (20lb) ©

Hard-pressed, strong white cheese. In thrifty rural economies, nothing can be wasted, and yet cheesemaking was in the past something of a hit or miss affair. However, rather than consign unsuccessful cheeses to the dustbin, in Greece they make them into Kaseri. The cheeses are dipped in hot water, then kneaded and shaped or moulded into large wheels. In fact, Kaseri is very similar to Provolone Dolce in texture and the Greeks prefer it to Mozzarella on pizza.

Kefalograviera 🐄 ⟩ 40% ⊖ Ⓑ

Similar to Graviera but a little more salty, and the cheese is usually slightly smaller. Generally speaking, the larger the whole cheese, the better the flavour.

Kefalotiri 🐄 ⟩ 40-55% ⊡ 6-8kg (13-18lb) Ⓑ

Close-textured, pale, slightly oily cheese, with variously sized holes, a thin, hard rind and a pronounced ewes' milk tang. Somewhat harder than Kaseri, it is used in cooking and eaten for breakfast or as an appetizer. Most of the Kefalotiri found outside Greece is Kefalograviera, since the original is considered too strong for foreign tastes.

Kopanisti

A veined cheese from the Aegean Islands made from cows' or ewes' milk. The fresh curds are roughly cut, put into cloths to drain for a few hours, then hand moulded into balls and left to dry. After a while the surface of the cheese becomes covered with mould, and this is worked back into the cheese with a quantity of salt. The cheeses are then left to ripen for a couple of months until they become soft, creamy and salty. Some of the best come from the island of Mykonos.

Ladotiri

Meaning 'oil cheese': a hard ewes' milk cheese rubbed with olive oil.

Manouri

Whey cheese from Crete and Macedonia. It is white and creamy and slightly firmer than Mizithra, shaped into ovals and waxed or packaged in foil. Eaten with honey as a dessert.

Metsovone

Highly prized hard cheese coated with beeswax, made from ewes' or goats' milk.

Mizithra 🐄 ☾ 20% Ⓑ

Whey cheese made from the by-products of Feta and Kefalotiri. Whole fresh ewes' or cows' milk is sometimes added to make it richer. Similar to Italian Ricotta, it is used in cooking and eaten fresh. It is occasionally preserved in salt and can be dried and used for grating.

Teleme(s)

Feta cheese from northern Greece.

KEY WORDS

Agelada cow	**Palio** mature
Elafro mild	**Pikantiko** piquant
Fresco fresh	**Provatina** ewe
Katsika goat	**Skliro** hard
Malako soft	**Tiri** cheese

HUNGARY see *Eastern Europe*. ICELAND see *Scandinavia*. INDIA see *Asia*.
IRAQ see *Middle East*.

Israel

The modern Israeli dairy industry is highly mechanized and efficient, dominated by Tnuva, a huge co-operative controlling over 80 per cent of milk produced. All cheese is made from pasteurized milk, mainly copying European types.

Atzmon
Soft, buttery, cows' milk cheese similar to Italian Bel Paese.

Bashan
Smoked sausage-shaped cheese with a shiny red rind. Made from mixed ewes' and goats' milk. Fairly piquant.

Duberki
Drained yoghurt shaped into balls. Dried or steeped in oil.

Ein-Gedi
Foil-wrapped Camembert type made from cows' milk.

Emek
Hard, full-fat, loaf-shaped cows' milk cheese with a red rind.

Gad
From G'vina Danit, meaning 'Danish cheese'. Springy yellow loaf with scattered small holes. Modelled on Danish Danbo.

Galil
Fairly strong ewes' milk green-veined Roquefort type.

Gewina Zfatit
Fresh, white, salty ewes' milk cheese. Lightly pressed in round baskets that leave a surface impression. Cows' and/or goats' milk may be added. Sometimes ripened until dry and hard.

Gilboa
Semihard, mild cows' milk loaf similar to Edam.

Gilead
Full-fat, drum-shaped ewes' milk *pasta filata* cheese.

Golan
Hard ewes' milk *pasta filata* cheese similar to Italian Provolone.

Jizrael
Hard, pressed cooked cheese with large holes like Emmental.

Kol-Bee
Loaf-shaped imitation Gouda made from cows' milk.

Tal Ha'Emek
Pasteurized copy of Emmental.

Thou shalt not seethe a kid in its mother's milk. Exodus 23.19. Jewish dietary laws forbid the mixing of milk, and therefore all dairy products, with meat. This means that animal rennet cannot be used in cheesemaking. Vegetable rennets are used instead to manufacture kosher versions of many cheese types, also acceptable to most vegetarians and widely exported from Israel.

The Ancient Romans considered the idea of drinking fresh milk rather nauseating. They preferred to consume milk in the form of cheese and even in those days there was an astonishing variety. They could choose from fresh, smoked or dried cheeses, cheeses coagulated with fig juice or flavoured with marjoram, mint and coriander, a Grana-type cheese called Lunar, ewes' milk cheeses and goats' cheeses from Liguria. Foreign cheeses were imported, such as English Cheshire, a ewes' milk cheese called Cythnos from Greece and two French cheeses, almost certainly Roquefort and Cantal.

Italians are just as enthusiastic about cheese today. They use it a great deal in cooking as well as eating it at the end of meals. The range of Italian cheese types is quite magnificent and each cheese is superb of its kind. Quite apart from native Italian inventiveness, the geography of the country lends itself to a wide variety of cheeses, stretching as it does from the sweet alpine pastures down the mountainous leg of Italy almost as far as Africa. Cows and sheep have flourished in different parts of the country for centuries in well-nigh perfect conditions. Even the swamps of central and southern Italy, barren in every other way, proved ideal for the water buffalo whose milk adds an unusual element to the cheese range.

There are approximately twice as many sheep as cows in Italy, mainly in the centre and south; their numbers decrease towards the north. The distribution of cows is almost exactly reversed and this pattern is closely reflected in the traditional areas associated with the two types of cheese. Lombardy (Lombardia), Piedmont (Piemonte) and the Po valley (in the north) are renowned for cows' milk types. Tuscany (Toscana), Lazio, Sardinia (Sardegna), Campania, Puglia, Sicily (Sicilia) and the whole of central and southern Italy produce marvellous ewes' milk cheeses, which become more *piccante* the farther south one goes. This is admittedly an oversimplified view of Italian cheesemaking — on a local level there is a plethora of variations and designations to wade through. The same cheese may be sold under several different names and one name may be applied to many cheeses which are often totally different in character.

Asiago 🎲 ➲ 34-44% ⊟ 8-15kg (18-33lb) Ⓒ

Originally a ewes' milk cheese from the wild and rocky pine-clad plateau of Asiago in the foothills of the Dolomites (Dolomiti), this cheese is now made from cows' milk throughout the province of Vicenza. There are two main types: Asiago d'allevo and Asiago pressato. Asiago d'allevo is made fom partly skimmed milk and is sold as a table cheese at four to eight months when medium-ripe (*mezzano*) or for grating when older (*vecchio*), aged up to two years. Aromatic yellowy buff paste with small, evenly scattered holes and a smooth hard, rind which ranges from straw-coloured to brown. Asiago pressato is a full fat cheese which ripens in about a month, best from June to September. Mild, with a delicate tang, it has a thin, supple, yellow rind.

Baccellone

Ewes' milk cheese similar to Ricotta, made in and around Livorno especially in spring. Eaten with fresh broad beans (*baccelli*).

Bagoss, Bagozzo 🎲 ➲ 35-40% ⊟ 18-25kg (40-55lb) Ⓓ

Basically a simple country cheese from Brescia, its production is small-scale and erratic. Made from partly skimmed milk, it has a hard, golden rind and a deep yellow, grainy interior. Some cheeses are uncooked: these tend to have a hint of the bitter herbs of the mountain pasture. The cooked type has a milder taste. Eaten as a table cheese after two months ripening, or allowed to mature for up to six months for a more piquant, harder cheese which is used for grating. Also known as Bresciano and Grana Bagozzo.

Bel Paese 🎲 ➲ 52% ⊟ 2kg (4lb) Ⓐ

This sweet, buttery cheese, pale yellow with a smooth springy texture and a shiny golden rind (often waxed), is a spectacularly successful 20th century invention created by Egidio Galbani in 1906 and made in Lombardy. It is an uncooked, pressed, quick-ripening cheese. The name (meaning 'beautiful country') derives from the book written by Abbot Antonio Stoppani, a friend of the Galbani family. His portrait, imposed on a map of Italy, appears on the foil wrapping in which the cheese is sold. The American version depicts a map of the western hemisphere. See *Crema Bel Paese, Italico*

Bettelmat

Traditional unpasteurized Fontina-type cheese from the Swiss border of Piedmont.

Bitto 🎲 ➲ ⊟ 10-30kg (22-66lb) Ⓓ

Made in summer in the alpine pastures of Sondrio, this simple rustic cheese is made from whole raw cows' milk, traditionally with a fifth part of goats' milk. It is a scalded, pressed, firm cheese with small eyes oozing whey, ripened for a month or so for use as a table cheese or up to three years for grating, becoming increasingly strong and aromatic.

Bocconcini, Bocconi Giganti see *Mozzarella*

Bonassai

Modern ewes' milk cheese developed at the Sardinian Livestock and Cheese Institute. Soft small square cheese with a thin pale wrinkled rind and creamy white interior with a yoghurt-like flavour.

Borelli see *Mozzarella*

Bra 🎲 30% 3.5kg (11lb) Ⓓ

From Piedmont, a dense, strong, straw to ochre-coloured salty cheese with a thick light brown rind made from partly skimmed raw cows' milk, sometimes mixed with ewes' and/or goats' milk, matured for six months. There is also a softer ivory-coloured version which is ripened for 45 days. Round or square, with an intense flavour; not a cheese for faint hearts or sensitive palates.

Branzi ⟩ 45-50% ▱ 1.5-2kg (3-4lb) Ⓓ

Traditional cheese from the Bergamo mountains made from whole raw cows' milk, to which a little goats' milk is sometimes added. It has a thin golden rind and a supple, straw-coloured holey paste with a faint lactic taste. Ripened for a month, or longer for a grating cheese.

Bresciano see *Bagozzo*

Brocotte see *Ricotta*

Bross, Bruss

Fiery speciality of Piedmont, made by pounding fresh or leftover cheese with the local brandy.

Burrata ★

Found only in Puglia, but worth seeking out. Strings of *pasta filata* cheese and cream are encased in a small ball of the same cheese. Made from cows' or buffalo milk. Must be eaten fresh.

Burrini ⟨⟩ ⟩ 45% 200-300g (7-10oz) Ⓑ

A speciality of southern Italy, Puglia and Calabria in particular. Small, pear-shaped, *pasta filata* cheeses, hand moulded around a pat of sweet butter, with a mild taste and a faint tang rather like Provolone Dolce. They are ripened for a few weeks only and eaten with bread spread with the buttery heart of the cheese. for longer keeping, especially for export, the cheeses are dipped in wax. Also known as Butirri, Butielli and occasionally Provole.

Cacetti

Small, pear-shaped Caciocavallo from Campania and Puglia. After moulding, the cheeses are dipped in wax and hung up by a loop of raffia attached at the narrow end to mature for about ten days.

Caciocavallo ★ ⟨⟩ ⟩ 44% 2-3kg (4-7lb) Ⓑ

Type of cheese prevalent throughout the eastern Mediterranean and the Balkans and known under a variety of similar names. Light straw-coloured and close-textured with, occasionally, a few holes scattered through the paste, and a smooth, thin, golden yellow or brownish rind. These spun-curd cheeses are moulded by hand into fat skittle shapes and ripened for three months or so for a table cheese (sweet and delicate) and longer for grating. The ripening method, whereby the cheeses are hung in pairs over poles as if on horseback (*a cavallo*) accounts for one theory as to the origin of the curious name. Another suggests that the cheese was originally made with mares' milk. If true, this would make Caciocavallo the oldest Italian cheese, dating back to the nomadic era when mares' milk was an occasional food (though whether there was ever a surplus that could be used in cheesemaking seems most unlikely). In any case, it was almost certainly known in Roman times. Columella in his classic treatise on agriculture *De Rustica* (AD 35-45) described precisely the method for making it.

Caciocavallo Siciliano ⟩ 42% ▱ 7-12kg (15-26lb) Ⓓ

Essentially the same as Caciocavallo except that goats' milk may be mixed with the cows' milk and the curds are pressed in oblong moulds rather than being shaped by hand. It is salted for about three weeks and then dipped in wax.

Caciofiore
A Caciotta from the Marches (Marche) made in winter from ewes' or cows' milk coagulated with vegetable rennet and tinted with saffron.

Caciotta ★   ▨ 45% 🖬 1-2kg (2-4lb) Ⓑ
Deliciously creamy, softish small cheese ranging in colour from white to golden yellow and in flavour from sweet and mild to lightly piquant. Factory versions made from pasteurized cows' milk tend to be rather bland. Otherwise, Caciotta can be made from any type of milk, since the term is less descriptive of a particular cheese type than an indication that this is a small cheese made from local milk by artisans and farmers in the traditional manner. These farmhouse versions show innumerable regional variations in flavour and shape. Some have smooth, firm, oiled rinds, others have the basket-work imprint typical of some Pecorinos. They are usually aged for ten days to a month. The best are said to be Caciotta di Urbino and Caciotta Toscana. Umbrian Caciottas may be flavoured with garlic (*agliato*), onion (*cipollato*) or truffle (*tartufato*). See *Caciofiore, Chiavara, Fresa*

Canestrato
Traditionally a ewes' milk cheese from Sicily, pressed in a wicker mould (*canestro*) which leaves its imprint on the outside of the cheese. The name is now used all over Italy for cheese made in these basket-work moulds. When the feminine form of the word is used (Canestrata or Incanestrata) it denotes a hard, matured ewes' milk Ricotta made especially for grating. See *Foggiano, Pecorino Siciliano*

Caprini
The name implies small goats' milk cheeses (from *capra*, goat), and some farms (especially in Sardinia) still make them. Those produced commercially in Lombardy are more often than not made from cows' milk. Eaten fresh or ripened.

Caprini di Montevecchia
Matured Lombardy Caprini, distinguishable by a thin covering of brownish mould.

Caprino Romano   see *Romano*

Casiddi
Small hard goats' or ewes' milk cheeses from Basilicata.

Casigliolo
Caciocavallo-type cheese made in Sicily. Also called Panedda and Pera di Vacca.

Casizzolu   ☼ ➤ 1-2kg (2-4lb) Ⓓ
Sardinian version of Provolone Dolce, where it is often eaten toasted over an open fire.

Castelmagno
Blue-veined cows' milk cheese similar to Gorgonzola. Named after a mountain village near Dronero, Piedmont.

Casu Becciu, Casu Iscaldidu, Casu Marzu
Descriptive but not very flattering names ('old', 'warm' and 'rotten') given to pungent crumbly cheeses made in spring from cows' or goats' milk in the Gallura region of Sardinia.

Chiavara
A Caciotta made from cows' milk near Genoa (Genova).

Ciccillo see *Provola*

Cotronese, Crotonese

Ewes' (or ewes' and goats') milk cheese made in small dairies near Crotone, Calabria. Sometimes flavoured with whole black peppercorns. Also known as Pecorino di Crotone.

Crema Bel Paese

A processed cheese spread but surprisingly acceptable even though a little metallic in flavour. See *Bel Paese*

Cremini

Originally the name for small, full-fat, fresh cream cheeses but now applied to any mild cheese spread (usually processed).

Crescenza 🐄 💧 48-50% 🧀 1-2kg (2-4lb) Ⓑ

Very fresh Stracchino from Lombardy. Cut into small rectangles and wrapped in greaseproof paper for sale. Rindless white cheese with a faintly acidulous flavour and lusciously creamy texture, it is ripened for a maximum of ten days and should be eaten as soon as possible after that. The best Crescenza reputedly comes from around Milan (Milano) and Pavia.

Dolcelatte 🐄 💧 50% 🧀 1-2kg (2-4lb) Ⓐ

Smooth, creamy, mild blue-veined cheese (the name, a registered trade mark, means 'sweet milk'). It is a factory-made, more easily digestible version of Gorgonzola. Sometimes labelled Gorgonzola Dolcelatte. A similar cheese made by a rival company is called Dolceverde. See *Torta Gaudenzio*

Emiliano 🐄 💧 32% 🧀 20-30kg (44-66lb) Ⓒ

Pale yellow Grana-type cheese from Emilia with a dark brownish-black oiled rind. Ripened between one and two years

Ercolini see *Provolone*

Fior di Latte 🐄 💧 44% Ⓑ

The official designation for Mozzarella made with cows' milk, meaning 'the cream of the milk'.

Fiore Sardo 🐑 💧 40% 🧀 1.5-4kg (3-9lb) Ⓓ

Traditional uncooked Pecorino from Sardinia with a characteristic convex shape, crumbly texture and a pronounced aftertaste. Aged for three months for a table cheese (golden rind) or more than six months for grating (dark brown rind).

Foggiano

Type of Pecorino (the ewes' milk is sometimes mixed with cows' or goats' milk), a speciality of Foggia, in Puglia. Also known as Canestrato di Foggia.

Fontal 🐄 💧 45% 🧀 10-16kg (22-35lb) Ⓑ

Cheese similar to Fontina which was, in fact, called Fontina until the Stresa Convention of 1951 protected the exclusive claims of the Valle d'Aosta. It is produced on an industrial scale throughout Piedmont and Lombardy but unlike genuine Fontina it is made largely from pasteurized milk, and has fewer eyes and a slightly darker rind.

Fontina ★ 🐄 💧 45% 🧀 8-18kg (18-40lb) Ⓑ

One of the best of the many excellent Italian cheeses, genuine Fontina comes only from the Valle d'Aosta high up in the Alps near the borders with France and Switzerland. Made from whole unpasteurized milk of one milking, it is a pressed, scalded, three-month-ripened cheese with a smooth, slightly elastic, straw-coloured paste that has sparse small round holes. The rind is an uneven light brown, thin and lightly oiled. Fontina has a delicate, nutty, almost honeyed flavour, somewhat like Swiss Gruyère but sweeter and more buttery. The best is made in mountain chalets between May and September when the herds pasture on the alpine meadows. In the winter months the milk is processed in small cheese factories in the valleys.

Formaggelle
Small, soft cheeses made from ewes', goats' or cows' milk in the mountains of northern Italy. In Liguria they may be called Formagetti. Usually eaten fresh, but sometimes lightly ripened.

Formaggini
Generic name for small cheeses. Usually refers to processed cheeses or spreads but can sometimes denote small, locally made cheeses.

Fresa
A mild, sweet Caciotta made in Sardinia from any type of milk.

Friulana see *Montasio*

Giganti see *Provolone*

Gorgonzola ★ 48% 6-12kg (13-26lb) Ⓐ
Italy's principal blue-veined cheese has enjoyed a deservedly high international reputation for generations. Originally a winter-made cheese, a Stracchino, it has the mild creamy paste typical of that wonderfully fertile family of Lombardy cheeses. Its greenish-blue mould gives Gorgonzola the sharp, almost spicy flavour which contrasts so agreeably with the delicacy of the paste. The naturally formed rind is coarse and reddish-grey in colour with powdery patches. Many decidedly apocryphal tales have arisen to explain its origins well over 1,000 years ago. One that seems plausible tells how migrating herdsmen travelling south to winter pastures stopped over at the village of Gorgonzola near Milan and paid the innkeepers with freshly made cheeses. The innkeepers stored them in their cool, damp cellars, which provided ideal conditions for natural mould formation (the caves at Valsassina and Lodi were later to fulfil the same purpose) and later served these 'mouldy' cheeses to their guests, apparently to their considerable satisfaction.

Nowadays Gorgonzola is still made in Lombardy, but all the year round and no longer at Gorgonzola itself. *Penicillium glaucum* is added to whole pasteurized milk of two milkings. After coagulation the curds are cut into small pieces and placed in wooden hoops to drain naturally, with the warm morning curds in the middle and the cool evening curds on the outside. The curds are salted and turned at regular intervals over a period of about two weeks, then ripened in a cool, humid environment for two to four months (a process that formerly took at least a year). The cheeses are usually sold wrapped in foil. Avoid any cheeses that are brownish or hard or that have a sour, bitter smell. See *Dolcelatte, Stracchino, Torta Gaudenzio*

Gorgonzola Bianco
Rare, unveined white Gorgonzola. Also called Pannerone.

Grana ★ 32% Ⓑ
The generic name Grana describes all those finely grained hard cheeses that originated in the Po valley before the advent of the

Romans. The most famous member of the group is undoubtedly Parmigiano Reggiano (Parmesan). All Grana cheese is made from partly skimmed milk and is matured in its distinctive drum shapes for at least a year. It is usually used as a grating cheese but when younger is also a delicious dessert cheese. Grana cheese should never be stored in the refrigerator; it keeps best covered with a cloth or greased paper in a cool cupboard. For grating, buy a chunk and grate it as and when you need it: this way it will release much more flavour and is ultimately more economical than the small packets of ready-grated cheese. In Italian cooking there is really no substitute for Grana. See *Emiliano, Grana Padano, Lodigiano, Parmigiano Reggiano*

Grana Bagozzo see *Bagozzo*

Grana Padano ★ 🥛 ● 32% ▭ 24-40kg (53-88lb) Ⓑ

For centuries the cheese-producing centres of the Po valley wrangled over whose name should be associated with the excellent Grana they produced. Piacenza, long famed for its cheese 'il piacentino' and considered the most deserving contender, finally lost the battle when a compromise solution was reached in 1955. The names Grana Padano and Parmigiano Reggiano were given legal protection and the characteristics and area of production (*zona tipica*) of each cheese were precisely delineated. The qualifying provinces for Grana Padano were Alessandria, Asti, Cuneo, Novara, Turin (Torino), Vercelli, Bergamo, Brescia, Como, Cremona, Mantua (on the left bank of the Po), Milan, Pavia, Sondrio, Varese, Trento, Padua, Rovigo, Treviso, Venice, Verona, Vicenza, Bologna (on the right bank of the Reno), Ferrara, Forlì, Piacenza and Ravenna. Grana Padano is made all the year round and matures more rapidly but, apart from that, its characteristics are basically the same as those of Parmigiano Reggiano. It is a pressed cooked cheese made from partly skimmed milk of two milkings. The ripening period varies from one to two years and the cheeses are sold at varying stages of their maturity. The paste is a pale straw colour darkening with age. The rind is thick, oily and very hard and can be black or yellow-ochre. See *Grana, Parmigiano Reggiano*

Groviera, Gruviera
The Italian version of Gruyère.

Incanestrato see *Canestrato*

Italico
The official designation invented in 1941 for semisoft delicately flavoured table cheeses similar to Bel Paese, sold under brand names such as Fior d'Alpe.

Lodigiano 🥛 ● 29% ▭ 30-50kg (66-110lb) Ⓒ
A Grana cheese produced around Lodi near Milan. The paste, typically hard and granular although more crumbly than Parmesan, is characterized by a slight greenish tinge. It is matured even longer than Parmesan, up to five years in some cases, and is extremely strong, even bitter. It is also prohibitively expensive. See *Grana*

Logudoro 🐑 ▨ 50% ▭ 2kg (4lb) Ⓒ
Mild sweet factory-made dessert cheese from Lombardy. The paste is creamy white and there is no rind apart from wicker mould marks. Ripened for three to four weeks.

Majocchino
Sicilian ewes' milk cheese made on a small scale in basketwork moulds. Whole black peppercorns are usually mixed with the curd.

Manteca, Manteche

Cheeses similar to Burrini but larger, with a lump of butter encased in a coating of *pasta filata*. The butter is usually whey butter made as a by-product of the cheese. Made in a variety of shapes (loaf, pear, ball, etc.) and sometimes smoked. The cheese jacket preserves the butter—a useful device in a hot climate before refrigeration was common. Originally from Basilicata.

Marzolino

Tuscan ewes' milk cheese (nowadays mixed with cows' milk), exported throughout Europe in the Middle Ages. Pale smooth cheese, shaped by hand into flattened balls, with a thin, straw-coloured rind and a distinctive strong flavour.

Mascarpone, Mascherpone ★ 85% Ⓑ

Delectable, virtually solidified cream, mildly acidulated by lactic fermentation and whipped up into a luscious velvety consistency. Originally produced in Lombardy only in the cool of autumn and winter but now available all year round. (Some is being made from buffalo milk in southern Italy.) Served fresh with fruit or sweetened and flavoured with cinnamon, powdered chocolate or coffee and liqueurs. See *Torta Gaudenzio*

Montasio 40% 5-10kg (11-22lb) Ⓓ

Produced in Friuli-Venezia Giulia, it is similar to Asiago, springy when two to five months old, hard and brittle after a year or two. Mild when young, it becomes nutty, then full and piquant. Straw-coloured with odd small holes and a dark golden rind. Originally a monastery cheese (devised by monks at Moggio in the 13th century), it is now made in small factories mostly in Udine and Veneto.

Morlacco 15kg (33lb) Ⓓ

Long-established mountain cheese from the Veneto area, made from partly skimmed milk. Ready after two weeks, although, like most of northern Italy's cheeses, it is often kept much longer for use as a cooking cheese. It is covered with greenish mould which gives a distinctive aroma, and the cheese itself is compact and white, with small holes.

Mozzarella 45% Ⓐ

The colonization of half the world by pizza chains has made Mozzarella the best-known Italian cheese after Parmesan and Gorgonzola. Melted on top of pizza it becomes quite palatable and is wonderfully stringy. In other respects, however, its flavour is one of the least interesting, especially if judged by the insipid factory product (often not Italian-made) available in most supermarkets. If you can find it, try the original Mozzarella di Bufala (made from the milk of water buffaloes usually mixed with cows' milk) which is still made in parts of the south. Softer, stickier and less rubbery than cows' milk Mozzarella, it has a stronger flavour and a more pronounced smell.

Mozzarella, which dates back to the 16th century, is a fresh *pasta filata* cheese, hand-moulded into creamy white balls and, in Italy, sold swimming in a bowl of whey. Ideally it should be eaten as soon as possible after buying, but it will keep for a day or two if it is moistened with a little fresh milk and put in the refrigerator. The best Mozzarella is reputedly that from Capua, Aversa and the Sele valley. A lightly smoked version called Mozzarella Affumicata is also available, and in Naples (Napoli) they sometimes flavour buffalo Mozzarella with cumin or caraway seeds (Borelli). Made in a variety of shapes—*ovoli* (eggs), *bocconi* (mouthfuls), *trecce* (plaits)—and given regional names such as Provatura in Puglia. See *Fior di Latte, Provola, Scamorza*

Murianengo
Rare blue-veined cheese made from cows' or goats' milk on the Italian-French border.

Nostrale, Nostrano
Any simple locally made rustic cheese. The name denotes not so much a particular cheese type as the fact that it is 'home-made' or made in the locality.

Ovoli see *Mozzarella*

Paglierina
Small, softish, fresh ivory-coloured cheese from Piedmont, usually somewhat sour-tasting. Sold on little straw mats (*paglia*, straw), they are often eaten dressed with oil and seasoned.

Palloni, Pancette, Pancettoni see *Provolone*

Panedda see *Casigliolo*

Pannarone, Pannerone see *Gorgonzola Bianco*

Parmesan
The translation of Parmigiano Reggiano is often used to describe the sickly dry (sometimes adulterated) ready-grated powder that bears no resemblance to the real thing.

Parmigiano Reggiano ★ 🏵 ➧ 32% 🗆 30kg (66lb) ⑧
The whole cheese is a truly magnificent sight: an enormous shiny brown drum with its name stamped vertically all over the sides. When split open (along the natural grain of the cheese using a special leaf-shaped knife), it reveals a beautiful straw-yellow grainy paste, brittle and crumbly with a superb fruity flavour that should never be bitter. It has been lauded by name for at least 700 years, but the Grana family of cheeses to which it belongs has a much more ancient provenance. It has long been valued for both medicinal and gastronomic purposes.

The making of Parmigiano Reggiano is strictly controlled. It has to be made between 1 April and 11 November with milk from the *zona tipica* (the provinces of Parma, Reggio Emilia, Modena, Mantua on the right bank of the Po and Bologna on the left bank of the Reno). Unpasteurized evening and morning milk are partly skimmed and then mixed together in huge copper cauldrons. The starter is added and the milk brought gradually up to a temperature of 33°C (91°F) when the rennet is added to coagulate the milk over a period of about 15 minutes. The curds are then broken up with a sharp rod (*spino*) into tiny grains, which are then cooked in the whey at 55°C (131°F), left to settle on the bottom of the vat, scooped out in a cheesecloth and pressed in a special mould (*fascera*). The cheeses are left in these moulds for several days and then salted in brine for about three weeks before being stored for at least one and no more than four years. The cheeses are sold at four stages of their maturation: *giovane* (young, after a year), *vecchio* (old, after two years), *stravecchio* (mature, after three years) and *stravecchione* (extra mature, after four years). Parmigiano is at the peak of perfection when it is *con gocciola*, which means that when the cheese is split open you can just see tiny tears of moisture glistening on the surface. It is a superb dessert cheese when young and as it gets older it is grated and sprinkled on pasta, risotto and innumerable other dishes. See *Grana*

Passito
Local Lombardy dialect (meaning 'past it') for Stracchino.

Pecorino ★

Generic name for ewes' milk cheeses (from *pecora*, sheep)—one of the most important Italian cheese families and particularly associated with central and southern Italy. A typical Pecorino is a hard-pressed, cooked, drum- or wheel-shaped cheese, made from whole or skimmed unpasteurized milk coagulated with sheep's rennet, and decidedly piquant in flavour. The farther south one goes, the more *piccante* the cheeses become. Any ewes' milk cheese can be called a Pecorino but over the centuries some have become more widely known and more important commercially than others, notably Pecorino Romano and Pecorino Siciliano.

Pecorino Pepato

A Pecorino (usually Siciliano) flavoured with whole black peppercorns, sometimes simply called Pepato.

Pecorino Romano ★   🐑 🌙 36% 🗋 6-22kg (13-48lb) Ⓑ

The most famous of the Pecorino cheeses and the legendary cheese made by Romulus, Pecorino Romano had its characteristics and *zona tipica* precisely laid down by the Stresa Convention of 1951. Made between November and June, the traditional area of production is Lazio, but this has now been extended to include Sardinia.

Pecorino Romano has always been a popular cheese both in Italy and overseas. Columella talks of it being exported in the first century AD and a considerable amount of the cheese produced today finds it way abroad, especially to the United States. It has a greyish-white close-textured paste and a smooth natural rind stamped by the consortium which checks its authenticity. (At one time it was rubbed with oil and wood ash.) It is ripened for a minimum of eight months, when the flavour is sharp and dry and goes particularly well with coarse country bread. Grated, it is an essential part of many regional dishes. It gives off a somewhat acrid smell when sprinkled on hot food, but this should be tolerated in the interests of authenticity; the flavour is not adversely affected.

Pecorino Sardo see *Fiore Sardo*

Pecorino Senese

A type of Pecorino Toscano made near Siena. The rind is rubbed with tomato paste or with olive oil and wood ash.

Pecorino Siciliano   🐑 🌙 40% 🗋 4-12kg (9-26lb) Ⓒ

Made in Sicily between October and June it has a dense, whitish-yellow paste with a few scattered holes. Strong flavour with characteristic ewes' milk tang. Also known as Canestrato and Incanestrato.

Pecorino Toscanello

Semisoft white ewes' milk cheese from Sardinia with a smooth white rind. Cheeses from the best pastures have some of the flavour of the thyme that grows there.

Pecorino Toscano   🐑 40-45% 🗋 1-3kg (2-7lb) Ⓒ

Until recently the name was given to any cheese made in Tuscany from ewes' milk, sometimes mixed with cows' or goats' milk. The name is now reserved for pure ewes' milk cheeses made between September and June (mixed milk cheeses are sold as Caciotta). Tuscan Pecorinos are smaller and usually milder than other Pecorinos, and may be sold soft and fresh (yellow rind) or firm and ripened for a few months (browner reddish rind). Toscanello is a slightly larger ewes' milk cheese which is ripened for at least six months.

Pepato see *Pecorino Pepato*

Pera di Vacca see *Casigliolo*

Piacintinu
Once a Grana cheese made in Piacenza. Now refers to a Sicilian Pecorino made in Messina and flavoured with saffron.

Prescinseua
Ligurian acid-curd cheese made from whole milk, drained in a cloth and used fresh in many local dishes.

Pressato 🐄 🌙 30% ⊖ 9-14kg (20-31lb) ©
Firm, pale yellow, cooked cheese with many uneven holes spread throughout the paste, made from partly skimmed milk. It was first developed in Vicenza as a variant of Asiago. Pressato is a more even-tempered cheese than Asiago and, at least locally, is now more popular. Unlike Asiago it is salted partly before and partly after being pressed, it ripens in a much shorter time—40 to 60 days—and is eaten only as a dessert cheese. The flavour is pleasantly sweet and fragrant.

Provatura see *Mozzarella*

Provola, Provole
Can be either unripened Provolone moulded into small balls or longer ripened Mozzarella. The cheese is soft, sweet and mild with a hard wax coating. Burrini are sometimes sold under this name and Provola is sometimes sold under a brand name (e.g. Ciccillo). To add to the confusion, a variety of other diminutives may be used (such as Provo-lette or Provolini), but they are all basically the same (literally, tiny Provoloni). Also available smoked (*affumicata*). Found mainly in the south, especially Campania.

Provolone ★ 🐄 🌙 44% 200g-30kg (7oz-66lb) ⑧
An uncooked, smooth, close-textured *pasta filata* cheese made from whole cows' milk coagulated with calf's rennet (Provolone Dolce) or lamb's or kid's rennet (Provolone Piccante). Originated in southern Italy, but production has now spread to the Po valley and with it the increasingly pervasive trend (much deprecated by connoisseurs) towards the mild (*dolce*) rather than the piquant (*piccante*) varieties. The former, aged for two to three months, is softer, mild and smooth with a thin waxed rind. The latter, aged from six months to two years, is darker in colour with small eyes, a tough hard rind and a stronger spicier flavour. Hand-moulded into multifarious shapes, and sold under a diversity of regional and descriptive names, such as Ercolini, Palloni, Silanetti, Sorrentini (the smaller ones) and Pancette, Pancer-toni, Salami, Giganti (the big brothers). The larger cheeses are sometimes smoked and are usually bound with rafffia or string and hung up in pairs on poles while waiting to be sold. The best come from Campania and Puglia.

Puina
Ricotta in the Venetian dialect, much used in cooking.

Quartirolo 🐄 🌙 26-50% ⊂⊃ ⑩
Uncooked pressed cheese from Lombardy. Nowadays it is made all year round from pasteurized whole or partly skimmed milk but at one time only in autumn from the fourth growth of grass, *erba quartirolo*, hence the name. Also known as Milan Stracchino. Sold when very fresh and pure white, or ripened for seven to eight weeks with a thin washed rind and pale paste.

Ragusano ✿ ➤ 44% 6-12kg (13-26lb) ©

From Ragusa, Sicily, whose flowery meadows produce fine-quality milk with a high fat content and give this *pasta filata* cows' milk cheese its particular flavour and aroma. It is shaped like a square cushion with cord marks from the custom of hanging pairs of cheeses over a support while ripening—up to six months as a table cheese, or longer, when the rind is rubbed with olive oil to produce a grating cheese with a strong, spicy flavour.

Raschera

Produced in the Alps around Cuneo from cows' milk, to which ewes' or goats' milk may be added. The best cheeses from alpine pastures include the words '*di alpeggio*' on the label. Round or square with a thin, reddish yellow rind and an elastic ivory interior with a few small holes. Rich and aromatic, best in summer and autumn.

Raveggiolo

A creamy white ewes' milk cheese with a slightly elastic texture. Eaten within a few weeks of making.

Ricotta ★

Traditionally a whey cheese, made as a by-product of other cheese-making, but nowadays whole or skimmed milk is sometimes added, giving a much richer product. It is white and mild with a fine, granular consistency and is usually shaped like an upturned basin with basket-work marks on the outside. Ricotta Romana, a pure ewes' milk cheese made from November to June, is highly esteemed, drier and more granular than others. There are three stages: the most familiar is fresh, bland, very soft, unripened and unsalted; *ricotta salata* or *canestrata*, common in Sicily, is salted and dried, like Greek Feta; *ricotta secca* is matured to a dry hard consistency and used mostly for grating. Sicily also specializes in Ricotta Infornata (baked until it is a warm brown), which may be fresh or ripened. In Puglia you may come across Ricotta Marzotica, ripened for a week in herb leaves and Ricotta Schianta, a strong flavoured preparation fermented in earthenware jars. In northern Italy ricotta is often smoked, and in Piedmont it is traditionally mixed with paprika. Fresh Ricotta (known as Puina in Veneto) is used a great deal in Italian cooking and is also often eaten sprinkled with powdered coffee, chocolate or sugar. Ricotta can also be called Brocotte. See *Canestrato*

Rob(b)iola

Another of those confusing designations that can mean a number of different things. The name has two possible derivations: from the Lombardy village of Robbio in Lomellina and from the Latin *rubium*, red, an indication of the reddish-brown rind typical of most Robiola cheeses. It usually means a soft, unpressed cows' or mixed milk cheese that ripens over a period of one to four weeks, when it acquires the characteristic red rind mould coating. This cheese resembles Taleggio and becomes gradually more piquant with age. Another rarer type, Piedmontese Robiola di Roccaverano, is more akin to Camembert, ripened for no more than a few weeks and becoming softer and creamier with age. Another traditional Piedmontese type is Robiola del Bec, Bec being the dialect word for goat. Basically similar to Robiola di Roccaverano, but ripened slightly longer and obviously stronger tasting. Connoisseurs prefer this type when made in October and November, the mating season of the goats.

Robiolette, Robiolini

Small cheeses from Lombardy, usually shaped into rolls or bars, slightly acid to taste and eaten with oil and seasoning.

Romano

Italians always distinguish between Pecorino Romano (made with ewes' milk), Caprino Romano (made with goats' milk) and Vacchino Romano (made with cows' milk). Pecorino Romano is the classic all-purpose cheese, but the cows' milk version often found outside Italy is also hard and sharp and good for cooking.

Salami see *Provolone*

San Gaudenzio see *Torta Gaudenzio*

Scamorza

From Abruzzo, a type of cows' milk Mozzarella. The word means 'dunce' in southern dialect and refers to the shape—like a pear, but with a distinct pointed 'head' formed by the cord used to hang the cheese during manufacture. Often smoked.

Scanno

Table Pecorino from Abruzzo. Traditionally eaten with fresh fruit. Black on the outside and buttery yellow inside. The flavour has a mildly burnt tinge.

Silanetti, Sorrentini see *Provolone*

Stracchino 🍴 🥛 48-50% 🧀 50g-4kg (1¾oz-9lb) Ⓑ

Stracchino is a generic term for a type of Lombardy cheese that was at one time made in the autumn and winter from the milk of cows that had come down from their summer alpine pastures to be wintered on the plains. The milk of these 'tired' cows (*stracche* in the Lombardy dialect) imparted a distinctive flavour to the cheese (as a result of the change of grazing). They were also quick-ripening cheeses that in the days before refrigeration could be made only in the winter. Nowadays these cheeses are made all year round and many different types come under the same etymological umbrella. Gorgonzola is a matured Stracchino. So are Quartirolo, Taleggio and some Robiola cheeses. Today, what is labelled Stracchino is a pale, meltingly soft cheese with a very light rind and a delicate fruity flavour. See *Crescenza*

Taleggio ★ 🍴 🥛 48% 🧀 2kg (4lb) Ⓑ

Named after a small town near Bergamo, this is an unpressed uncooked cheese of the Stracchino type. The paste is creamy and supple with a thin pinkish-grey rind that should not appear cracked or broken. The cheese ripens in about 40 days, when the flavour is mild and fruity. Under perfect conditions some cheeses can be ripened for twice as long: the flavour deepens, the cheese becomes plumper, more aromatic and the paste a deeper yellow. These and Taleggio made with unpasteurized milk are especially prized.

Toma, Tuma

Made in the mountainous regions of Valle d'Aosta, Piedmont and Liguria from cows' milk, sometimes mixed with goats' or ewes' milk. Uncooked pressed cheeses of varying fat contents and sizes, from 2 to 6kg (4-13lb). Usually aged for about three months and best in summer and autumn, when sweetly nutty, slightly tangy, with a pale smooth paste. Some are aged for a year, becoming deep golden and piquant. In Sicily the name is used for fresh curds moulded in a basket.

Tomini

Small cheeses from the same regions as Toma. Usually eaten while bland, fresh and white, dressed with olive oil, pepper and salt at the end of a meal.

Torta (San) Gaudenzio ★

One of several trade names for Gorgonzola con Mascarpone: alternate layers of these two cheeses pressed together like a gâteau. (Sold as Torta Dolcelatte in Britain.) The mixture of Gorgonzola and Mascarpone is a traditional one, originating in the Trieste area, where it may also be flavoured with anchovy and caraway seeds. Other tortas now come with layers of walnuts or basil.

Toscanello see *Pecorino Toscano*

Trecce, Treccia see *Mozzarella*

Tuma see *Toma*

Vacchino Romano see *Romano*

Vezzena

Rare Grana-type cheese related to Asiago though very much sharper and more granular, and without the holes. The paste ranges from white (winter-made cheeses) to yellow (summer-made). Eaten after six months as a table cheese and after a year or more for grating. Also called Veneto, Venezza.

KEY WORDS

Affumicato smoked	**Giovane** young
Bufala buffalo	**Molle** soft
Cacio old word for cheese	**Mucca** milk cow
Capra goat	**Pecora** ewe
Dolce mild	**Piccante** piquant
Duro hard	**Vacca** cow
Formaggio cheese	**Vecchio** old
Fresco fresh	**Zona tipica** area of production

Latin America

Cheesemaking was unknown to the indigenous Amerindians before the Europeans arrived in Latin America some 500 years ago, and the European cattle and sheep brought over by the colonizers have been bred for meat rather than dairying. Most of Latin America falls within the tropical zone, not renowned for its cheeses. Simple fresh cheeses are commonplace and versions of popular European types are made on a commercial basis. Untemperamental long-keeping cheeses like Dutch Edam and Gouda have proved widely adaptable throughout Latin America, and Argentina makes imitations of several Italian types including Parmesan, Mozzarella and Romano.

Añejo (Mexico)
Dry salty goat cheese, ripened for eight months. Sometimes covered with chilli powder and called Queso Enchilado.

Asadero (Mexico)
Literally 'good for roasting', a slightly acidic *pasta filata* cheese made from whole cows' milk. From the south. Also called Oaxaca.

Bernina (Colombia) 🐄 💧 50% 250g (9oz) ©
Piquant cheese ripened for about a week. Foil-wrapped.

Bola see *Prato*

Campesino (Paraguay)
Fresh, lightly pressed, salty cows' milk cheese.

Catupiri (Brazil)
Rennet-curd cows' milk cheese eaten with quince marmalade.

Chanco (Chile) 🐄 💧 50% ⊂⊃ 6-10kg (13-22lb) ©
Smooth, mild buttery cheese with a golden-brown rind made mostly from pasteurized milk. Also called Mantecoso.

Chihuahua (Mexico)
Soft, sourish cows' milk cheese much used in cooking.

Cincho (Venezuela)
Fresh acid-curd ewes' milk cheese like Spanish Villalón.

Coalhada (Brazil)
Fresh creamy cows' milk cheese usually eaten with sugar.

Coyolito (El Salvador) 🐄 💧 ⊂⊃ 20-22kg (44-48lb) ⒟
Coarse, piquant, pressed cheese washed with brine and coconut milk during a three-week ripening period.

Crema (Argentina) 🐄 💧 55% ⊂⊃ 3.8kg (8½lb) ©
Fresh soft cream cheese ripened for about a week.

Cuajada (Venezuela)
Creamy cows' milk cheese wrapped in maize or banana leaves.

Gaucho (Argentina)
Semihard cows' milk cheese made from skimmed milk.

Hoja (Puerto Rico)
Brined cows' milk cheese thinly rolled and folded in layers.

Llanero (Venezuela)
Strong, crumbly, grating cheese from the *llanos*, huge plains stretching south of Caracas into Colombia.

Maduro (Costa Rica)
Semihard low-fat cheese made from pasteurized cows' milk.

Mano (Venezuela)
Pasta filata cows' milk cheese wrapped in banana leaves.

Mantecoso (Peru, Chile)
In Peru a popular farm-made soft cheese. In Chile a semihard cheese similar to Port Salut. See *Chanco*

Minas (Brazil) 🐄 💧 30-45% 🧀 500g-2kg (18oz-4lb) ©
Bland, slightly sour acid-curd cheese made in small factories in Minas Gerais from whole pasteurized milk. Sold either fresh (*frescal*) or pressed and partly ripened (*curado*). Used in cooking and eaten with fruit or preserves.

Oaxaca see *Asadero*

Patagras (Cuba) 🐄 💧 40% 🧀 5kg (11lb) ©
Springy, mild, firm cheese with a red waxed rind similar to Gouda. Made from whole or partly skimmed pasteurized milk.

Pera (Colombia)
Small, fairly hard spun-curd cheese made from partly skimmed cows' milk and stuffed with candied fruit.

Petacones (El Salvador)
Hard-pressed cows' milk cheeses ripened for about two weeks.

Prato (Brazil) 🐄 💧 46% ©
One of the most popular Brazilian types. Mild cheese with small holes and a deep golden waxed rind. Ripened for six to seven weeks. A spherical version is known as Bola.

Quartirolo (Argentina, Brazil) 🐄 💧 50% 🧀 3.8kg (8½lb) ©
Fresh cheese which develops a fruity flavour on keeping.

Quesillos (Chile, Paraguay)
Small, fresh cows' milk cheeses wrapped in banana or maize leaves.

Queso Blanco
Generic term for fresh white cheese produced throughout Latin America from whole or skimmed milk or whey.

Queso Enchilado see *Añejo*

Reino (Brazil)
Hard cows' or goats' milk cheese, similar to aged Portuguese Serra.

Requeijão (Brazil)
Acid-curd skimmed cows' milk cheese. The common factory-made type is a bland cheese with a thin soft rind. Requeijão de Sertão refers to the traditional type which is firmer, with a drier rind.

Suero (Costa Rica)
Low-fat cheese made from buttermilk.

Middle East

Good pasture is often difficult to find so the most important milk-producers are goats and ewes. Cheeses—mostly white brined types—are simple but very popular, especially for breakfast.

'Akawi (Lebanon)
Fresh, soft, white cows' milk cheese, shaped into cakes.

Baida, Beda (Egypt)
A white pressed cheese made from skimmed cows' or buffalo milk. Eaten fresh or cured in its own whey.

Beyaz Peynir (Turkey)
Literally 'white cheese', made of ewes' or goats' milk. Eaten fresh or ripened in brine for several months. Similar to Greek Feta.

Biza (Iraq)
Fresh acid-curd cheese made from hand-skimmed ewes' milk. Flavoured with garlic, onion or carob. Also called Fajy.

Danni (Egypt)
Ewes' milk cheese from northern Egypt. Eaten after three days or ripened in its whey for four to five months.

Dil Peyniri (Turkey)
Hard, round, spun-curd cheese made from any type of milk.

Damietta, Domiati, Dumyāti (Egypt)
Cows' or buffalo milk cheese. Unusually, the milk is salted before, rather than after renneting. Sold fresh, soft, white and mild — or ripened for four to eight months in salted whey or brine when it becomes darker and much more tangy. Packed in tins for export.

Edirne (Turkey)
Soft fresh ewes' milk cheese made in the north-west.

Fajy see *Biza*

Gebna, Gibne, Jibne
Simple cheese found all over the Middle East, traditionally made by nomads. Ewes', goats' or camels' milk is coagulated with animal or vegetable rennet. Eaten fresh.

Gravyer (Turkey)
Turkish imitation of Gruyère.

Jubna (Saudi Arabia)
Fresh, white, round, heavily salted cheese made from ewes' or goats' milk. Eaten after pressing or preserved in brine.

Kareish (Egypt)
Acid-curd very salty cheese made from skimmed cows' or buffalo milk. Eaten fresh or ripened in brine.

Kasar, Kaser (Turkey)
Pressed semihard ewes', cows or mixed milk cheese.

Kashkawān (Lebanon, Syria)
Pressed spun-curd cheese made from goats' milk, similar to Italian Caciocavallo. Ripened for six to seven weeks.

Labna (Lebanon)
Soft, fresh acid-curd cheese made from strained yoghurt (any milk).

Labniya (Syria)
Sour-milk curds thickened with rice or barley meal, flavoured with herbs and steeped in oil. It can be called cheese—but only just. Most Syrian cheeses are made at home for domestic use.

Lor, Lour (Turkey, Iraq)
Unpressed cheese made from ewes' milk whey mixed with whole milk—eaten fresh.

Meira (Iraq)
Semihard to hard cheese made from ewes' milk, pressed between heavy stones and ripened in sheepskins for up to a year.

Mihaliççik (Turkey)
Semihard ewes' milk cheese salted in a brine bath for two weeks and ripened for about three months.

Mish (Egypt)
Fresh goats' milk 'started' with a piece of mature Mish and salted, spiced and aged for about a year in earthenware pots. Extremely salty.

Qareshie (Lebanon)
Crumbly soft white cheese made from any milk. Eaten very fresh, salted or unsalted, with sugar or jam.

Roos (Iraq)
Strong, salty cheese made from ewes' or goats' milk near Ain Kawa and Haj Omran. Moulded and pressed by hand into grapefruit-sized balls and ripened for about six months.

Salamura (Turkey)
Strong white goats' milk cheese ripened in brine.

Shankleish (Lebanon)
The king of Lebanese cheeses begins life as Labna, but is strained repeatedly, spiced, shaped into balls and dried in the sun, then rolled in dried thyme. Made with great care in the north of the country.

Tel Peyniri (Turkey)
Same as Dil Peyniri but usually made from skimmed ewes' milk.

Tulum Peyniri (Turkey)
Semihard pressed cheese made of partly skimmed ewes' or goats' milk mixed with olive oil or yoghurt. Ripened for about four months in a sheepskin or goatskin bag (a *tulum*). Dry, strong and pungent.

Van Peyniri (Turkey)
Goats' milk cheese from Lake Van. Fresh, white and crumbly when young, becoming brown and powdery with age. Stored in goatskin bags. May also be herb-flavoured. Eaten for breakfast.

Zukra (Lebanon)
Named after the tribe that first made it, Zukra is a soft goats' cheese sold in goatskin drums in which it is stored with Qareshie to keep it moist. Even if you don't buy the whole drum, you will be given some of the softer cheese along with the Zukra.

MOROCCO see *Africa*

The Netherlands

Dutch cheeses, although few in number, have achieved a spectacular commercial success. The Netherlands are, in fact, by far the largest exporters of cheese in the world, a position they have held for centuries. At an early date Dutch cheesemakers developed cheeses with exceptional keeping qualities, ones that were easily transportable and reliable rather than exotic—cheeses typified by Gouda and Edam. Both are now among the most copied cheese types in the world, along with English Cheddar, French Camembert and Swiss 'Swiss'. The tangy spiced cheeses have proved less popular abroad, although much liked by the Dutch themselves.

Cheesemaking in the Netherlands is heavily industrialized. Fewer than 100 fully automated factories turn out nearly 500 million kg (approximately 1,100 million lb) of cheese each year with a bare minimum of staff. Computerized cheesemaking has led to a decline in the number of farmhouse producers, most of whom make Gouda in its many varieties. There are very few local cheeses: some ewes' milk cheeses on the island of Texel and in the province of Friesland and some goats' milk cheeses in Ankeveen, Noord-Holland and Aarle-Rixtel, Brabant.

Amsterdammer see *Gouda*

Arina ♦ ⅅ 48% ⊟ 4kg (9lb) ©
Creamery-made, Gouda-style pure goats' milk cheese. Quite strong. Coated in special plastic cheese coating.

Commissiekaas see *Edam*

Dietkaas
Low fat (20 to 48 per cent) or low salt cheese distinguished by a 'D' on the control stamp. Often a Gouda-type, but any cheese can be made this way.

Edam (Edammer) ★ ໋ ⅅ 40% ○ 880g-6.5kg (30oz-14lb) Ⓐ
Its bright red coating of paraffin wax makes Edam the most immediately recognizable cheese in the world (although in the Netherlands itself the cheeses are sold with the natural golden rind uncovered). Its equally distinctive spherical shape occurs because the cheese firms quickly before the interior has time to settle. Edam is smooth and supple with a slightly acidulous aftertaste, sold young at about six weeks old, or after six months to a year, when it becomes stronger, drier and saltier (mature cheeses are coated in black wax for export).

Edam originated in the town of Edam at least 600 years ago and by the late 17th century about 454,000 kg (1,000,000 lb) of cheese was being exported every year, much of it to the Dutch colonies. Now nearly all factory-made, Edam may be flavoured with herbs, peppercorns or cumin seeds. The normal size weighs around 2kg (4lb). There is also a smaller Baby Edam, a stronger, double-sized Commissiekaas (sold as Mimolette in France and coloured deep orange with annatto), and Middelbaar, a rare heavyweight at 6.5kg (14lb).

Fricotal see *Maasdam*

Friese Nagelkaas ໋ ⅅ 20-40% ⊟ 7-9kg (15-20lb)
Surprisingly, the homeland of the ubiquitous black and white Friesian cattle has not produced many original cheese types. Nagelkaas (literally 'nail cheese') is a rather coarse, hard-pressed, long-ripening cheese made from skimmed milk sometimes mixed with buttermilk and studded with cloves and cumin seeds. The paste

is grey-white, dry and extremely spicy and piquant after a minimum of six months' ageing. The rind is tough and hard, especially in well-matured cheeses. Also sold under the names Friese Kanterkaas and Friesian Clove.

Gouda (Goudsche) ★ 🏵 🌑 48% ⊖ 2.5-20kg (5½-44lb) Ⓐ

The most important Dutch cheese, accounting for over two-thirds of the total production, which originated in Gouda in the 13th century. Made from full milk, it is a pressed uncooked cheese with a firm straw-coloured paste scattered with small irregular holes or a few large ones depending on the type of starter culture that has been used. The young cheeses, aged for one to four months, are very mild and buttery, but mature Goudas, sometimes ripened for as long as three years, are darker in colour and much tangier, with a fuller, richer flavour and a more pronounced spicy aroma. Farmhouse Goudas are made from unpasteurized milk, and have the word *Boeren* (*boer*, farmer) stamped on the rind. Farmhouse Goudas with cumin are quite common, and there are also versions flavoured with nettles, mustard seeds, herbs, peppercorns, garlic and dill.

Gouda is produced in various sizes. The smallest, Baby Gouda or Lunchkaas, is usually eaten young, after four weeks' ripening. Amsterdammer, ripened for four to eight weeks, is a small, softer, creamier Gouda with a higher moisture content than usual and a distinctive shiny orange rind. Roomkaas is a soft, smooth Gouda enriched with cream (60 per cent fat); it usually weighs around 5kg (11lb). A range of 'light' cheeses which look and taste similar to Gouda, but have a fat content of around 30 per cent are sold under various brand names.

Kanterkaas see *Friese Nagelkaas*

Kernhem (Kernhemse) ★ 🏵 🌑 60% ⊖ 2kg (4lb) Ⓑ

Washed rind cheese reminiscent of traditional monastery cheeses but recently invented by the Netherlands Institute of Dairy Research. It is lightly pressed and ripened for about four weeks in cool humid conditions, during which time it is regularly turned and the rind washed with water. The paste is creamy and golden, with a full, rich flavour. Kernhem is classed by the Dutch as a *meshanger* cheese—one that clings to the knife when cut.

Kwark

Soft, white, lightly drained fresh curd cheese. Magere Kwark is made from skimmed milk and the fat content is practically nil.

Leerdammer see *Maasdam*

Leiden, Leyden (Leidse) ★ 🏵 🌑 20-40% ⊖ 3-8kg (7-18lb) Ⓑ

Pressed, uncooked crumbly, rather salty cheese made from partly skimmed milk and buttermilk and flavoured with cumin seeds. Modern cheesemaking hygiene forbids the traditional practice of treading the cumin into the curds: feet have been replaced by machines. Leiden is ripened for at least three months. Factory-made cheeses have natural yellow rinds (40 per cent fat) or are red waxed (20 per cent) but farmhouse Leidens have their rinds rubbed with annatto (at one time a mixture of vegetable dye and beestings was used), making them a deep, glowing orange-red. Farmhouse Leiden (stamped with the words *Boeren Leidse* and a pair of crossed keys, the arms of the city of the city of Leiden) has a legal minimum fat content of 20 per cent (although usually higher in practice) and is drier and sharper than the factory version.

Lunchkaas see *Gouda*

Maasdam 🐄 🌙 45% ⊖ 6-12kg (13-26lb) Ⓑ
A factory-made, recently developed cheese similar to Swiss Emmental. Ripened for at least four weeks. The flavour is sweetish and mildly nutty. Commonly sold under trade names such as Westberg, Leerdammer, Fricotal and Meerlander.

Meikaas 🐄 🌙 48% ⊖ 2.5-5kg (5½-11lb) Ⓒ
'May cheese' is a type of Gouda made when the cows first go out to pasture in the spring. It is aged for a minimum of six weeks, and is often available until December.

Mimolette see *Edam*

Mon Chou 🐄 🌙 73% ⊗ 100g (3½oz) Ⓒ
Rich, creamy, factory-made cheese with a mild, faintly acid flavour. Sold wrapped in foil; of recent origin.

Nagelkaas see *Friese Nagelkaas*

Pompadour 🐄 🌙 50% ⊖ 4kg (9lb) Ⓑ
Trade name for a young, smooth, creamy Gouda-type cheese flavoured with garden herbs (parsley, celery and garlic). Waxed for export. Similar cheeses sold under different brand names may be flavoured with peppercorns or caraway seeds.

Roomkaas see *Gouda*

Subenhara
Trade name for a cheese similar to Pompadour.

Texel
Rare, fresh ewes' milk cheese from the island of Texel. Rumour has it that the flavour of this cheese is, or at least was, a result of steeping sheep's droppings in the milk before coagulation.

Westberg see *Maasdam*

Witte Meikaas 🐄 🌙 48% ⊖ 2.5-5kg (5½-11lb) Ⓓ
Fresh white curd cheese with a high moisture content, made from whole milk and rather acid in flavour. The name means 'White May', and the cheese is made on farms in the spring. Sold mainly in Amsterdam.

KEY WORDS

Belegen 4-6 months old	**Komijne** cumin
Boerenkaas farmhouse cheese	**Oude** over 9 months old
Extra belegen 6-9 months old	**Ryp** mature
Geit goat	**Schaap** ewe
Jong 4-8 weeks old	**Vers** fresh
Jong belegen 2-4 months old	**Volvet** full fat
Kaas cheese	**Zacht** soft
Koe cow	

NEW ZEALAND see *Australasia*

North America

UNITED STATES

North America has not, on the whole, been kind to cheese, although more cheese and more types of cheese are made there than anywhere else. Supermarkets are swamped by the mass of anesthetized, homogenized, artificially coloured and flavoured, pre-packed, ready-sliced, ready-shredded, ready-grated—it sometimes seems ready-digested—cheese food and cheese products. The national obsession with health has made low-salt, low-fat and low-cholesterol more popular than ever. Cheese manufacturers are making efforts to offer these modified versions to well-known types of cheese. Low fat Cheddar, Munster and Swiss cheeses have been around for years. Increasingly available are low-fat Jarlsberg, Gouda and some Monterey Jack cheeses. Synthetic enzymes are used to make Kosher and vegetarian cheeses. Regional cheeses with character and fine flavour are abundant in farmers markets and farmstands across the country. Many small manufacturers are offering mail-order services to devotees who search out alternatives to the bland, tasteless products found in most supermarkets. Specialist or "farmstead" cheesemakers, using cows' or goats' milk are burgeoning. Some are making fine original American types, others good foreign imitations. Cheese lovers are importing many fine European cheeses. The strict laws enforcing pasteurization have been relaxed somewhat. Raw milk can be used in the making of cheese, provided that it is ripened for at least 60 days at correct temperatures. After some recent outbreaks of ill health related to contamination by imported raw-milk cheeses, the guidelines are stricter than even a few years ago. However, many of the finest cheeses in the world are available in America. Fancy food stores can provide the enthusiast with a wide array of imported and domestic products of the finest quality.

American

A term loosely used to mean American-made Cheddar. It represents over 70 per cent of America's gigantic production, was the first cheese brought to America (by the Pilgrim Fathers), the first to be made there and the first to be industrialized. Early farm-made cheeses were much praised by travellers, but the factory-produced Cheddars found in every grocery store gave the cheese its nicknames—'store cheese' and 'rat cheese'. It may be bland or strong and is often heavily dyed with annatto and waxed black, red or orange. The various names under which the cheese is sold such as Barrel, Mammoth, Daisy, Picnic, Flat or Twin, Young American, Longhorn (salami-shaped) refer usually to the size or shape of the whole cheese, but there are also regional variants with different flavours, aromas and textures. Cheddar is made throughout America, but the best-known cheeses are those from Vermont, New York State, Oregon and Wisconsin. The Amish communities in Pennsylvania and Monterey Farms in California make raw milk Cheddars which tend to be quite dry and sharp-tasting. See *Colby, New York State, Pineapple, Tillamook, Vermont*

American Bleu or Blue

Cows' milk cheeses blued with *Penicillium roquefortii*. Blues are made in many states. See *Maytag, Treasure Cave, Oregon Blue*

Braided Cheese

Of Armenian origin, strips of fresh *pasta filata* cheese plaited or twisted together. Very white, rubbery and quite tasteless unless flavoured with caraway or nigella seeds (*Nigella damascena*, better known as Love-in-a-mist). Very popular at parties: not only does it look like a plate of spaghetti, it is also low in fat. Also called String, Rope or Syrian Cheese.

Brick ★ 🐮 🔪 50% 🧀 2.5kg (5½lb) ©

Truly original, a lightly pungent sweetish cheese with numerous holes in a very pale supple paste. Many think of it as a cross between Limburger and Cheddar, but it is really much more like Tilsiter than anything else. It was invented in the 1870s by a Swiss cheesemaker in Wisconsin, where most of it is still made. The name derives from its shape or, some say, from the traditional practice of pressing it with bricks. The rind is smeared with a culture of *Bacterium linens* and regularly wiped with a cloth dipped in brine during the three-month ripening. The resulting aroma is distinctly spicy but not overpowering compared to other washed rind cheeses. The reddish natural rind is sometimes removed and the cheeses waxed before they are sold. Sometimes described as 'the married man's Limburger'—it is a milder cheese.

Chantelle

Trade name for a full-fat, mild sliceable cows' milk cheese with a springy yellow paste similar to Italian Bel Paese. Coated in red wax.

Chèvre

Goats' milk cheeses of all shapes, sizes and ages, both domestic and imported, have become tremendously popular in America in recent years. Laura Chenel, owner of California Chèvre, studied techniques in France and now makes many varieties: delicately flavoured 150g (5oz) Chabis and Banon; 225g (8oz) Pyramides and Sainte Maure logs; and stronger 1.5kg (3lb) Fourmes, aged for months rather than days. Sallie Kendall, also in California, makes a goat Camembert, an extra-rich white mould-ripened cheese called Chevrefeuille, and a crumbly Chèvre Bleu, sold young, although flavour develops with age. Westfield Farm in Massachusetts make a goats' milk Blue Log in 225g and 1kg (8oz and 2lb) sizes—the blue mould is sprayed on to the outside of the log so the paste is not as salty as a blue cheese. Coach Farm in Colombia County, New York State, makes excellent goats' cheeses, from buttons to aged 2kg (4lb) logs, under the expert care of a French cheesemaker. Goats' milk Cheddars are made in Iowa and California, and there are numerous local makers throughout the United States. See *Monterey Chèvre, Taupière*

Colby 🐮 🍶 50% 🧀 ©

From Colby, Wisconsin, a Cheddar variant first made in 1882 by Ambrose and J.H. Steinwand. The curd is not 'cheddared' which makes the paste more open, moist and sliceable than an ordinary Cheddar. It is dyed deep orange yellow and waxed or vacuum packed in variously sized blocks or rounds. The flavour is mild and rather sweet. A popular everyday cheese.

Coldpack

A very big seller across the United States, made by blending cheese with wine, brandy, spices and flavourings. The mixture is not heated as in the case of processed cheese, hence the name. Usually sold in ceramic pots and sometimes called Cheddar Spread or Potted Cheese.

Cottage Cheese

Incredibly popular with dieters and cooks. Fresh soft white granular cheese made from skimmed milk coagulated with or without rennet. All Cottage Cheese is legally required to have a moisture content of not more than 80 per cent; it must be made with skimmed milk and have a fat content of not less than four per cent. Cheeses with one to four per cent fat must be labelled 'low fat'. The large curd type is known as popcorn or California style; mashed, it becomes country or creamed style. Pot Cheese is similar, with large curds, but is firmer than Cottage Cheese, having been pressed. Any of the types may be flavoured with fruit, herbs or spices.

Craigston
Unpasteurized Camemberts are not allowed in America, but this superb cheese, made in Wenham, Massachusetts, is cured to make it as close as possible to a raw milk Camembert from Normandy.

Creole
Rare fresh cows' milk cheese from Louisiana. Traditionally sold as one large curd bathed in thick cream.

Delico
An excellent, well-established Brie-type cheese made in Illinois. Sold in Mid-west shops and by mail order.

Farmer
Fresh white cheese similar to Cottage Cheese but firmer and higher in fat (12 per cent). Made with whole milk, lightly pressed and enriched with cream.

Liederkranz 🐄 💧 50% 🧀 125g (4oz) ©
America's most famous indigenous cheese has not been made for several years. A soft, moist, washed rind cheese invented by Emil Frey in New York in 1892. Frey was apparently trying to duplicate the popular Bismarck Schlosskäse then being imported from Germany but which arrived in poor condition after the long Atlantic crossing. The new cheese turned out to be a considerably milder, less pungent form of Limburger with a rich velvety golden paste and a very pale brown bacterial crust.

Maytag Blue ★ 🐄 💧 ⊖ 2kg (4lb) ©
One of America's best cheeses, Maytag is named after the washing machine company which paid for its development at Iowa University. Between Gorgonzola and Roquefort in flavour, it has a creamy smooth white paste with heavy blue veining and a distinctive 'blue' flavour. It is aged in caves while the mould develops.

Minnesota Blue see *Treasure Cave*

Monterey Chèvre
Fresh white goats' milk cheese with a creamy texture, yet which is low in fat, cholesterol and salt and lactose-free. Sold in tubs.

Monterey Jack 🐄 💧 50% ⊖ 4.5-5kg (10-11lb) ©
Distantly related to Cheddar, but developed in the 1840s from a cheese made by Spanish missionaries in Monterey, California. Creamy, whole milk versions are made made in various parts of California (Monterey and Sonoma); ripened for around six weeks they can be rather bland. Wisconsin Jacks tend to be made in blocks from partly skimmed milk and are slightly stronger tasting. Dry Jack, aged for nine months or more, was first made during World War II when cheesemakers were looking for an alternative to Parmesan. It is a hard, nutty, tangy grating cheese made in 3.5kg (8lb) wheels and coated with a mixutre of cocoa, pepper and vegetable oil.

New York State
Unpasteurized New York State Cheddars are truly excellent, and are

often aged for one to two years. The curing rooms are very dry, so the cheeses (both white and annatto-coloured) tend to be crumbly and sharp tasting. Coon County and Herkimer are notable cheesemaking areas within New York State.

Oregon Blue 🏵 🎀 🖘 2kg (4lb) Ⓓ
Creamy yellow cheese, lightly veined with blue, yet with a tart flavour. Made with buttermilk. Most is sold on the West Coast.

Philadelphia
Brand name of America's best known cream cheese which originated in New York State in the late 19th century. Probably the biggest-selling packaged cheese in the world.

Pineapple
Cheddar, hung to ripen in a net, which produces pineapple shapes and markings. First made in Litchfield, Connecticut in the 1840s. The paste is dry and grainy with a sharp tang. The surface may be treated with shellac making it brown and shiny and even more like a pineapple. Rarely seen nowadays.

Pot Cheese see *Cottage Cheese*

Potted Cheese see *Coldpack*

Ricotta
American Ricotta is smooth and moist and, unlike the original Italian whey cheese, uses the curds as well. Made with whole or partly skimmed milk and generally low in sodium.

Rope Cheese see *Braided Cheese*

Rouge et Noir 🏵 🎀 45-50% 🖘 225g (8oz) Ⓒ
Mould-ripened cheese from California, looking very like Camembert.

String Cheese, Syrian Cheese see *Braided Cheese*

Taupière ★ 🍴 🎀 300g (10oz) 🌱 Ⓓ
A superb, dome-shaped cheese coated with ash, aged for two or three months. Made by Laura Chenel in California.

Teleme
Similar to a creamy Monterey Jack; a young cheese made in small quantities in California.

Tillamook
Cheddar made in Oregon and sold mainly on the West Coast. Aged for three to seven months. Tangy, full-flavoured and moister than the New York State Cheddars. Made in 18kg (40lb) blocks and 1kg (2lb) salt-free forms. Sometimes unpasteurized.

Tradition de Belmont 🏵 🎀 🖘 I and 2kg (2 and 4lb) Ⓒ
Brie-style cheese from Wisconsin, sold younger and milder than French Bries.

Treasure Cave 🏵 🎀 🖘 2.3-2.7kg (5-6lb) Ⓓ
The oldest commercially made American blue cheese, widely available in supermarkets. Made in Minnesota and aged in caves for three to four months. White, rather salty blue-veined cheese. Also known as Minnesota Blue.

Vermont ★

Some of the best American Cheddars, moister than the New York State versions, are made in Vermont. The Cabot Co-operative Creamery uses unpasteurized milk to make 1.5kg (3lb) wheels. Other names to look for, especially when in the area, are Shelburne and Crafton. Some, aged up to two years, are known as Private Stock. Vermont cheesemakers occasionally spice their cheeses with caraway or flavour them with sage, which may be real chopped sage or chlorophyll juice extracted from green maize.

CANADA

Given the sizeable French population it is strange that the French appear to have had very little influence on Canadian cheesemaking. Early French settlers on the Isle of Orléans made Fromage Raffiné to a soft cheese recipe brought from France, although this is no longer made. The late 1860s saw the establishment of cheese factories all over Canada. These were particularly suited to the production of Cheddar, which found a ready market in Britain and the United States. Canada is still known for its excellent Cheddar, two of the best being Black Diamond and Cherry Hill, both ranked by experts alongside the otherwise incomparable English farmhouse cheeses. Canadian Cheddars are certainly among the best Cheddars to be found in supermarkets, especially in Britain, where they will be well aged after their sea journey. Most Canadian Cheddars are not pasteurized, but heat treated to a slightly lower temperature for reasons of hygiene.

As in Europe, religious orders took up cheesemaking and developed some of the lastingly successful types. Oka—a fine semisoft, surface-ripened, mild creamy cheese with a distinctive odour—was first made in 1893 by a monk from Entrammes (see *France*), who took his expertise to a Trappist community near Montreal (Oka cheese is now a commercial concern). Benedictine monks at the Abbey of St Benoît du Lac in Quebec created Ermite (Hermit), Canada's creamy blue cheese, in 1943, and still make this and several other European-type cheeses. A vast range of European styles of cows' and goats' milk cheeses are also made.

NORWAY see *Scandinavia*. PARAGUAY, PERU see *Latin America*.
POLAND see *Eastern Europe*.

Portugal

Cheesemaking in Portugal is relatively unsophisticated compared with other western European countries. Factory production is a fairly recent phenomenon. In general, mainland cheeses are made of ewes' milk and, to a lesser extent, goats' milk. Cows' milk types are mostly confined to the Azores. A number of foreign cheeses are also made. (See map on p.132).

Alcobaça 🐑 🌓 55% ⊖ 200g (7oz) Ⓓ
Serra-type cheese with a very white paste, from Alcobaça.

Azeitão ★ 🐑 🌓 45% ⊟ 200-250g (7-9oz) 🌿 Ⓓ
Mild, slightly sourish, pale, creamy cheese with a soft, smooth, yellow rind. Coagulated with vegetable rennet (*Cynara cardunculus*) and ripened for three to four weeks. Best eaten in winter and spring. A variant of Serra and of ancient origin, made in Azeitão, a small village near Setúbal.

Cabreiro
Smooth white cheese made in Castelo Branco from mixed ewes' and goats' milk. Eaten fresh or ripened in brine.

Castelo Branco ★ 🌓 45-50% ⊖ 1kg (2lb) Ⓒ
Made from ewes' or mixed ewes' and goats' milk in Castelo Branco. The paste is white and smooth with a light scattering of small holes. Eaten after three or four weeks' ripening when strong and peppery, or fresh, when it is sold as Queijo Fresco de Castelo Branco.

Castelo de Vide
Serra-type cheese of limited production and variable quality.

Evora ★ 🌓 45% ⊖ 90-150g (3-5oz) Ⓒ
Very strong salty cheese made from ewes' milk, occasionally mixed with goats' milk. Yellowy white and crumbly with a darker hard crust. Ripened between six and 12 months and becoming harder with age. From Evora, Alentejo.

Ilha ★ 🐄 🌓 45% ⊖ 5-10kg (11-22lb) Ⓒ
Made in the Azores on the islands of São Jorge, São Miguel, Terceira and Pico (*ilha*, island). A firm-bodied pale yellow cheese with a hard natural crust almost certainly introduced to the islands by English immigrants. The flavour ranges from mild to mellow and nutty depending on age, and is similar to Cheddar, if slightly tangier. Ripened between one and three months and eaten up to six months old. Both pasteurized and unpasteurized versions are available.

Nisa
Farm-made Serra-type cheese. Rare and of variable quality.

Pico 🐄 🌓 45% ⊖ 500g (18oz) Ⓓ
From the island of Pico in the Azores, a pale smooth cheese made from unpasteurized milk. Creamy and fairly piquant. Ripened for three to four weeks. Best in winter and spring.

Queijo Fresco
Fresh, moist, creamy cheese made from any type of milk.

Queijo Seco
Fresh cheese cured in brine. Greyish, crumbly and salty.

Rabaçal ★ 45% ⊟ 1kg (2lb) ©

Fresh white curd cheese made from ewes' and goats' milk in the province of Coimbra. Occasionally ripened for a month or so, when it becomes firmer and stronger. Often eaten for breakfast and at the beginning of meals.

Requeijão 🐄 ⟲ ⊟ 100-200g (3½-7oz) ©

Very mild fresh whey cheese similar to Italian Ricotta, made as a by-product of ewes' milk cheese production. The whey is heated to 75°C (167°F), the coagulated solids skimmed off and then placed in straw baskets to drain. Eaten for breakfast or before meals. Keeps for a maximum of five days.

Saloio ⟲ 45% ⊟ 30-50g (1-1¾oz) ⑩

Once made from ewes' milk but now increasingly from cows' milk, a fresh white cheese with a slightly sourish flavour. Generally available only in restaurants and served before meals. Made near Lisbon. The name means 'country bumpkin'.

São Jorge 🍲 🌶 45% ⊟ 3-5kg (7-11lb) ©

A variety of Ilha made from unpasteurized milk. Crumbly with a piquant flavour. Ripened for two to three months.

Serpa ★ 🐄 45% ⊟ 1.7-2kg (3½-4lb) 🌿 ⑩

Variety of Serra, dating back to the Roman occupation. Made at Serpa, Alentejo, a pale soft to semihard cheese with a sharp peppery flavour. Coagulated with vegetable rennet and ripened for four to six weeks. A longer ripened version (five months or more) is sold as Serpa Velho and is very hard and strong-tasting. Best eaten from December to April.

Serra 🐄 🌶 45% ⊟ 1-2kg (2-4lb) 🌿 ©

Portugal's most famous cheese is an ancient type, farm-made in the Serra da Estrêla and at Manteigas, Celorico da Beira, Gouveia, Seia and Guarda. It has a pale yellow buttery paste with sparse small holes and a soft, smooth, golden rind. The flavour is mildly lactic and rather refreshing. Coagulated with vegetable rennet and ripened for four to six weeks. Sometimes aged further (five months or more) and sold as Serra Velho. Best between December and April. A harder and inferior factory-made version is sold as Tipo Serra.

Tomar 🐄 🌶 45% ⊟ 30-40g (1-1½oz) ⑩

Small, firm, tangy cheeses made near Tomar, north-east of Lisbon. Pale and crumbly with small holes and a tough grey-yellow crust. Ripened for at least two to three weeks. Often preserved in olive oil.

KEY WORDS

Cabra goat	**Queijo** cheese
Curado ripened	**Seco** dry
Fresco fresh	**Vaca** cow
Ovelha sheep	**Velho** aged

PUERTO RICO see *Latin America*. ROMANIA see *Eastern Europe*.
SAUDI ARABIA see *Middle East*.

Scandinavia

DENMARK

Its temperate climate and predominantly lowland terrain make Denmark an ideal dairying country, yet it has few original cheese types. Nevertheless, Danish cheeses are immensely successful in foreign markets—two-thirds of Danish production is exported to over 100 countries. Most of these cheeses are efficient copies of foreign types which now carry Danish names, thanks to the Stresa Convention of 1951. Some are even displacing similar indigenous cheeses in their country of origin. (Danish Feta, for example, is exported in vast quantities to the Middle East.)

The Danish Ministry of Agriculture sets the highest possible standards of quality control, particularly for exported cheeses. Some would say they go too far in permitting cheese to be made only from pasteurized cows' milk. (An exception applies to some blue cheeses: aiming for an improved texture, they are heat-treated to a lower temperature.) Cows are by far the most important dairy animal; goats' milk cheese is made for local consumption only.

Blå Castello ♔ 🐄 70% 150g and 1kg (5oz and 2lb) Ⓑ

Invented in the 1960s, a crescent-shaped cheese with sharply defined dark blue internal veining and a downy white surface mould. Rich, creamy yet quite solid in texture; mild tasting.

Danablu ♔ 🐄 50-60% ▢ 3kg (7lb) Ⓐ

Danish Blue was invented in the early 20th century as a substitute for Roquefort. A huge commercial success—although quite different from Roquefort. It can be rather dry and is often very sharp and salty. The paste should be clear and white.

Danbo ♔ 🌙 45% Ⓑ

A descendant of Samsø. Rather bland with a springy pale yellow paste scattered with a few cherry-sized holes. Made in various shapes and sizes and often coated in red or yellow wax. Usually ripened for about five months (factory versions as little as six weeks) and occasionally spiced with caraway seeds.

Esrom ★ ♔ 🐄 45-60% ▱ 1.5kg (3lb) Ⓑ

Washed rind cheese once known as the Danish Port-Salut but actually closer in character to German Tilsiter. The paste is pale and creamy with lots of irregular holes and slits. It has a sweet, rich flavour and a definite spicy aroma when fully aged. Esrom lovers insist that the rind should be eaten with the cheese.

Havarti ★ ♔ 🌙 30-60% ▱ 4.5kg (10lb) Ⓐ

Named after the farm owned by Hanne Nielsen, pioneering 19th-century cheesemaker who scoured Europe in search of new techniques and, almost single-handed, revitalized the then moribund Danish cheese industry. Her greatest success was Havarti, once known as Danish Tilsit. It is a supple, creamy, washed rind cheese with innumerable irregular holes throughout the paste. Fairly full-flavoured at about three months old, it becomes stronger and more pungent with age. The 60 per cent fat version is richer, slightly softer and may be flavoured with caraway seeds. It has no rind and is usually vacuum packed in blocks or drums.

Hingino ♔ 🌙 32-40% ▱ 2.5kg (5½lb) Ⓒ

Hard, dry, piquant grating cheese, a modern invention inspired by Italian Canestrato. Mainly exported to Greece and the Middle East.

Maribo 🐄 🌢 45% ⊖ 14kg (31lb) Ⓑ

Fuller in flavour than Samsø-type cheeses, Maribo has a firmer, drier paste scattered with numerous irregular holes. Ripened for about four months. Usually coated in yellow wax.

Mycella 🐄 🌢 50% ⊖ 5kg (11lb) Ⓑ

Once known as Danish Gorgonzola, the veins are greenish-blue and the paste creamy yellow. Mild for a blue cheese.

Rygeost ★

Smoked acid-curd cheese encrusted with caraway seeds. Traditionally eaten around a bonfire on Midsummer's Eve. A naturally smoked cheese made on the island of Fyn, rare nowadays.

Saga

Mild, very creamy, rather solid Brie-type cheese. Reputedly invented to avoid the disappointing chalky centre often found in Brie. Available plain, blue, or coated with chives. Formerly known as Dania.

Samsø 🐄 🌢 45% ⊖ 14kg (31lb) Ⓑ

The everyday all-purpose Danish cheese, supposedly inspired by Emmental; it has the holes, though not so many nor so large, but the consistency of the paste is more reminiscent of Edam. It can be sold fairly young (about eight to ten weeks old), when it is mild and sweet, or aged for several months more to become stronger and more pungent. Named after the island of Samsø and the ancestor of many Danish cheese types. A cheese called Svenbo is more convincing as an Emmental lookalike. See *Danbo*

FINLAND

Lakes and pine forests account for a large part of the land area of Finland and a third of the country lies north of the Arctic Circle so it is surprising to find that dairying is its most important form of agriculture and that it has a well-established cheesemaking tradition. Cheese types that were being made in the Middle Ages are still available today. The techniques used to make some of these traditional cheeses are notably idiosyncratic: the addition of eggs to the curds, for example, and the habit of baking fresh cheeses before an open fire. Such cheeses are mostly farm-made on a small scale but can still be found in specialist stores like the Juustovakka chain of cheese shops. The bulk of Finland's cheese industry is controlled by three co-operatives of which Valio is the largest. The most important export cheese is the Finnish version of Emmental, usually sold as 'Finnish Swiss' and considered second only to the Swiss original.

Aura

Strong-tasting, blue-veined, factory-made cows' milk cheese often described in Finland as 'Roquefort'.

Emmental

Introduced to Finland in 1856 by a Swiss cheesemaker, Rudolf Klössner, with such success that an 'invasion' of a hundred or more of his fellow-countrymen followed in the years up until the end of World War I. Klössner is said to have started the first batch of Emmental by waving a pine branch over the milk—a branch now on show at the Sippola-Gardens creamery, Finland's oldest cheese factory. Finnish Emmental is made from pasteurized milk. A high-quality product, it is sold at three stages of its maturity: after three months (blue stamp), after six months (red stamp) and after nine months (black stamp). Much of it is exported, especially to the United States.

Ilves see *Munajuusto*

Juhla
The Finnish version of Cheddar.

Juustoleipä ★ 🏵 🌙 40% 250g (9oz) ©
Rectangular or wheel-shaped fresh cheese made mostly on farms. After coagulating the milk, the cheesemaker drains and presses the curds by hand on to a special wooden plate and then roasts the cheese in front of an open fire. A speciality of central Finland and Lapland, especially Kajaani and Ostrobothnia. The name means 'cheese bread'. Often served for dessert, baked with cream and covered with cloudberries (*lakka*) . May be used in coffee instead of milk. Also called Leipäjuusto.

Kappeli
Strong, aromatic, washed rind cheese similar to German Romadur.

Kesti
Type of Tilsiter flavoured with caraway seeds.

Korsholm see *Turunmaa*

Kreivi
Mellow cheese similar to German Tilsiter.

Kutunjuusto ★ 🍖 🌙 30% 🌥 200g (7oz) Ⓓ
Rare cheese from Tampere in western Finland. Mild, smooth and fresh, it is made on isolated farms.

Lappi
Similar to Dutch Edam but with a much higher fat content and usually ripened for a longer period.

Leipäjuusto see *Juustoleipä*

Luostari
Semihard cows' milk cheese similar to Port-Salut.

Mazurka see *Turunmaa*

Munajuusto ★ 🏵 🌙 40% 🌥 1kg (2lb) ©
Literally 'egg cheese'. A farmhouse cheese from the south and south-west, made in an unusual way. One or two eggs are added to about six litres of milk, which is then coagulated by heating. After the whey is drained off, the curds are lightly pressed in a wicker basket. The egg yolks give the cheese a wonderful golden colour. There is also a factory version sold under brand names, the best known being Ilves. Like Juustoleipä the fresh cheese can be roasted in front of a fire or grilled. The surface of the cheese becomes speckled with brown and will keep longer than the usual few days.

Polar
Very mild hard cheese with large holes.

Salaneuvos
A type of Gouda.

Turunmaa ★ 🏵 🌙 50% 🌥 6-10kg (13-22lb) ©
Originating in the 1500s from the south-west of Finland, a rich, slightly sharp cheese, deliciously creamy and smooth-textured. Nowadays

almost entirely factory-made. Ripened for two months. Usually eaten for breakfast. The name means 'Turkuland' and derives from Finland's oldest city. Often sold under brand names such as Korsholm and Mazurka.

ICELAND

Although Iceland's climate is milder than its name suggests (its shores are washed by the warm waters of the Gulf Stream), the terrain is not conducive to large-scale dairy farming. Snowbound volcanic peaks, rivers of solidified lava, icy glaciers and hot springs make for spectacular scenery but not for good grazing land. Nevertheless, Icelanders consume a considerable amount of cheese, mostly similar to other Nordic types. There are two factory-made 'blues' (Akureyri, Gradaost). Whey cheeses of the Swedish Mesost variety are very popular, and include a soft, spreadable type (Mysingur) and a harder sliceable one (Mysuost). An imitation Swiss cheese (Odalsost) and Edam (Braudost) are also widely available, as are, to a lesser extent, versions of Gouda, Tilsiter, Port-Salut, Camembert and other popular European cheeses.

Sheep flourish in even the hardest environments and have been the standby of Icelandic farmers since the island was first colonized in the 19th century. Skyr, Iceland's fresh, white, skimmed-milk cheese, was traditionally made from ewes' milk though cows' milk is more often used nowadays. The milk is soured with a starter consisting of a piece of the previous batch of cheese and then coagulated with rennet. The rennet used to be obtained by soaking pieces of vell in whey. The vell also contained traces of lactic bacteria, including those active in yoghurt-making, placing Skyr somewhere between a yoghurt and a cheese. These bacteriological conditions are now reproduced artificially in the factories where most Skyr is made. It has a very soft, almost liquid consistency and is consumed in great quantities usually mixed with milk or cream and sprinkled with sugar.

NORWAY

Norway is the most mountainous country in Scandinavia. Coupled with its extraordinarily ragged coastline, deeply indented with steep-sided fjords, this means that the proportion of cultivable land is extremely limited and the potential for good grazing land not much greater. However, unusually difficult conditions often produce ingenious responses, which is certainly true of Norwegian cheeses.

Bifost
Mild, white, fresh goats' milk cheese. Also called Hvit Gjetost.

Fjordland
Factory-made block using partly skimmed cows' milk. It has a pale smooth paste with unevenly distributed large round holes. Full nutty flavour faintly reminiscent of Emmental.

Gammelost ★   ☼ 🌑 5% ▢ 3kg (7lb) ❀ Ⓑ
'Old cheese'; an ancient type and as intimidating in appearance as the Vikings who reputedly enjoyed it. It is an excellent keeping cheese (ideal, perhaps, for long sea voyages) and was traditionally made in summer for winter use. The pitted hard brown crust makes it look at least a century old but in fact the entire making and ripening process takes only a month. Skimmed milk is coagulated with lactic bacteria and heated. The curds are heavily pressed, moulded and then boiled in whey for several hours. The cheeses are left to dry for a day or so and then pierced with *Penicillium*-coated needles or broken up,

kneaded with *Penicillium* spores, remoulded and re-pressed. During the ripening period another mould, *Mucor*, grows on the surface, producing a long soft fuzz that is regularly worked back into the cheese by hand. This growth is now artificially induced, although in the past it developed spontaneously from minute traces either left in the moulds from the previous batch of cheese or impregnated in the walls of the dairy. Traditionally the cheeses were stored in straw scented with juniper berries. The result of all this, not surprisingly, is an extremely potent cheese, sharp, strong and aromatic with some blue-green veining in a brownish-yellow paste, quite unique—but an effective antidote to the rigours of a northern winter. Virtually inedible unless sliced very thinly.

Gjetost ★ ● 38% 🧀 250-500g (9-18oz) Ⓑ
A whey cheese made from a mixture of cows' and goats' milk or entirely from goats' milk. In the latter case it is marked *Ekte* (genuine) Gjetost. Often sold as Gudbrandsdalsost, after the Gudbrand valley where it is made. Apart from the milk base the manufacturing process is virtually the same as for Swedish Mesost although the finished product is somewhat darker in colour. Eaten for breakfast, shaved into thin slices, and on spiced fruit cake at Christmas. The appropriate accompaniment is said to be hot coffee or chilled *akevitt*.

Hvit Gjetost see *Bifost*

Jarlsberg ★ 🌣 ● 45% ⊖ 10kg (22lb) Ⓑ
Based on an old Norwegian type but re-invented in the 1950s and now extremely popular. Mellow, slightly sweet flavour and an elastic texture rather similar to Dutch Gouda. The paste is golden yellow with variously sized round holes. Factory-made from pasteurized milk and ripened for six months. A great deal is exported, particularly to the United States.

Knaost see *Pultost*

Mysost
Whey cheese made entirely from cows' milk. See *Gjetost*, *Sweden* (*Mesost*)

Nøkkelost 🌣 ● 45% ⊖ 12kg (26lb) Ⓑ
A milder copy of Dutch Leiden. *Nøkkel* means 'keys', recalling the crossed keys emblem of Leiden cheese.

Norbo 🌣 ● 45% ⊖ 5kg (11lb) Ⓒ
Recently invented; bland, golden, with holes, yellow rind.

Norvegia 🌣 ● 45% 🧀 5kg (11lb) Ⓒ
Rindless, vacuum-packed factory product. A very good melting cheese.

Pultost ★
Tangy cows' milk acid-curd cheese ripened for three weeks. Made all over Norway with numerous local variations. Buttermilk, cream and spices (usually caraway seeds) may be added. Also called Knaost or Ramost depending on the particular area.

Ridder 🌣 ● 60% ⊖ 2kg (4lb) Ⓑ
A new variety similar to Saint-Paulin with an orange, lightly washed rind and a rich buttery paste.

SWEDEN

Cheese is eaten a great deal in Sweden, at breakfast time and as part of the ubiquitous *smörgåsbord*. Indigenous types are mostly of the semihard, fairly bland variety, though strongly spiced cheeses are also popular. Most interesting of all are the brown whey cheeses—regarded as 'cheese' only by popular consent. Whey cheeses are excluded from most official definitions of cheese since curds form no part of the manufacturing process. These cheeses are not matured in the usual sense yet they cannot be termed 'fresh' since they keep extremely well without refrigeration.

Ädelost 🐄 🥛 50% ⬭ 2-3kg (4-7lb) Ⓒ

An imitation Roquefort made with pasteurized milk. Sharp and salty. Ripened for at least four months.

Billinge

Milder version of Herrgårdsost. Firm, white, with round holes.

Buost

Low-fat, greasy, semihard cows' milk cheese from Jämtland.

Drabant

Bland, innocuous type of Herrgårdsost ripened in foil—a good breakfast cheese for fragile constitutions.

Getmesost

Mesost (whey cheese) made with goats' milk whey.

Getost 🐐 🥛 30% ⬱ 500g (18oz) Ⓓ

Literally 'goats' cheese', one of the few Swedish cheeses that are still occasionally farm-made. Ripened for a month.

Graddost 🐄 🥛 60% ⬳ 250g (9oz) Ⓒ

Similar to Denmark's cream Havarti, a firm but very creamy mild cheese with many small holes.

Greveost 🐄 🥛 45% ⬭ 14kg (31lb) Ⓒ

The Swedish version of Emmental, but softer, paler and with huge round eyes. Nutty tasting and ripened for about ten months.

Herrgårdsost ★ 🐄 🥛 30-45% ⬭ 12-18kg (26-40lb) Ⓑ

Literally 'manor cheese' or 'home cheese', once produced on small farms. Originally from West Gotland, it is now factory-made all over Sweden. Basically a Swiss type, slightly softer than Gruyère with a sparse scattering of small holes, it is a pressed cooked cheese ripened for four to seven months. The rind is usually waxed yellow. The low-fat version (30 per cent) is made from partly skimmed milk and ripened for about four months only.

Hushållsost 🐄 🥛 30-45% ⬭ 3kg (7lb) Ⓒ

'Household cheese', one of Sweden's oldest and most popular types, is smooth, mild and creamy with a faintly acidic edge. The paste is straw-coloured, either with small, round, regular holes or with irregular holes and slits. Ripened for one to three months.

Kaggost

Semihard, mild cows' milk cheese with a springy creamy yellow paste sometimes spiced with cumin seeds and cloves. Wheel-shaped, ripened for one to three months and mild apart from the spices.

Kryddost ★
'Spiced cheese'; a Svecia type spiced with caraway seeds and cloves but matured for several months longer. Traditionally served with crayfish at special parties held during the crayfish season from August 8 onwards.

Lapparnas Renost
Hard smoked cheese from Lapland made with reindeer milk. Extremely rare since reindeer produce very little milk, and seemingly liked only by Lapps, who dunk it in coffee to make it palatable.

Mesost ★ 🐄 🐐 10-20% 🧀 1-8kg (2-18lb) Ⓑ
'Whey cheese' made by heating whey (a proportion of whole milk, cream or buttermilk is usually added nowadays) to precipitate the residual protein matter. For a whey cheese like Italian Ricotta the process stops at this point. For Mesost the boiling continues until the liquid is reduced considerably and the solids condense into a sticky brown mass caused by caramelization of the milk sugar (lactose). This is then poured into moulds, cooled, cut up into blocks and packed in foil or boxes. Extra sugar and spices are sometimes added. Whey cheese with cream added may be soft and spreadable, but more usually Mesost is firm and close-textured, light tan in colour with a bitter-sweet flavour.

Prästost 🐐 🐄 50% 🧀 12-15kg (26-33lb) Ⓒ
'Priest's cheese', made in Sweden for 200 years. Now mostly factory-made, often from a mixture of pasteurized and unpasteurized milk. Also called Prestost, Saaland Pfarr.

Starkost
'Strong cheese' is a hard aromatic variety from West Gotland. Also known as Västgötaost.

Sveciaost 🐐 🐄 30-45% 🧀 12-16kg (26-35lb) Ⓒ
'Swedish cheese', the everyday cheese eaten in vast quantities and available in many forms and varying fat contents, spiced or unspiced, young and mild or mature and extremely piquant. These factors are endlessly permutated to produce an extended family of cheeses suiting virtually all tastes.

Västerbottenost 🐐 🐄 50% 🧀 20kg (44lb) Ⓒ
'West Bothnian cheese', invented in the mid-19th century and still exclusively made in West Bothnia. A strong-tasting friable cheese ripened for about a year. Sometimes spiced.

Vastgötaost see *Starkost*

KEY WORDS

Flødeost (Denmark) cream cheese

Halvfet (Norway) 30 per cent fat

Helfet (Norway) 45 per cent fat

Hytteost (Denmark) cottage cheese

Juusto (Finland) cheese

Kvartfet (Norway) 20 per cent fat

Ost (Denmark, Norway, Sweden) cheese

Ostur (Iceland) cheese

Spain

Apart from Switzerland, Spain is the highest, most mountainous European country (only about two-thirds of the land can be said to be productive in any real sense) but within the overall pattern of plateau and mountain ranges there are dramatic contrasts in climate and terrain. Travelling south, the warm, wet, densely wooded slopes of Galicia and the wild peaks of Asturias and the Basque provinces give way abruptly to the broad, flat, intensely arid *meseta*, a high dusty plateau where almost nothing grows easily. Further south still it becomes bakingly hot and the landscape looks truly North African with the esparto-covered hills sloping down to the Mediterranean. Ewes' milk cheeses are found all over the country, while cows' milk types are confined to the wetter north and goats' milk cheeses to the mountain ranges. Cheesemaking is relatively uncommercialized and

IS VASCO • Roneal

NAVARRA

PIRINEOS

Soria

Lérida •

CATALUNA

Barcelona •

ARAGON

Tronchón •

Teruel •

• Cuenca

Castellón
de la Plana •

Puzol •

Valencia •

VALENCIA

HA

• Albacete

Alicante •

MENORCA

Mahón

ISLAS BALEARES

Palma •

MALLORCA

500 m

200 m

many cheeses are simply named after their place of origin. This has
some notable advantages: most of the indigenous cheeses are still
made from unpasteurized milk by individual farmers in the
traditional way, thus retaining their unique qualities. Unfortunately
this also means that many of these cheeses are found only in limited
quantities and in their particular area of production. Few Spaniards
have a wide knowledge of Spanish cheeses. Many cheeses look the
same and are often sold falsely as Manchego. Equally confusingly,
many cheeses are sold by brand name rather than generic type. The
Denominación de Origen (DO) labels protect standards and promote
pride in traditional cheese types. Many Spanish cheeses are stored in
olive oil or rubbed with olive oil as a way of preserving them or to
improve their appearance.

Afuega'l Pitu
Fresh or slightly ripened farmhouse cows' milk cheese from central and western Asturias, made with raw milk. Conical or pumpkin shaped, with marks from where the cloth was knotted at the top. After long, slow coagulation, the uncut curds are spooned into moulds and drained for a day. Sometimes flavoured (and coloured) with red pimento, when it is called Rojo del Aramo. Thin rind, compact white (or orange) cheese with a granular texture and slightly piquant taste, exceptionally creamy on the palate.

Alicante ✦ ♾ 37% ⊟ 150-500g (5-18oz) Ⓓ
Smooth, white fresh rennet-curd cheese with a clean milky flavour. The curds are squeezed by hand and pressed into decorative wooden moulds. Sold locally in Alto Vinalopó.

Aragón see *Tronchón*

Aralar see *Idiazabal*

Arangas see *Cabrales*

Armada ✦ ♾ 69% 1.5-3kg (3-7lb) Ⓓ
A curious, sharp, almost bitter cheese made from beestings. Shaped like a triangular column, the paste is greyish-white, often dry, cracked and crumbly. The rind is hard, yellowy and rather oily to touch. Ripened for about two months. Made in the province of León in spring and summer. Also known as Sobado and Calostro.

Los Balanchares
The name given to a range of soft goats' milk cheeses made on Doña Mencia farm in Baena, Córdoba. They vary in size and shape—some are soft logs, some are ash-coated and others are preserved in herbs and olive oil. Widely available throughout Spain.

Beyusco see *Queso de los Beyos*

Burgos ★ ♾ 58% ⊟ 1-2kg (2-4lb) Ⓒ
A fresh rennet-curd cheese, originally made in winter and spring from raw ewes' milk, but now a less interesting, well packaged blend or pure cows' milk cheese made all year round all over Spain. The paste is white, smooth and very mild with just a hint of saltiness. It keeps for about two days after making. Often eaten for dessert with sugar and honey. Also known as Requeson.

Cabrales ★ ♾ 45% ⊟ 1-5kg (2-11lb) Ⓑ
Spain's major veined cheese is made mostly with cows' milk, sometimes mixed with ewes' or goats' milk, on mountain farms in Asturias, mainly around Cabrales, Arangas and Peñamellera Alta. The best cheeses are said to be made in spring and summer, when milk from all three animals is used. It is a strong-smelling cheese with a powerful flavour. The paste is an uneven dull white with yellow-brown patches and irregular blue-brown veining. The rind is greyish-red and crusty, traditionally wrapped in sycamore leaves but nowadays often in foil. Ripened in natural limestone caverns for at least two months, aficionados prefer it at six months old, almost totally blue and '*con gusanos*' (with maggots).

Cádiz ✦ ♾ 51% ⊟ 1.5kg (3lb) Ⓓ
Medium-pressed, firm white cheese with an agreeably mellow flavour. After draining, it is pressed into plaited esparto baskets so that its hard golden rind shows the marks of the mould—the design is

the same as the moulds for Manchego. Eaten fresh or ripened for about three months. Best from winter to early spring.

Calostro see *Armada*

Camerano ♦ ⟳ 45% ⊖ 200-800g (7oz-1¾lb) Ⓓ
Fresh, white cheese with a mildly acid flavour, basket-moulded and ripened for 24 hours. From the Sierra de Cameros, Logroño. Best from winter to mid-summer. Also called Queso Fresco de Montaña.

Cantabria ⛰ ⟆ 45% ⊖ 400g-2.7kg (14oz-6lb) Ⓒ
A DO cheese from the mountainous north. Lightly pressed to make a dense, rich, creamy-textured ivory cheese with a soft pale rind. Sold young, after seven to ten days.

Cebrero ★ ⛰ ⟆ 50% 2kg (4lb) Ⓒ
Oddly shaped—a drum with an overhanging rim, like a thick-stalked mushroom—this pressed firm cheese has a buttery aroma, creamy close-textured paste and a fairly sharp rustic flavour— almost like yoghurt. The rind is firm and crusty with white streaks radiating from the centre of the 'lid'. It is ripened for three to four days. Made in Lugo in the Cebrero mountains near the Portuguese border and sometimes sold under its Portuguese name Queixo do Cebreiro.

Cervera ♦ ⟳ 67% 1-2kg (2-4lb) Ⓓ
Fresh white cheese rather like Burgos and Villalón, with a milky flavour and the characteristic aroma of sheep's cheese. The shape is variable; more often than not the cheeses are roughly pressed by hand into a lopsided disc. Should be eaten immediately. Made in the Valencia area and also known as Queso Fresco Valenciano.

Cuajada
A fresh, very smooth, milky-tasting cheese sold in small tubs. Originally from northern Spain; now made industrially throughout the country from ewes' and goats' milk.

Entzia see *Idiazabal*

Estrella see *Oropesa*

Flor de Esquera see *Queso Castellano*

Gamonedo ⟆ 33% ⃞ 2-5kg (4-11lb) Ⓓ
Similar to Cabrales, made in the mountain province of Asturias from cows' milk mixed with smaller quantities of ewes' and goats' milk. It has a very lightly veined white paste with many tiny pinpoint holes and a thick, brownish-yellow, coarse dry rind that is sometimes covered with fern fronds. Very strong-smelling with an intensely piquant flavour. Smoked over a period of ten to 20 days and ripened in natural caves for at least two months. Also known as Gamoneu.

Gorbea see *Idiazabal*

Grazalema ♦ ⟆ 51% ⊖ 2-4kg (4-9lb) Ⓓ
A hard-pressed pale yellow cheese with small, variously shaped eyes clustered in the middle of the paste and a striated, golden, oily rind. Has a pleasantly fresh, clean smell and a taste rather like Manchego. Traditionally moulded in esparto baskets although tin moulds are becoming increasingly common. It is doubly salted, first in brine for 48 hours and then buried in a vat of salt for 24 hours before being ripened from two to three weeks up to 90 days.

Gutierrez Oveja Seco see *Queso Puro de Oveja*

Guzman see *Queso Castellano*

Iberico see *Queso Iberico*

Idiazabal ★ 🐏 💧 45% 🗆 1-3kg (2-7lb) 🌿 ©
Now protected by a Denominación de Origen, Idiazabal must be made in a defined area in the Basque country from the milk of Laxta and Carranzana sheep. May be unpasteurized; sometimes made with vegetable rennet. A pressed, dense, white to ivory cheese with a hard pale yellow rind. Made from winter to summer. Matured for at least 60 days. Some cheeses are smoked ten days before being sold: these have an orange-brown rind. The defined area includes Aralar, Entzia, Gorbea, Orduña, Urbia and Urbasa—cheeses made in these areas to the set standards may be sold as Idiazabal or under their local names.

León 🐏 💧 52% 🗆 600g-1kg (1¼-2lb) Ⓓ
A mellow cheese with a close-textured white paste and a rough, hard, yellowy rind. Made in Oseja de Sajambre.

Mahón ★ 🐄 💧 38% ⬭ 1-4kg (2-9lb) Ⓑ
A DO cheese from the island of Menorca. It is made from September to June and is sold at various stages of maturity: fresh (to be eaten within ten days); semicured (matured for a minimum of two months); cured (five months); and old (ten months). The rind is hard, greasy and yellowy brown and the cheese is slightly granular, ivory-coloured with irregular holes and a salty flavour (due to the pastures). Commercial cheeses are cushion shaped, in imitation of the centuries-old farmhouse method of moulding the cheese in a cloth, pegged at the top and pressed in on itself, leaving an indentation on top of the cheese. After salting, the cheeses are matured for a month, then rubbed with oil and paprika and matured further. Farmhouse cheeses are made with unpasteurized milk, and only sold after two months.

Málaga 🐐 💧 58% 🗆 2kg (4lb) Ⓓ
The most common of several similar goats' milk cheeses made in Andalucía and Extremadura, lightly pressed with a dense creamy white paste and a pleasant goaty flavour. The pale, buff-coloured rind shows the impression of the mould. Ripened for five days.

Manchego ★ 🐏 💧 50% 🗆 2-3.5kg (4-8lb) Ⓑ
Spain's most famous cheese is made in the plain of La Mancha and, according to the DO rules, can be made only from the milk of La Manchega sheep. The best Manchego is said to be that from around Ciudad Real, but Toledo, Albacete and Cuenca are also important centres. It is a beautiful cheese, with a firm, ivory paste, sometimes dotted with small eyes, and a hard rind impressed with plaited esparto marks along the sides. The top and bottom retain the elaborate patterns of the cheese press (where the cheese remains for six to seven hours). During the ripening period, the surfaces become covered with a greenish-black mould that is usually cleaned off before the cheeses are sold. The taste, depending on the age of the cheese, is salty, slightly to distinctly piquant and melting on the palate. Manchego is sold at various stages of maturity, but usually not before 13 weeks (*curado*), then over three months (*viejo*) and *en aceite* (in olive oil, when it is ripened for at least a year and has a rough blackish rind).

Mató
Fresh, unsalted, soft curd cheese from Catalonia (sold in tubs or from a block like Italian Ricotta). Several small producers still make this

cheese from boiled goats' milk and plant rennet; modern methods use cows' milk or blends, with calf's rennet. Pure white and junket-like, with a texture that breaks up as you cut it and a light, milky taste.

Morón
Fresh cheese made of a mixture of cows' and ewes' milk, or sometimes of goats' milk alone. After ripening for 24 hours, it is creamy, white and soft with a clean lactic aroma and mild flavour. May be further aged in a vat of olive oil, after which it is rubbed with paprika. It is then firmer and spicier. From the town of Morón de la Frontera in the province of Sevilla.

Orduña see *Idiazabal*

Oropesa 🐄 🐑 46% ⊖ 2kg (4lb) Ⓓ
Similar to Manchego, made in Toledo. Rather darker in colour with a harder, thicker rind. Ripened for about three months and rubbed with olive oil. Also called Queso de la Estrella.

Paramo de Guzman see *Queso Castellano*

Pasiego prensado 🐄 🐑 49% ⊖ 1-1.5kg (2-3lb) Ⓓ
Made in the Valle de Pas in Santander, usually from whole milk but sometimes from partly skimmed milk mixed with ewes' milk. A pressed cheese with a creamy, mild, white paste and a smooth, shiny, yellow rind. Ripened for one to two weeks.

Pasiego sin prensar 🐄 🐑 8% ⊖ Ⓓ
Literally 'unpressed Pasiego', made from cows' milk sometimes mixed with ewes' milk and coagulated with lamb's rennet. Shaped into an irregular disc, it has a thick, brownish rind with white powdery streaks. The flavour is mild, milky and slightly sweet. Eaten fresh.

Pata de Mulo see *Villalón*

Patela see *Ulloa*

Pedroches 🐄 🐑 52% ⊖ 2-3kg (4-7lb) Ⓓ
Rich golden, slightly pungent cheese with a hard yellow rind impressed with esparto plaits round the sides. Rather piquant with a touch of saltiness. Ripened for one to two months and then stored in olive oil. Made in the Valle de los Pedroches.

Perilla see *Tetilla*

Picón
Creamy yellow blue-green veined cheese with a pungent aroma; the taste is not as strong as you would expect and is not too salty. It is made in the same way as Cabrales, and with similar blends of milk, but comes from the western part of the Picos de Europa mountains. It comes wrapped in maple leaves—the only material to hand when the shepherds wanted to move the cheeses in and out of the caves in which they mature—and beneath the leaves is a strong smelling sticky brownish layer. Also known as Queso de Bejes, Queso de Trenso and Queso de los Picos de Europa. Queso de Valdeon is a similar cheese, made in León.

Plasencia
Semihard goats' milk cheese from Extremadura. Pale, creamy paste with a firm golden rind. Rather mellow in flavour. Ripened for a minimum of four months. There is also a smoked version.

Puzol 🐄 ☽ 50% ⊝ 300g-2kg (10oz-4lb) Ⓓ
Fresh, mild white cheese which should be eaten within two days. Also called Queso Fresco Valenciano.

Queso de los Beyos ☽ ⊝ 500g-1kg (18oz-2lb) Ⓓ
Made from whole unpasteurized cows', ewes' or goats' milk, but never blended. A farmhouse cheese from western Asturias, mainly made in spring and summer, it is rubbed with dry salt, then ripened for at least two weeks. It is about 12cm (5in) tall with a slightly wrinkled dusty white rind. Inside the cheese is thick, golden yellow, rich and buttery. Occasionally sold smoked. Also called Beyusco.

Queso Castellano ★ 🐏 ☽ ⊝ 1.5-3kg (3-7lb) ©
A superb pressed full fat cheese made in Old Castille from raw or pasteurized ewes' milk. Its production method is the same as for Manchego, but different pastures and climate make a distinctive cheese, often held in higher esteem than Manchego. It is matured for at least two months and has a slightly oily, waxy rind, ranging from light grey to dark brown. It is very dense and grainy, with a well-balanced flavour and a long, clean aftertaste. Different producers give their cheeses different characteristics. Names to look for are Flor de Esquera and Paramo de Guzman, which is sometimes tinned in olive oil.

Queso de la Estrella see *Oropesa*

Queso Fresco de Montaña see *Camerano*

Queso Fresco Valenciano see *Cervera, Puzol*

Queso de la Garrocha 🐐 ☽ ⊝ 1kg (2lb) Ⓓ
Soft, compact cheese with blue-grey velvety mould on rind. Nutty, goaty aroma and light creamy flavour. Matured for three to six weeks and made in Catalonia.

Queso Iberico ☽ ⊝ 3kg (7lb) ©
Recently established DO to cover cheeses made in central Spain from a blend of cows', ewes' and goats' milk. Made and presented in the same way as Manchego, it is Spain's most widely available and least expensive cheese. Often known as 'Manchego blend', it is identified by brand names such as Record, Garcia Baquero, Los Claveles and Carvel. Matured from 15 days to six months. Younger cheeses may be sold with a natural white rind or black wax coat; matured cheeses have a darker natural rind or may be painted brown or black.

Queso de los Ibores 🐐 ☽ ⊝ 500g-1.5kg (18oz-3lb) Ⓓ
Made in the province of Cáceres. The local pastures are rich in herbs, giving the milk (sometimes pasturized) an intense aroma. Made mainly from autumn to spring and eaten fresh or matured for 15 days to three months. Clean-tasting creamy cheese with a natural rind rubbed with olive oil or pimento.

Queso do los Montes San Benito de Huelva 🐄 ☽ 51% ⊝ ⚘ Ⓓ
A hard-pressed cheese, coagulated with vegetable rennet, with a smooth, dry, tawny rind and a buttery paste. Ripened for three weeks and eaten up to two months afterwards, or, if stored in olive oil, up to two years. Made in the province of Huelva.

Queso del Montsec 🐐 ☽ ⊝ 2kg (4lb) Ⓓ
Also known as Formatge Cendrat as it is coated with wood ash. A farmhouse cheese, usually unpasteurized, from the village of Clua in the Montsec hills, Lérida. Available all year, abundant in winter and

summer. Ripened for two to three months, it is close textured and creamy, with a touch of piquancy and a pronounced aftertaste.

Queso de Peñamellera 🐄 ⊟ 500g (18oz) Ⓓ
Farmhouse washed rind cheese from western Asturias. Made all year, especially in spring, from unpasteurized cows' or ewes' milk, or a mixture. Ripened for about two weeks, it has a wrinkly, orange, oily rind, a strong aroma and slightly bitter flavour.

Queso de la Peral 🐄 ⊟ 2kg (4lb) Ⓓ
Blue-veined cheese made with pasteurized cows' milk mixed with ewes' cream and *penicillium* spores. Matured in caves and made only in the village of San Jorge de la Peral, Asturias. The paste is very solid, creamy yellow, piquant but not too strong and very palatable.

Queso Puro de Oveja
Pure ewes' milk cheese is seen throughout Spain, looking and tasting very like Manchego, but not entitled to the name because the production zone or breed of sheep do not meet DO requirements. Gutierrez Oveja Seco, for example, is from sheep from different regions. Many Manchego producers make a cheese that is not entirely from La Manchega sheep and is not so expensive as genuine Manchego.

Queso del Tietar ★ 🐑 🐄 ⊟ Ⓑ
A farmhouse cheese from the province of Avila, made all year, but mainly in spring and summer. Very aromatic, with a hard, blue-grey rind with a light sprinkling of mould. The cheese has a high fat content and is firm yet springy, with a mild, creamy taste.

Queso de Valdeon see *Picón*

Quesucos 🐄 46% ⊟ 100g-3kg (3½oz-7lb) Ⓓ
Unpressed cheeses made from various milks in Santander. Usually mild, sometimes smoked, mostly produced in summer.

Requeson see *Burgos*

Rojo del Aramo see *Afuega'l Pitu*

Roncal ★ 🐑 🐄 60% ⊟ 2kg (4lb) ©
An uncooked pressed cheese made between December and July, and matured for at least four months. Within the hard rind is a rich, pale yellow cheese with irregular small holes. A DO cheese from Navarra.

San Simón 🐄 🐄 40% 1-2kg (2-4lb) ©
Smoked pear-shaped cheese from Lugo with a creamy paste, a glossy golden rind and a mildly acid flavour. Sold after two to four weeks.

Sierra de Zuheros 🐑 🐄 ⊟ 1kg (2lb) ©
Pressed crumbly cheese made in Manchego-style moulds, either with a pale rind, or rolled in paprika, which gives it a distinctive spicy taste.

Sobado see *Armada*

Soria 🐑 🐄 55% 500g-1kg (18oz-2lb) Ⓓ
Smooth, white fresh cheese similar to Camerano but with a slightly darker firmer crust and a saltier flavour. Moulded in wicker baskets.

Tetilla 🐄 🐄 40% 1kg (2lb) ©
A flattened pear-shaped cheese with a pleasantly clean, slightly sour, salty flavour and an elastic texture. Ripened for two to three weeks.

Made in Galicia all year round, but best from autumn to early spring. Also called Perilla.

Torta del Casar 🦃 🐑 57% ⊖ 1kg (2lb) 🌿 Ⓓ

A quick-ripening cheese made mostly in spring around the town of Cáceres. The cheese has a soft, rich, golden paste and a dry, darker rind; it is best eaten after two to three weeks, when the rind becomes cracked and streaky. It is coagulated with vegetable rennet.

Torta de la Serena 🦃 🐑 52% ⊖ 1kg (2lb) 🌿 Ⓓ

Cheese rather like Pedroches, coagulated with vegetable rennet and moulded in esparto hoops. The paste is quite soft, rich and yellowy with numerous variously sized holes. Made in Badajoz.

Tronchón 🐑 45% 600g-1.5kg (1¼-3lb) 🌿 Ⓓ

Formerly farm-made from raw ewes' milk, nowadays the dairies use a blend of cows' and goats' milk. Springy, very pale cheese darkening at the edges with a glossy, butter-coloured rind and a well-balanced, rather salty flavour that melts on the tongue. The curds, coagulated mostly with animal rennet but occasionally with thistle flowers, are shredded, drained and placed in circular dish-shaped moulds. They are then ripened for about a week and a crater forms on the top. Made in Castellón de la Plana and Teruel. Also known as Aragón.

Ulloa 🐄 🐑 45% ⊖ 1kg (2lb) Ⓒ

A mild cheese with a white paste and a springy yellow rind. The curds are scooped into cheese cloths, moulded and lightly pressed before being ripened—anything from two weeks to six months. Best in autumn and winter. Made in the provinces of La Coruña, Lugo and Pontevedra. Also called Patela.

Urbasa, Urbia see *Idiazabal*

Valdeteja 🐐 🐑 72% ⊖ 1kg (2lb) Ⓓ

Fairly sharp, white cheese with a pronounced goaty smell. The rind is dry, crusty and yellow-orange. It is ripened for two to three weeks.

Villalón ★ 🦃 🐑 54% ▭ 500g-2.5kg (18oz-5½lb) Ⓒ

Fresh, white, mild, slightly sour cheese, hand-pressed and steeped in brine for two to three hours, usually eaten immediately, but occasionally ripened for longer periods. From Villalón de Campos, Valladolid. Also called Pata de Mulo.

Zamorano ★ 🦃 🐑 ⊖ 3kg (7lb) Ⓑ

Made and presented in a similar way to Manchego, but the milk must come from Churra sheep in Zamora. The production method uses lower temperatures and it is generally matured for longer (from three to nine months)—originally in wine cellars, which gave the cheese a special aroma. The flavour is very full and intense, with a great bite.

KEY WORDS

Anejo aged	**Oveja** ewe
Blando soft	**Picón** piquant
Cabra goat	**Prensado** pressed
Curado medium-ripened	**Queso** cheese
Duro hard	**Suave** mild
En aceite in olive oil	**Vaca** cow
Fresco fresh	**Viejo** mature

SWEDEN see *Scandinavia*

Switzerland

The Swiss once used cheese as currency. Artisans, workers and priests in the Middle Ages were paid partly in cash and partly in fine Swiss cheeses—a form of coinage that could not be debased nor depreciate with time. Early exports were, no doubt, based on the same bartering principles. Cheeses were taken over the Alps into Italy and exchanged for rice, spices and wine. This eminently civilized form of trade has now gone but the Swiss still place a justifiably high value on their own cheeses, which were recognized as superb even in Roman times. The climate, the richness of the milk and, above all, fine cheesemaking skills transmitted from generation to generation have all contributed to the generally excellent quality of Swiss cheese. The Swiss have also been especially inventive in their cheese cookery. Apart from the famous *fondue* and *raclette*, they make marvellous cheese soups, puddings, soufflés and huge cheese tarts, *Käsewahe*.

Agrini
Small, soft, cylindrical goats' milk cheeses with white rind flora. From Ticino.

Alpkäse
Generic term for hard or semihard mountain cows' milk cheeses. Mostly wheel-shaped with tough dry rinds and variously sized holes. There are innumerable regional variations such as Berner, Bündner, Frutigtal, Tessiner and so on.

Anniviers see *Raclette*

Appenzell(cr) ★ ☼ ❂ 50% ⊖ 6-8kg (13-18lb) Ⓑ
Delicious cheese with a powerful flavour, made from unpasteurized milk. The paste is smooth and dense, scattered with a few pea-sized, perfectly round holes. The rind, washed with spices and white wine or cider, is hard and thick. Ripened for three to six months. Originated in the canton of Appenzell in the 8th or 9th century. See *Rasskäse*

Bagnes see *Raclette*

Bellelay see *Tête de Moine*

Berner Alpkäse see *Alpkäse*

Binn see *Raclette*

Bratkäse ☼ ❂ 45% ⊖ 1-1.5kg (2-3lb) ©
Grilling cheese similar to Raclette but usually eaten with bread. Made from pasteurized or unpasteurized milk, it has a rich buttery yellow paste with many variously sized holes and a firm, dry rind. Ripened between six and ten weeks. These cheeses were traditionally roasted on the end of a stick over an open fire. The best are said to be those from Nidwalden and Obwalden.

Bündner Alpkäse see *Alpkäse*

Chascöl
Grisons dialect for cheese. Typically a hard wheel-shaped cheese.

Chaux d'Abel ☼ ❂ 45% ⊖ 6-8kg (13-18lb) ©
Smooth, sweetish, pale yellow cheese with a few irregular holes and a rust-coloured, firm, dry rind. Made near Neuchâtel.

Conches see *Raclette*

Emmental(er) ★ ☆ ➍ 45% ⊖ 60-130kg (132-286lb) Ⓐ

Commonly known throughout the world as 'Swiss' cheese and imitated in many other countries, Emmental accounts for over one third of Swiss cheese production. Genuine Swiss Emmental (stamped 'Switzerland' all over the rind) is made only from unpasteurized milk in both dairies and small farms. It is a pressed cooked cheese instantly recognizable by the round walnut-sized holes evenly distributed throughout the dense golden paste. Though firm, it has a melt-in-the-mouth texture and a mild, distinctly nutty taste.

The name comes from the Emme valley near Bern where it originated. It takes about 1,000 litres of milk (the average daily yield of 80 cows) to make one 80kg (176lb) cheese. Evening and morning milk are mixed and coagulated with rennet. At the same time a culture of propionic acid producing bacteria is added to the milk. The curds are cut with a cheese harp, shredded into minute pieces, then 'cooked' in the whey for about half an hour. The mass of curd is then wrapped in a cheesecloth and lifted into a wooden hoop to drain. It is turned and pressed several times, soaked in a brine bath for one or two days and then taken to special cellars for ripening. It is during this ripening period of between four and ten months that the famous holes are formed. The number, size and shape of the holes depend on a host of factors: the scalding temperature of the curds, the level of salting, the temperature and humidity of the ripening store, the length of ripening, the number of times the cheese is turned during the ripening and so forth. The precise level of all these factors is itself determined by the way each batch of curds is 'working'—something that can only be judged by expert cheesemakers with years of experience. It is not surprising therefore that Emmental is generally considered to be one of the most difficult cheeses to make successfully, nor that the Swiss, with their centuries of experience, remain unimpressed by their innumerable would-be competitors. 'Anyone can make the holes,' they say, 'but only the Swiss can make the cheese'.

Etivaz
A type of Gruyère made in Etivaz.

Fribourg see *Vacherin Fribourgeois*

Frutigtal see *Alpkäse*

Glarnerkäse see *Alpkäse*

Glarner Kräuterkäse see *Sapsago*

Gomser see *Raclette*

Grüner Käse see *Sapsago*

Gruyère ★ ☆ ➍ 45% ⊖ 20-45kg (44-99lb) Ⓐ

Like Emmental, a pressed cooked cheese, although Gruyère wheels are much smaller and have straight rather than convex sides. The holes are also smaller, roughly pea-sized, and much more sparsely scattered through the paste. The rind is a coarse reddish brown labelled all over with the word 'Switzerland' to indicate a genuine unpasteurized Swiss product. For Gruyère the curds are cut less finely, scalded at a higher temperature, pressed harder and longer and ripened at a lower temperature but for the same period (four to ten months), producing a drier, firmer cheese with a more pronounced sweetish flavour and a typically nutty aroma. It is an excellent cooking cheese (even better than Emmental). Gruyère, which originated in the town of the same name in the 12th century, should be kept wrapped in a cloth dampened with salt water.

Hasliberg see *Alpkäse*

Haudères, Heida see *Raclette*

Hobelkäse see *Sbrinz*

Illiez see *Raclette*

Justistal see *Alpkäse*

Kräuterkäse see *Sapsago*

Maggia
Semihard unpasteurized cows' milk cheese made in Ticino.

Mutschli 🂠 🌙 45% ⊟ 500g-5kg (18oz-11lb) ©
Originally a mountain cheese now made all over Switzerland from pasteurized and unpasteurized milk. Fragrant, sweet-tasting with irregular holes and a warm, slightly rough, golden crust.

Nidelchäs 🂠 🌙 55% ©
Small, often oval-shaped, creamy cheese with a white bloomy rind. Sometimes known as Rahm-Käsli.

Nidwaldner Bratkäse, Obwaldner Bratkäse see *Bratkäse*

Orsières see *Raclette*

Paglia
Creamy blue-veined cheese similar to Italian Gorgonzola. Ripened on beds of straw. Made in Ticino.

Piora ★ 🂠 🌙 45% ⊝ 8-16kg (18-35lb) ⓓ
Delicate rich cheese with many small holes. Made in Ticino. Vero Piora is made on the Alp Piora itself; Tipo Piora is made on other mountains in the same area; Uso Piora is made from a mixture of cows' and goats' milk. All are ripened for about six months.

Raclette ★ 🂠 🌙 45-50% ⊝ 5-10kg (11-22lb) ⓑ
Literally 'scraper', the name given to a family of semihard cheeses mostly from the canton of Valais. Cheeses made locally, from unpasteurized milk, are quite different to factory-made Raclette. A firm, buttery cheese, it has a golden paste with a few small holes and a rough grey-brown rind deeply impressed with the name of the cheese. The flavour is full and fruity. Eaten as it is or particularly suitable for use in the traditional Swiss dish also called *raclette*. To make *raclette* a whole cheese is sliced in half and the cut surface placed before an open fire. As the cheese melts it is scraped on to a dish and eaten immediately with potatoes boiled in their skins, pickled onions and gherkins. There are many types of Raclette cheese, among them Anniviers, Bagnes, Binn, Conches, Gomser, Haudères, Heida, Illiez, Orsières, Simplon and Walliser.

Rahm-Käsli see *Nidelchäs*

Rasskäse
A type of Appenzeller made with skimmed milk, giving it a very low

fat content of around 16 per cent. Much darker, sharper and more pungent than ordinary Appenzeller.

Royalp ☼ 🌑 45% ⊖ 4-5kg (9-11lb) Ⓑ

Introduced in the 19th century and known as Tilsit in Switzerland and Royalp abroad. More like Appenzeller than German Tilsiter, it is firmer with far fewer, more regularly shaped holes. It is ripened for two to four months and has a rather mild flavour with a spicy piquant aftertaste. The unpasteurized version is marked with a red label; the pasteurized version has a green label.

Saanen ☼ 🌑 40-45% ⊖ 15-30kg (33-66lb) Ⓒ

Made in the Saanen valley in the Bernese Oberland since the 16th century. A very hard cheese similar to Sbrinz, it has a deep yellow brittle paste with many tiny pinpoint holes and is usually shaved with a cheese plane. Generally ripened for two to three years but will keep indefinitely.

Sapsago ☼ 🌑 3% 100-200g (3½-7oz) Ⓑ

A cheese with many names and few uses: Grüner Käse, Glarner Kräuterkäse, Kräuterkäse, Schabziger, or simply 'Green Cheese'. Whatever the name, it is a rock hard, pale green cheese, shaped like a cylinder tapering slightly at the top, strong and spicy to taste. Made of skimmed milk or whey heated with lactic acid or vinegar to precipitate the proteins. The solids are then heavily pressed, ground up and mixed with powdered herbs and pressed again into special moulds to produce the characteristic shape known as 'Stöckli'. It was introduced into the canton of Glarus by monks at least 500 years ago. The curious flavour and colour comes from blue melilot (*Melilotis coerulea*), a herb brought back from Asia Minor by crusaders and still only found in the area in which the cheese is made. Sapsago is a condiment cheese, used only for grating onto bread or local dishes. Sold wrapped in foil or powdered in cartons.

Sbrinz ★ ☼ 🌑 45% ⊖ 20-45kg (44-99lb) Ⓑ

Probably the cheese that Pliny knew in the 1st century AD as *caseus helveticus*, 'Swiss cheese'. Sbrinz is the most ancient of Swiss cheeses and there has been a vigorous Italian market in it for many centuries. It is generically related to Italian Grana cheese, being a long-ripened, extra-hard, pressed, cooked cheese used mostly for grating and very spicy and piquant in flavour. Similarly, it is said to be easily digestible and has some reputation as a medicament. Made only from unpasteurized milk and only in Central Switzerland: in Lucerne, Unterwalden, Schwyz and Zug. The name derives from the village of Brienz in the Bernese Oberland. It is ripened (stored, unusually, on edge) for 18 months to three years. In Ticino it may appear under the name Sulle Spalle, reflecting in the local dialect how such cheeses were once transported on muleback through the Saint Gotthard Pass on their journey to Italy. It is an excellent grating cheese and also melts extremely well, making it ideal for cooking. It is frequently also eaten as an appetizer shaved into paper-thin curly slivers (*rebibes*). In this form it (and other hard cheeses similarly treated) is sometimes referred to as Hobelkäse (from *Hobel*, a carpenter's plane). Sbrinz is the best known (and the best) of a large family of extra-hard cows' milk cheeses.

Schabziger see *Sapsago*

Schwyzer

Hard cows' milk cheese made in Central Switzerland either in the mountains (*fromage d'alpage*) or the valleys (*fromage de campagne*).

Sedrun
Semihard wheel-shaped goats' milk cheese with a thick dry greyish crust. Ripened for a maximum of five months. Dry matter fat content is 45 per cent.

Sérac
Fresh cows' milk whey cheese similar to Italian Ricotta—a by-product of the mountain cheeses. Occasionally ripened or seasoned with herbs and spices. Fat content is usually at least 15 per cent.

Séré ♔ ☽ 125-500g (4-18oz) ©
Fresh cheese like German Quark made from whole or skimmed pasteurized milk. There are three types: *maigre* (0-15 per cent fat), *gras* (40 per cent fat), *à la crème* (50 per cent fat).

Simplon see *Raclette*

Spalen (Schnittkäse), Sulle Spalle see *Sbrinz*

Spycher
Low fat semihard drum-shaped smooth yellow cows' milk cheese with a soft brown rind.

Tessiner see *Alpkäse*

Tête de Moine ★ ♔ ♪ 50% ☐ 500g-2kg (18oz-4lb) ⑧
A monastic cheese traditionally made only from summer milk and on sale when the first leaves of autumn begin to fall, through until March. It is a smooth, spicy, fruity, pressed, uncooked cheese ripened for four to six months in cool cellars. The paste is straw yellow and the rind rough and rather greasy to touch. It was invented by monks at Bellelay Abbey who later taught the method to local farmers. The name (meaning 'monk's head') derives, some say, from a tax levied by the abbey whereby the farmers would provide one cheese for each monk during the season. Others say it refers to the tonsured appearance of the cheese when it is served in the traditional way: with the top sliced off and the rind cut away to a depth of about 2cm (¾in) all round. The cheese is usually sliced into thin curls with a special knife and eaten with pepper and powdered cumin. Also called Bellelay.

Tilsit Suisse see *Royalp*

Toggenburger Ploderkäse ♔ ♪ 15% ⊂⊃ 7-13kg (15-29lb) ✿ ©
Made in the Alps north of the Walensee, a cube-shaped white-pasted slightly granular cheese made from skimmed milk coagulated by lactic fermentation. It is Switzerland's only sour milk cheese. The milk is usually soured naturally, then heated and the curds allowed to drain in the moulds without pressing. During the six month ripening period the cheeses become covered with a fat layer (*Speckschicht*)—not actually fat but a thick bacterial smear.

Tomme Vaudoise ♔ ♫ 45-50% ⊝ 100-180g (3½-6oz) ©
From the canton of Vaud, north of Lake Geneva, small quick-ripened cheeses made mostly in small dairies from pasteurized or unpasteurized milk. The paste is pale yellow and supple with a lightly crumpled covering of white mould which becomes streaked with red as the cheeses mature. Very mild, faintly spicy and sometimes flavoured with cumin. Ripened for about a week.

Urner
Low-fat hard cows' milk cheese from Central Switzerland.

Vacherin Fribourgeois ⚅ 🐄 45% ⊖ 6-10kg (13-22lb) Ⓑ

Quite a different cheese from Vacherin Mont d'Or but often confused
with it. This is a mountain cheese, one of the oldest in Switzerland,
dating back to the 15th century. Made only in the canton of Fribourg
from pasteurized or unpasteurized milk and cured for three to four
months. Smaller and softer than Gruyère, it has a pale yellow paste
with many small holes and slits and a mild, sourish taste. The rind is
pinkish brown and rather coarse.

Vacherin Mont d'Or ★ ⚅ 🐄 50% ⊖ 200g-3kg (7oz-7lb) Ⓑ

Justly famous, a marvellous cheese when at its best, it has a rich velvety texture and a faintly resinous flavour. Made in the Vallée de Joux
near the border with France. The French make the same cheese but
after legal wrangles have been obliged to rename their version
Vacherin du Haut-Doubs (although it is still commonly known as
Mont d'Or). It is a winter cheese, made with the milk from the last
hay crop when the fat content is higher than usual. Moulded in a strip
of pine bark, it is cured in a humid atmosphere for about three months
and sold in wooden boxes (in which it is also customarily served). The
paste is a dull yellow and has the consistency of thick clotted cream.
The crust, pale reddish brown rather like lightly baked bread,
becomes gently crumpled when the cheese is à point. Served traditionally, this crust is removed in one piece and the inside scooped out
with a spoon. If the cheese is sliced, the cut surfaces should be protected with a small sheet of glass or wood to prevent the paste flowing
out of the crust. A whole Vacherin Mont d'Or makes a wonderfully
luxurious dessert cheese.

Walliser see Raclette

Ziegenkäse

Meaning 'goats' cheese' and made in various parts of Switzerland, it
may be soft, semisoft or semihard, and may now be mixed with a certain percentage of cows' milk.

SYRIA, TURKEY see Middle East. TUNISIA see Africa.

USSR

At the time of writing, the USSR is suffering widespread food shortages; Moscovites will read this with either acute nostalgia or cynicism. Rough and ready processed cheeses are often all that is available. Nevertheless, according to official information there are more than 150 cheeses being manufactured in the Soviet Union and foreign travellers might have more luck than natives in finding them. Some interesting indigenous cheeses come from the European fringes of Russia, from Trans-Caucasia (especially Armenia, home of early cheesemaking) and from the mountain ranges along the Chinese and Mongolian borders. The Russian for cheese is Sir.

Altaisky, Altay 🐄 🌘 50% ⊖ 12-20kg (26-44lb)

Hard-pressed cooked cheese with medium-sized holes and a slightly sweet, nutty taste.

Bukovinsky 🐄 🌘 45% ⊖ 2-3kg (4-7lb)

Creamy, slightly sour-tasting cheese with irregular eyes.

Chanakh

A Caucasian brined cheese with a lactic taste; made from cows', ewes' or goats' milk or a blend.

Daralagyazhsky

Semihard Armenian cheese made from ewes' or goats' milk.

Desertny Bely 🐄 🌘 50% ⊖ 500g (18oz)

Factory-made cheese with white rind flora, ripened for a week.

Dorogobuzhsky 🐄 🌘 45% ⊂⊃ 500g (18oz)

Oily, spreadable cheese with a damp reddish rind. Ripened for about six weeks. Piquant and strong-smelling.

Dorozhny 🐄 🌘 50% ⊖ 1-2kg (2-4lb)

Washed rind cheese with a tender, buttery consistency, strong aroma and sharp flavour.

Estonsky 🐄 🌘 45% ⊔ 2-3kg (4-7lb)

Hard mild cheese with a waxed rind. Ripened for one month.

Gornoaltaysky ★ 🌘 50% ⊔ 10-15kg (22-33lb)

Strong grating cheese made from ewes' or cows' milk and ripened for three months. Occasionally smoked.

Kalininsky 🐄 🌘 50% ⊖ 600g-1kg (1¼-2lb)

Soft buttery cheese in a pungent washed crust.

Karpatsky 🐄 🌘 50% ⊖ 12-18kg (26-40lb)

Swiss-type cheese with large holes from the Carpathian region, sometimes known as Panonio.

Kobiisky

Salty, Feta-like cheese from northern Caucasia, made from cows', ewes' or goats' milk.

Kostromskoy 🐄 🌘 45% ⊖ 5-12kg (11-26lb)

Mild factory-made cheese with a red waxed rind.

Krasnodarsky

Firm washed rind cows' milk cheese from the Black Sea region.

Latviisky 🏭 🌙 45% ⬭ 2kg (4lb)
Strong, smelly, washed rind cheese ripened for two months.

Litovsky 🏭 🌙 30% 4-6kg (9-13lb)
Melting consistency and irregular holes within a hard rind.

Medynsky
Soft, supple cows' milk cheese, similar to German Limburger.

Moskovsky
Hard-pressed cows' milk cheese ripened for four months.

Motal
White, brined ewes' or cows' milk cheese, farm-made in the Caucasus
and ripened for about three months.

Osetinsky
Caucasian brined cheese, best made with ewes' milk, but some made
with cows' milk. Also called Tushinsky.

Rossiisky 🏭 🌙 50% ⊖ 5-18kg (11-40lb)
Factory-made chese with a mild, lactic, slightly crumbly paste.

Sirok
Acid- or rennet-curd cheese made from cows' milk.

Smolensky
Soft washed rind cheese up to about 1kg (2lb) in weight. Can be made
from any milk, usually cows', having an almost mushroomy flavour.

Sovietsky 🏭 🌙 50% ⊖ 12-16kg (26-35lb)
Piquant rather rubbery cheese with pea-sized holes made in the Altai
mountains and ripened for about four months.

Stepnoi 🏭 🌙 45% 7-9kg (15-20lb)
Grainy, rather greasy cows' milk cheese much the same as German
Steppenkäse. Strong, sometimes spiced with caraway.

Suluguni
Small brined cheeses from southern Russia. Ewes' or cows' milk.

Tvorog, Twarog
Fresh cheese made from sour milk, much used in cooking. Sometimes pressed in wooden forms.

Uglichesky
Dutch-type cows' milk cheese with a lactic taste.

Volzhsky
Latvian washed rind cheese with a strong aroma and flavour.

Yaroslavsky
Firm, holey cows' milk cheese, mild when young, but nutty and pronounced if left to mature.

Yerevansky ★
A semihard white brined ewes' milk cheese. Ripened in tins.

VENEZUELA see *Latin America*. YUGOSLAVIA see *Eastern Europe*. UNITED STATES
see *North America*.

Buying, storing and serving cheese

All cheeses are temperamental to a greater or lesser extent and can be
ruined by careless handling. Since cheese is a relatively expensive
commodity, care in buying, storing and serving it makes sound
economic sense as well as being gastronomically rewarding.

BUYING CHEESE

The first essential is to find a reputable cheesemonger where you can
find cheeses in excellent condition. A wide selection is not the only
criterion. A few well-chosen cheeses displayed with care and
attention to their particular characteristics may well be a better
indication of a good shop than a huge indiscriminate array. Many
shops unfortunately stock far too many cheeses without having the
turnover to justify it and cheeses left on the shelf for too long will
inevitably deteriorate. A shop where you are allowed, even
encouraged, to taste before you buy is almost bound to be a good one.
It shows that the retailer has every confidence in his own product.

Unless you are prepared to place yourself entirely in the hands of
your cheesemonger, you will need to know something about the
desirable and undesirable features of each cheese. Some guidelines
have been given in the listings in this book. The nature of the paste,
the rind, the eyes or the veins all hold clues to the condition of a
particular cheese. Examine the label if there is one. Many cheeses are
now subject to legal protection and most countries have stringent
rules concerning the labelling of food products generally. The
presence or absence of information can tell you a great deal about the
origins, authenticity and composition of a cheese: for example
whether it is farmhouse- or factory-made, pasteurized or
unpasteurized, the fat content, the type of milk and so on.
Remember that it is nearly always better to buy pieces cut from a
whole cheese rather than pre-packed sections. Cheese should always
be cut properly, either with a wire cutter or a special knife, and then
be covered with plastic wrap or metal foil.

STORING CHEESE

If possible, avoid the problem of storage altogether and buy only as
much cheese as you can eat on that day or the next. Most good
cheesemongers are better equipped to store cheese properly than the
average household. On the whole refrigerators and freezers do
nothing for cheese, although fresh cheeses must be kept in the
refrigerator. Soft cheeses (Brie, Camembert, etc.) can be stored for a
day or so in the warmest part of the refrigerator (the vegetable drawer
is best). Semihard and hard cheeses should be stored in a cool
cupboard for preference. Cheeses should always be wrapped closely
and separately (to avoid mingling flavours). Greaseproof paper, foil or
plastic wrap are ideal in most cases, but some cheeses (Granas, for
example) are better wrapped in a damp cloth. Although not
recommended, most cheeses can be frozen without too much loss of
flavour or texture. Wrap well and freeze in portions that you will be
able to finish at one sitting, as defrosted cheese develops a bitter taste
after 24 hours.

SERVING CHEESE

Cheese is served for breakfast in Germany, the Netherlands and
Scandinavia and in many Middle Eastern countries. In Portugal it is
frequently eaten before the main meal as an appetizer. In some
countries, such as Greece, sliced cheese is served with a meal as a side

dish, and in Russia it is customary to eat whenever you drink—a piece of cheese is often the most convenient morsel.

In England, Stilton or Cheddar are traditional with port after dinner, accompanied by fruit and nuts. The French express great horror at any departure from their normal practice, which is to serve the cheese after the salad and before the dessert. This makes sense, as you can continue drinking the wine served with the main course without a sweet interruption. A selection of three or four cheeses is usual at a private dinner, and bread or plain biscuits should also be served. Some cheeses (generally fresh ones) are not usually served as part of a cheese board, but are eaten with fruit or sugar; others are used only or mostly for cooking.

Far more important than what you serve it with is the temperature at which you serve cheese. All cheeses, even fresh ones, need to be taken out of the refrigerator some time before being served (up to an hour for soft cheeses, longer for hard ones) in order to develop their flavour to the full. Be extra careful with soft cheeses: they are apt to liquefy if kept in a warm room for too long. Hard cheeses under the same conditions tend to become harder and may sweat. Serve only as much cheese as is likely to be eaten at any one time, to avoid returning it to the cold store: cheeses do not take kindly to frequent oscillations of temperature.

WHAT TO DRINK WITH YOUR CHEESE

The words cheese and wine are firmly associated, yet you cannot match all cheeses with all wines.

Wine country often produces cheese, making local partnerships an intriguing possibility: try Valençay and Sancerre, Munster and Alsace Gewürztraminer. Stick to the humbler wines, the *vins de pays*, the Italian country wines. Great wines, even from a cheese district, somehow have less in common with local food than the small wines destined for everyday drinking. Fine wines need a restrained partner and will be overwhelmed by strong, pungent cheeses. The cheeses of England and northern France marry well with their local drinks—try Maroilles with strong beer, Cheddar or Caerphilly with cider.

Outside the great wine- and cheese-producing countries of France, Italy and Spain, there are no hard and fast rules—and it is fun to experiment. Personal preference will come into the final decision, but a little consideration of the character of both partners should act as a guide. An assertively flavoured cheese needs a wine to match. With a strong mature Cheddar, a hefty red wine (such as Châteauneuf-du-Pape) or a nutty oloroso sherry both work well. Choose full-bodied fruity reds to accompany washed rind cheeses. Softer reds and dry fruity whites go with most goats' milk cheeses, bearing in mind that the more piquant cheeses will stand up to more powerful flavours in the wine. Soft cheeses, and those of finer taste, call for more elegance in the wine. White rind cheeses work well with Chardonnay wines, whether from Burgundy, Australia or California. Young Cheddar, along with Jarlsberg, Edam and mild Brie, complements even the finest Burgundies and clarets.

Try sweet wines with the fattier cheeses, especially blues. Sauternes is traditionally drunk with Roquefort in France. Think twice before falling for the classic combination of Blue Stilton and vintage port. Good port—when it is to be found—is an experience that needs no complement. The same goes for a decent Stilton. Drink port with Stilton by all means, but choose a relatively young nutty tawny, a good fruity ruby or a late-bottled kind. The cheese needs the sweetness and strength a fortified wine brings, but can somehow overbalance the delicate structure of a fine vintage port.

Glossary

Acid-curd milk coagulated by lactic acid rather than rennet

Annatto Bixa orellana, a West Indian plant that produces a commonly used cheese dye

Beestings another name for Colostrum

Bloom soft downy mould growth on the surface of the cheese

Blue, blue-veined cheeses with internal moulds, usually blue or green, spreading through the paste

Brined cheese cheese ripened in a solution of water and salt

Buttermilk milk left after cream has been made into butter

Cheddaring blocks of curd repeatedly stacked and turned to facilitate draining and mat the curd particles

Coagulation the clotting of milk by rennet or lactic acid

Colostrum the first milk produced by a cow after calving

Cooked after coagulation the temperature of the whey is raised above the renneting temperature (see p. 6), thus 'cooking' the curds and producing a harder, drier cheese

Coryne bacteria the reddish-brown smear that develops on the surface of washed rind cheeses

Evening milk milk obtained from an animal during the evening milking (usually richer in fat than morning milk)

Eyes another word for the holes in some cheeses

Farmhouse made on the farm, not necessarily from raw milk

Flora the mould growth on the surface of cheeses like Camembert

Fresh unripened

Lactation period the period during which mammals secrete milk

Lactic acid acid produced when milk sours

Lactose milk sugar

Macerated cheese cheese steeped in alcohol and sometimes mixed with herbs and spices

Monastery cheese cheeses traditionally made by monks

Morning milk milk obtained during the morning milking

Pasta filata a method of cheesemaking that involves immersing the curd in hot water or whey and kneading it until it becomes elastic

Paste the interior of a cheese, the part that is eaten

Pasteurization a method of partially sterilizing milk (see p.5)

Penicillium candidum the fungus responsible for the growth of white surface moulds on Camembert-type cheeses

Penicillium glaucum responsible for the veining of Gorgonzola

Penicillium roquefortii responsible for the veining of Roquefort

Plastic curd synonym for pasta filata

Propionic acid its action during ripening produces the holes in holey cheeses

Raw milk unpasteurized milk

Rennet a coagulant usually obtained from the fourth stomach or vell of an unweaned calf, sometimes from other animals, occasionally from plants. Now also grown from microbes (yeast or fungus)—acceptable to vegetarians

Rennet-curd milk coagulated by rennet

Skimmed milk from which the cream has been removed, thus lowering the fat content. Milk may be fully or partly skimmed

Spun curd synonym for pasta filata

Starter a culture of lactic acid bacteria added to the milk before renneting to increase its acidity

Surface-ripened cheese ripened by surface moulds

Vell see Rennet

Washed rind cheeses bathed in water, brine or alcohol during the ripening period producing reddish bacterial surface smears

Whey the liquid separated from the curds in cheesemaking

Whole milk with all its fats intact—in other words not skimmed

Recommended cheese shops

England

The Cheeseboard
1 Commercial Street
Harrogate
North Yorkshire HG1 1UB
Tel: 0423 508837

The Cheese Hamlet
706 Winslow Road, Didsbury
Manchester M20 0DW
Tel: 061-434 4781

The Cheese Shop
17 Kensington Gardens
Brighton
East Sussex BN1 4AL
Tel: 0273 601129

The Fine Cheese Co
29 Walcot Street
Bath BA1 5BN
Tel: 0225 483407

James & John Graham Ltd
Market Square, Penrith
Cumbria CA11 7BS
Tel: 0768 62281

Harrods Ltd
Knightsbridge
London SW1X 7XL
Tel: 071-730 1234

Jeroboams
51 Elizabeth Street
London SW1W 9PP
Tel: 071-823 5623

Langmans Fine Cheeses
13 Wood Street
Stratford-upon-Avon
Warwickshire CV37 6JF
Tel: 0789 415544

The Mousetrap
2 St Gregory's Alley
Pottergate
Norwich NR2 1ER
Tel: 0603 614083

Neal's Yard Dairy
Neal's Yard, Covent Garden
London WC2H 9DP
Tel: 071-379 7646

Paxton & Whitfield Ltd
93 Jermyn Street
London SW1Y 6JE
Tel: 071-930 0259

Rippon Cheese Supplies
26 Upper Tachbrook Street
London SW1V 1SW
Tel: 071-931 0668

Wells Stores
29 Stert Street, Abingdon
Oxfordshire OX14 3JF
Tel: 0235 535978

Ireland

Magills
14 Clarendon Street, Dublin 2
Tel: 713830

Scotland

Valvona & Crolla Ltd
19 Elm Row
Edinburgh EH7 4AA
Tel: 031-556 6066

Wales

The Farmhouse Cheese Shop
Carmarthen Provision Market
Carmarthen, Dyfed

France

Androuët Maîtres Fromagers
41 rue d'Amsterdam
75008 Paris
Tel: 48.74.26.90

La Ferme Saint-Hubert
21 rue Vignon
75008 Paris
Tel: 47.42.79.20

La Fromagerie Philippe Olivier
43-45 rue Thiers
62200 Boulogne-sur-Mer
Tel: 21.31.94.74

La Maison du Fromage
62 rue de Sèvres
75007 Paris
Tel: 47.34.33.45

United States

Cheese of all Nations Inc.
153 Chambers Street
New York, NY 10007
Tel: 732-0752

Ideal Cheese Shop
1205 Second Avenue
New York, NY 10021
Tel: 688-7579

Dean & DeLuca
560 Broadway
New York, NY 10012
Tel: 431-1691

Zabar's
2245 Broadway
New York, NY 10024
Tel: 787-2000

Index

Page numbers refer to main entries for each cheese; italicized numbers denote other references.

157

INDEX

Acknowledgements

The author and publishers would like to thank the following people and organizations for their invaluable help:

Abbey Farm (Shropshire); Agrexco Agricultural Export Co. Ltd.; The Arab-British Centre; Embassy of the Argentine Republic; Stephen Arloff; Atalanta U.K. Ltd.; Australian Dairy Corporation; Austrian Foreign Trade Office; Austrian Institute; Dra. Manuela Barbosa; Belgian Embassy; Joseph Berkmann; Brazilian Embassy; Embassy of the People's Republic of Bulgaria; Canadian High Commission; Crowson & Son Ltd.; Cuisine Magazine; Danish Dairy Board; Royal Danish Embassy; DMK Ltd.; Dutch Dairy Bureau; Emberton Bros.; English Country Cheese Council; Food and Wine from France; George Foster; Chris Foulkes; French Dairy Farmers Ltd.; Galbani (London) Ltd.; Central Marketing Organisation of German Agricultural Industries; Cilla Gibbs; The Great Britain-USSR Association; Greek Embassy; Hungarian Embassy; Icelandic Embassy; Italian Institute for Foreign Trade; Catherine Jackson; Katsouris Brothers Ltd.; Lorraine Major; Milk Marketing Board; Ernesto and Miranda Mussi; National Dairy Council; Royal Netherlands Embassy; New Zealand Dairy Board; Auguste Noel Ltd.; Norway Trade Centre; J.M.Nuttall & Co.; Paxton & Whitfield; Portugese Government Trade Office; Peruvian Embassy; Major Patrick Rance; Lizz Rawson; Caroline Schuck; Brian and Irene Smith; Spanish Chamber of Commerce; Spanish Embassy; Spanish Institute; Stilton Cheesemakers' Association; Swedish Embassy; Swiss Cheese Union; Valio Finnish Cooperative Dairies' Association; Venezuelan Embassy; Dr. Gerta Vrbova.

For this revised edition we would also like to thank:

Abergavenny Fine Foods Ltd; Pierre Aubin, Agriculture Canada; Robin Ayrdon; Belgian Office for the Promotion of Agricultural and Horticultural Produce; Bermic Cheese Specialists; Gill Brogden; Mario Burmo, Anthony Bryant Ltd; Daryl Burton; Ian Chilvers; Alastair Clark; Karen Craig; Paul Dymond; Edward Edelman, The Ideal Cheese Shop (New York); Hennart Frères; Janine Gilson, Foods From Spain; Handmade Cheeses of Scotland; Juliet Harbutt; Randolph Hodgson; Simon Johnson, McDonald & Johnson (Sydney); Elisabeth Lambert Ortiz; Monika Lavery; Carolyn Lockhart, Australian Gourmet Traveller Magazine; Trevor Maxwell, The Swedish Table; Ross McCallum; Cyril McDonnell, National Dairy Council (Ireland); Olivia Mills, The British Sheep Dairying Association; Jytte Nipper, Danish Dairy Board; Seva Novgorodsev; Don Philpott; Jeremy Probert; Philip Rippon; Anthony Rowcliffe & Son Ltd.; The Scottish Gourmet; Malcolm Seamark, New Zealand Dairy Board; Specialist Cheesemakers' Association; Alexa Stace; Leila Tannous; David Taylor; Sophie Vallejo; Emmerentia Van Wyk, National Co-operative Dairies (South Africa); Welsh Food Promotions Ltd; Doris Wood.